NEW TOWNS IN AMERICA

Reston, Virginia

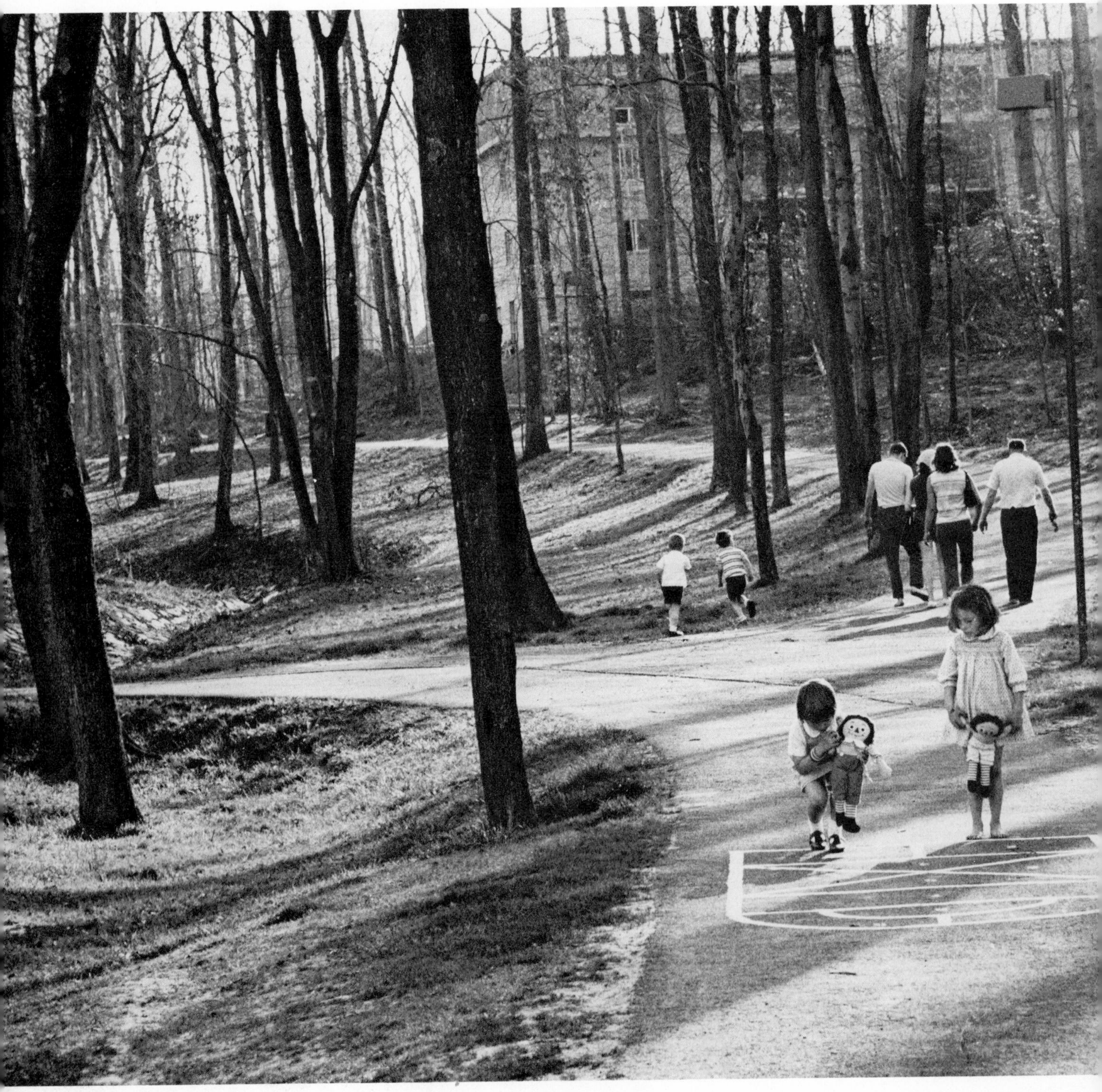

The American Institute of Architects

NEW TOWNS IN AMERICA
The Design and Development Process

Edited by JAMES BAILEY
Foreword by CARRELL S. McNULTY JR., FAIA

A WILEY-INTERSCIENCE PUBLICATION

JOHN WILEY & SONS
New York · London · Sydney · Toronto

The publication of this book was made possible through a Demonstration Grant awarded by the U.S. Department of Housing and Urban Development under the provisions of Sections 501 and 502 of the Housing Act of 1970 in furtherance of Section 701(b)(12) U.S.C. 1701 et al.

NEW TOWNS IN AMERICA: THE DESIGN AND DEVELOPMENT PROCESS.
Published by The American Institute of Architects. Printed in the United States of America. 1973. For information address The American Institute of Architects, 1735 New York Avenue, N.W., Washington, D.C. 20006.

Library of Congress Catalog Number 73-77292

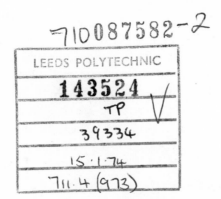
Design/Production: Hubert Leckie
Maps: Susan Lehmann

ISBN 0-471-00975-X

FOREWORD

Although there is a danger in using the term "New Town" because it may associate us too closely with the British experience, the title "New Towns in America" was chosen deliberately because it conveys a hint of the objectives to be sought in building new communities in our present society. It serves as a link to our past heritage of new-town construction. It also serves to convey an image of the appropriate urban scale; that of a highly personal community.

The idea for the book arose from a deep conviction on the part of The American Institute of Architects' Urban Planning and Design Committee that the profession needed to be made aware of this important new area of practice. It was a response to the recent passage of Title VII, the New Communities Section of the 1970 Housing Act, and, more important, to the work of the AIA Task Force on National Growth Policy, whose first report is printed verbatim in this volume.

To provide the basic material for the book, the committee held a Conference on New Communities in Washington, D.C., November 3-6, 1971, in which more than 350 professionals participated. Approximately 25 papers covering all aspects of the topic were distributed in advance of the conference, and tapes were taken of all seminars and plenary sessions.

Perhaps no one book can reflect all aspects of a topic as broad as that contained in the concept of a new town, and this book is no exception. The essay approach was deliberately chosen in order to convey to the utmost the variety of issues and attitudes current in the creation of what is, indeed, a very fluid art. It is not a verbatim report of the conference, but rather a synthesis of what took place. Not every participant or every paper has been included, nor are those that are presented in their original form. Rather, those chosen were included to reflect the breadth of the subject. Each was edited and organized to fit the requirements of a book, with little or no regard for their sequence at the conference. Some material was eliminated altogether, not because the authors had nothing interesting or important to say, but because their remarks were either duplicated by others (a common and often useful occurrence in the free-wheeling atmosphere of a conference) or covered issues outside the framework of the book.

This book owes much to the many participants in the conference, not only the speaker-authors, but the audience as well, which contributed so much to the seminar discussions. Special credit should be given to the members of the AIA Urban Planning and Design Committee's subcommittee on new communities, whose members gave of their time through many meetings in order to structure the conference and plan for the book. This group was composed of George Kostritsky, Carl Feiss, Ralph Warburton, George Pillorgé, and the writer.

Neither the conference nor the book would have been possible without the tireless efforts of Michael Barker, then AIA Director of Urban Programs, who served not only as conference director, but also as the "glue" that held it together.

If, as the committee hopes, this book can contribute to the understanding of new-town development, it will form only the first in a series covering urban and regional issues of importance to the profession.

Carrell S. McNulty Jr., FAIA

CONTENTS

LIST OF COMPARATIVE NEW TOWN PLANS

THE AUTHORS

THOMAS LUDLOW ASHLEY has been a Democratic member of Congress, representing Ohio's Ninth District, since 1955. As a member of the House Banking and Currency Committee's Subcommittee on Housing, he authored Title VII of the 1970 Housing Act and was instrumental in the passage of many landmark housing and urban development bills. Before his election to Congress he served with Radio Free Europe and as general counsel to Formed Steel Products.

DANIEL BRENTS, AIA, is an associate and planner for Envirodynamics Inc., architects and planners of Dallas. He served for three years as an associate of RTKL Inc., Baltimore, where he was project director for eight new-community developments ranging in size from 100 to 1,500 acres. His 10 years of practice in architecture, urban design, and planning has also included the Yerba Buena Convention Center in San Francisco while with the firm of John Bolles Associates.

DAVID A. CRANE, AIA, AIP, became dean of the Rice University School of Architecture in 1972 after serving as a professor of urban design at the University of Pennsylvania. He is also a principal in the firm of David A. Crane & Partners, which he founded in 1959. His many projects, both practical and theoretical, have brought him an international reputation in urban design. He has lectured extensively and authored more than a dozen articles and papers on architecture and urban design.

PHILIP DAVID is a professor of urban land development in the Department of Planning and Urban Studies of the Massachusetts Institute of Technology and a former associate professor at Harvard's Graduate School of Business Adminis-

tration. He has held many corporate positions, including those of chairman of the board of Cavanagh Leasing Corporation, president and director of Enterprise Research and Development Corporation, and vice president of Gulf States Land and Industries Inc. He is a member of the Inter-University Policy Committee of the Harvard/MIT Joint Center for Urban Studies.

CARL FEISS, FAIA, AIP, is a planning and urban design consultant practicing in Washington, D.C. He frequently lectures on architecture and city planning. He served as a special consultant to the National Commission on Urban Problems and the White House Conference on Natural Beauty. He has contributed articles to *Architectural Forum, Progressive Architecture, Architectural Record,* and *Law and Contemporary Problems.* He is a member of the board of trustees of the National Trust for Historic Preservation.

KNOWLTON FERNALD JR, FAIA, is a vice president for planning of the commercial and community development division of Cabot, Cabot & Forbes Inc. He is responsible for all the design functions on such projects as large-scale community developments, office complexes, and commercial centers. He is a former vice president for planning, architecture, and engineering for Laguna Niguel Corporation, where he had similar responsibilities.

HERBERT M. FRANKLIN is in private law practice in Washington, D.C., where he is of counsel to the firm of Frosh, Lane & Edson. He is also the consultant director of a two-year metropolitan housing project for the Potomac Institute. He has been an executive associate and vice president of the National Urban Coalition, and director of the urban redevelopment division of Urban America Inc.

ROBERT GLADSTONE, AIP, is president and founder of Gladstone Associates, economic and planning consultants of Washington, D.C. His extensive career in consulting, business management, and economic research has been conducted with a number of private and public organizations. He is the economic consultant for Columbia, Md., and has done economic analyses for several other new towns. He has authored many articles and research papers dealing with real estate economics and urban development.

SAMUEL C. JACKSON joined the Washington, D.C., law firm of Stroock, Stroock & Lavan in 1972 after serving three years as HUD's Assistant Secretary for metropolitan development. Before joining HUD, he was for three years a member of the Equal Employment Opportunity Commission. He carried out a private law practice in Topeka from 1957 to 1965.

JAMES MCKELLAR is an urban designer with the Philadelphia firm of David A. Crane & Partners. His special interests are large-scale project development, facilities systems programming and design, project development procedures, and environmental analysis and urban research. He has worked on several major projects, including an investigation into the total scope of environmental quality in the city of Albuquerque, N.M., and its environs, involving recommendations for action programs and procedures for environmental improvement.

WILLIAM NICOSON is a consultant on urban affairs practicing in Washington, D.C. He joined HUD in 1969 and in

1970 became the first director of its Office of New Communities Development, a post which he held until 1972. He is a member of the Bar in Washington and New York State. He has also practiced law in Paris.

GEORGE J. PILLORGÉ, AIA, AIP, is vice president and studio director of RTKL Inc., Baltimore. He has been the principal in charge of many large-scale commissions, including Montgomery Village, Spring Park New Community, and Canton New Community. He has conducted a macro-transportation impact study for the city of New Orleans, and a central business district study for Jacksonville, Fla. His projects have been published in several professional journals both here and abroad.

RALPH RAPSON, FAIA, is a practicing architect and head of the University of Minnesota School of Architecture. His works, which have brought him numerous awards, range from custom houses to large-scale civic, educational, and residential projects. He was formerly head of the Department of Architecture of the Institute of Design, Chicago, and an associate professor of architecture at MIT.

MALCOLM D. RIVKIN, AIP, is president of Rivkin/Carson Inc., development planners of Washington, D.C. The firm's activities range from market and feasibility studies to the preparation of housing programs and association with architects on programming and implementation of complex development projects. He has been a consultant on new communities to the U.S. Department of Transportation and on regional planning to the United Nations. He was formerly director of urban and regional development for Robert R. Nathan Associates Inc.

LLOYD RODWIN, AIP, is head of MIT's Department of Urban Studies and Planning and director of its special program for urban and regional studies. A specialist in planning theory and developing countries, he served as director of the Guayana Project of the Harvard/MIT Joint Center for Urban Studies, as well as consultant to the United Nations, the Organization for European Economic Cooperation, and many other governmental and private agencies in Central and South America, Canada and Europe. His publications include *The British New Towns Policy* and *Nations and Cities: A Comparison of Strategies for Urban Growth.*

ARCHIBALD C. ROGERS, FAIA, AIP, is chairman of the board of RTKL Inc., Baltimore. He is the 1973 first vice president and 1974 president-designate of The American Institute of Architects, as well as chairman of the Institute's National Policy Task Force, whose report appears elsewhere in this book. In 1966, he developed guidelines for a team approach to highway planning which led to the establishment of the Urban Design Concept Team to plan Baltimore's expressway system. His extensive public and professional service has included positions as chairman of the 1970 Indian-American Symposium on Architecture and Urban Design, a member of the Governor's Council on the Arts in Maryland, and chairman of the AIA Committee on Urban Design. He is currently a visiting lecturer at Virginia Theological Seminary.

GEORGE ROMNEY is chairman of Concerned Citizens Movement Inc., a non-profit membership organization devoted to the improvement of the quality of life in the U.S. He resigned as Secretary of the U.S. Department of Housing and

Urban Development in 1972 after serving four years. From 1963 to 1969 he was Governor of Michigan. He is the former president, chairman, and general manager of American Motors.

LAWRENCE SUSSKIND is an assistant professor in the Department of Urban Studies and Planning at MIT. He is codirector of two research projects dealing with alternative development strategies for the Boston region and national urban growth strategies. He is a doctoral fellow at the Harvard/MIT Joint Center for Urban Studies and has served as a consultant to the Massachusetts Department of Community Affairs.

ROBERT TENNENBAUM, AIA, AIP, is vice president for urban design and architecture, and a member of the board of directors of RTKL Inc., Baltimore. He is responsible for the management of urban design, land planning, and architectural projects for the organization. Under his direction, major new-community projects have been developed in New York, New Jersey, Maryland, Texas, and Florida. Before joining RTKL he was chief architect and planner with The Rouse Company for six years in Columbia, Md.

ALAN M. VOORHEES is president of Alan M. Voorhees & Associates Inc., transportation consultants. He has assisted in the planning of such new towns as Columbia, Reston, Fort Lincoln, and Canberra, Australia. He has been involved in a large number of planning programs, including those for such metropolitan areas as Los Angeles, St. Louis, Boston, Washington, Baltimore, Houston, Detroit, Minneapolis/St. Paul, Miami, and Seattle. He has also conducted extensive research in urban travel and the factors affecting urban growth.

RALPH WARBURTON, AIA, AIP, is dean of the University of Miami's Department of Architecture and Architectural Engineering; a senior partner in the firm of Ferendino, Grafton, Spillis, Candela, architects, planners, and engineers of Coral Gables, Fla., and a consultant in urban design to the U.S. Department of Housing and Urban Development. He previously served for five years as a special assistant for urban design at HUD. He has served as professional adviser for the HUD Design Awards program since 1968.

RAYMOND L. WATSON, AIA, is executive vice president and a director of the land development division of The Irvine Company. His responsibilities include the operations of the departments of planning, residential development and management, commercial development and management, and multifamily development and management. He is also a director and vice president of the Irvine Industrial Complex and chairman of the board and president of Community Cablevision Company, both wholly owned subsidiaries of The Irvine Company. He is a guest lecturer at the University of Southern California and the University of California's Riverside, Irvine, and Los Angeles campuses.

Westlake Village, California

I. THE EVOLUTION OF AMERICAN NEW TOWNS

Every new town, for better or worse, is an expression of the "stream of history," states Archibald C. Rogers in Part II of this volume.

The new towns, past and present, whose master plans are reproduced on the following pages, are no exceptions. Some, like Savannah and Washington, were inspired individual attempts to superimpose the idealism of a hopeful new country onto familiar European planning and architectural prototypes. Others, like Pullman, Ill., set out to uplift the lot of the workingman (and keep him loyal) by giving him an inspired—and inspiring—living environment. Still others, like Radburn, Baldwin Hills Village, and the Greenbelt towns, tried to show Americans that the Garden City was a better alternative than sprawl.

Each of these new communities was indeed part of the "stream of history," but the question is, How important a part? Certainly none of them was in the mainstream. Their influence on the growth and development of our nation—as well as on their own expansion—has been infinitesimal. While Savannah and Washington's original plans may remain more or less intact, there is little relationship between them and the chaotic development that has grown outward from them. And while Radburn, Baldwin Hills, and the Greenbelt towns are still with us (and still demonstrating the wisdom of their original concepts), the forces that have produced suburban sprawl have taken little notice of them.

Today's new towns are yet another attempt to influence the mainstream of U.S. urban development—though there are those who argue that, unfortunately, they are *in* the mainstream. Sociologist Herbert Gans, speaking before a meeting of the American Jewish Committee, has said that the current crop of new towns are "little more than slightly superior suburbs" based on old political, economic, and social power mechanisms. (Most of the authors in this volume acknowledge this condition, and they propose a number of techniques and methods for overcoming it.)

Is there any reason to hope that the new wave of new towns can make a difference in the pattern of unplanned agglomeration that has been gaining momentum for decades? If, like their predecessors, they are merely to be built as good examples that others, having seen the light, will follow, then the answer is almost certainly no. But if they become an important element in a plan for national urban growth that will improve the quality of community life, then new towns will at long last be more than dreams for utopians to cling to.

A concern for the "stream of history," Rogers states, "is not an excuse for nostalgic romanticism, even though there are ennobling elements of the past that can be reinterpreted for the present. Nor is it an excuse for a brutal futurism that can alienate society. Rather, it is an opportunity for honest experimentation with new forms and systems in which the community itself can participate."

PHILADELPHIA, PENNSYLVANIA 1685

William Penn and his surveyor general, Captain Thomas Holme, were primarily responsible for planning the first large American city to be laid out on a grid pattern, setting a precedent that virtually all other American cities followed. Drawn for a flat site lying between the Schuylkill and Delaware Rivers, the plan focuses on a 10-acre central square where the City Hall, topped by a statue of William Penn, now stands. Emanating from the square are the two major thoroughfares of the plan, Broad and High Streets, which bisect the city. Four other squares of similar size form the only other open space contained in the plan. The plan later underwent many subsequent revisions, including the addition of streets within the generous-sized city blocks laid out by Penn and Holmes.

Total acres: 1,200

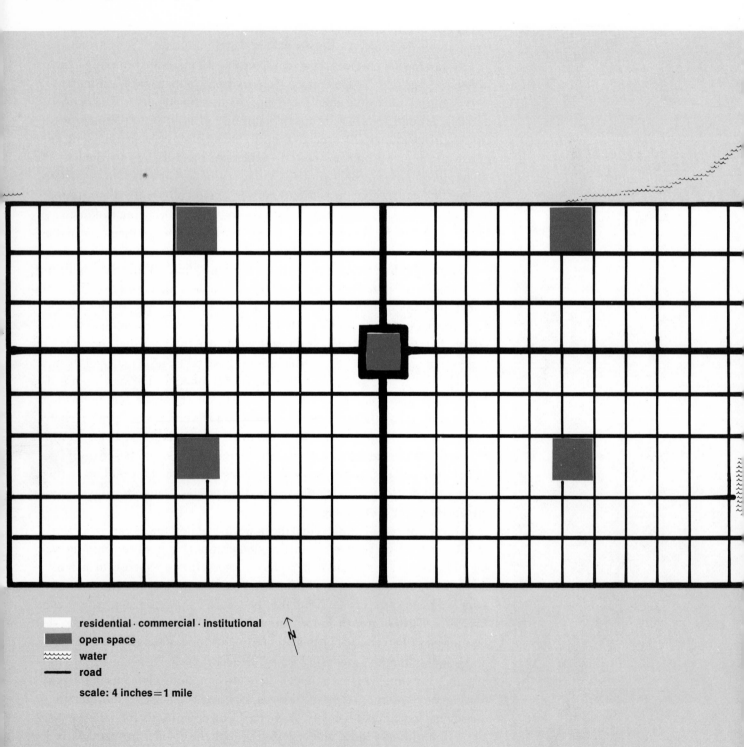

☐ residential · commercial · institutional
■ open space
〰 water
▬ road

scale: 4 inches = 1 mile

NEW ORLEANS, LOUISIANA 1722

The plan of the original part of New Orleans, which remains substantially intact today as the famous Vieux Carré, is one of the earliest and best examples of French colonial town planning in America. Jean Baptisti, Sieur de Bienville, who earlier had planned Mobile, and Adrien de Pauger, an engineer, laid out the site as a walled settlement fronting on a deep bend of the Mississippi. Its focal point is the *place d'armes*, now Jackson Square, which the planners placed at the river's edge behind the central section of a long quay. The *place* served not only as a parade ground, but also as an appropriate setting for the new town's principal building, the church, which faces the square on its inland side. As the city enlarged, the old walls were demolished and replaced by the present-day Canal Street, North Rampart Street, and Esplanade Avenue.

Total acres: 320

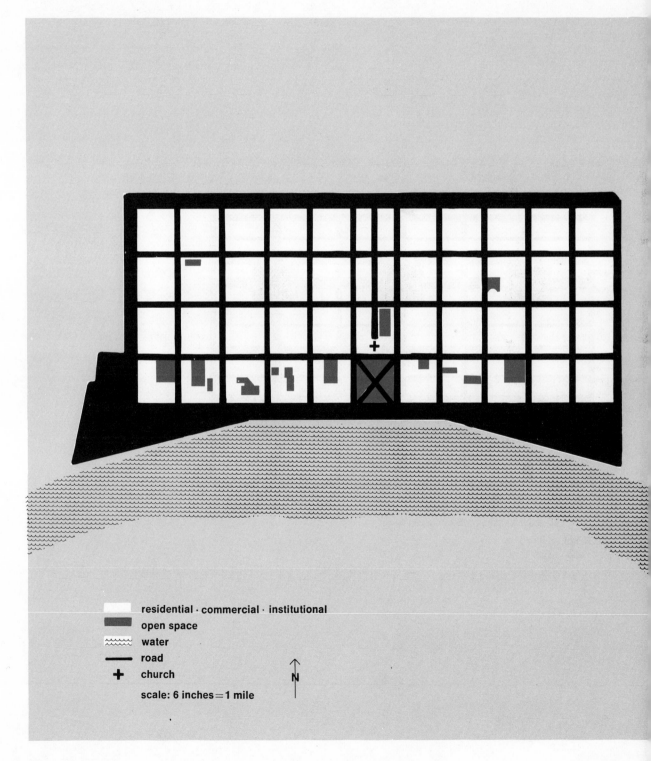

▫ residential · commercial · institutional
▪ open space
〜 water
— road
✚ church

scale: 6 inches = 1 mile

N

3

SAVANNAH, GEORGIA 1733

Savannah was founded and planned by James Oglethorpe, a member of the British House of Commons, who had brought 114 imprisoned debtors and impoverished persons to start a new life in America. Oglethorpe's original plan covered two square miles that now forms the center of the modern city. Its basic module is a "ward" composed of an open square, local streets, 40 house lots 60 by 90 feet, and, fronting the square on two sides, trustee lots for churches, stores, and other public and semipublic uses. The main streets were 75 feet wide, with minor streets half as wide and lanes at the rear of the house lots 22½ feet wide. Fifteen additional wards were added to the original six before the Civil War. After that, Oglethorpe's unique concept was abandoned and the city continued to expand on a standard gridiron system.

Total acres: 1,280

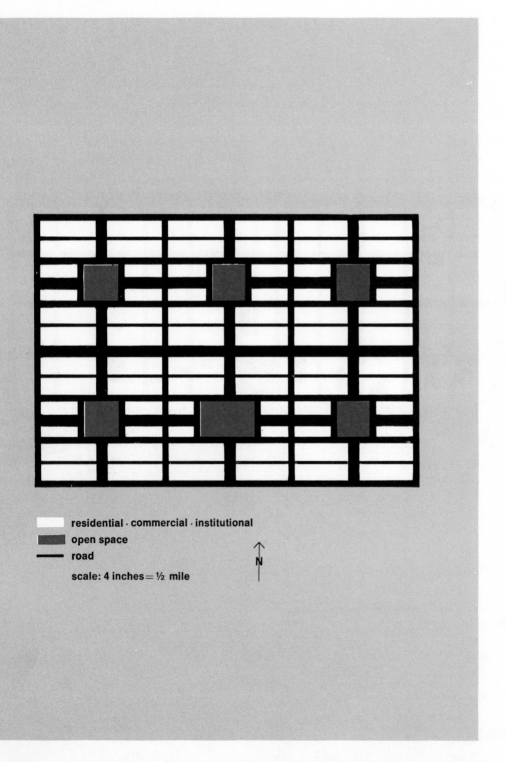

■ residential · commercial · institutional
■ open space
— road

scale: 4 inches = ½ mile

N

WASHINGTON, D.C. 1791

Major Pierre Charles L'Enfant's grandiose plan for the nation's capital is perhaps the most ambitious ever prepared for an American city. Laid out under the watchful eye of Washington and Jefferson, the plan embodies L'Enfant's familiarity with, and admiration of, Versailles and Paris. It introduced new planning concepts to this country that had an influence on many later city plans. The plan is basically a grid system on which are superimposed broad, tree-lined radial avenues intersecting at circles where

L'Enfant envisioned majestic fountains and parks. Though the plan has undergone many changes, it has been followed to a far greater degree than many other plans for American cities and towns. This is largely due to the fact that L'Enfant's composition was "rediscovered" in the late 19th Century, and the plan was again used a guide to the city's growth.

Total acres: 5,700

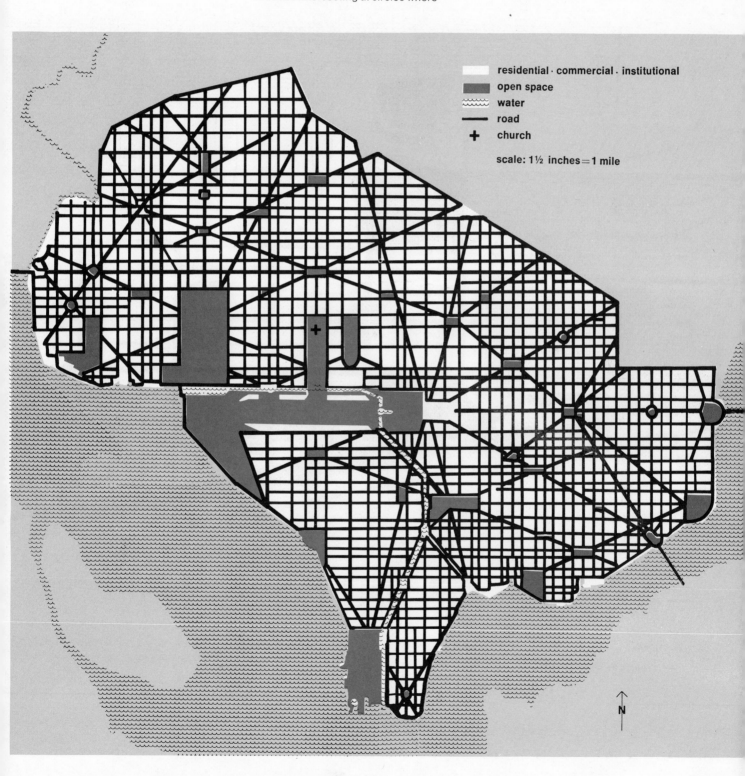

residential · commercial · institutional
open space
water
road
church

scale: 1½ inches = 1 mile

N

PULLMAN, ILLINOIS 1880

Sleeping-car manufacturer George Pullman established his company town on Lake Calumet 12 miles south of Chicago. The plan, by Architect Solon S. Beman and Landscape Architect Nathan F. Barrett, was the first since that of Williamsburg to pay as much attention to the design of the individual buildings as to the layout of streets, parks, and building sites. Though it follows the basic grid pattern, the plan avoids monotony by treating streets as enclosed ways lined with row houses or apartments. The major open spaces are a large park and public square situated between the Pullman factory and the railroad station, and a market square intersected by four streets. The Pullman Company maintained complete ownership of land and all the buildings until 1894, when the Supreme Court ordered the company to divest itself of all but its manufacturing property. After that the town began to decay, and only in recent years have projects been undertaken to restore some of the original character.

Total acres: 300

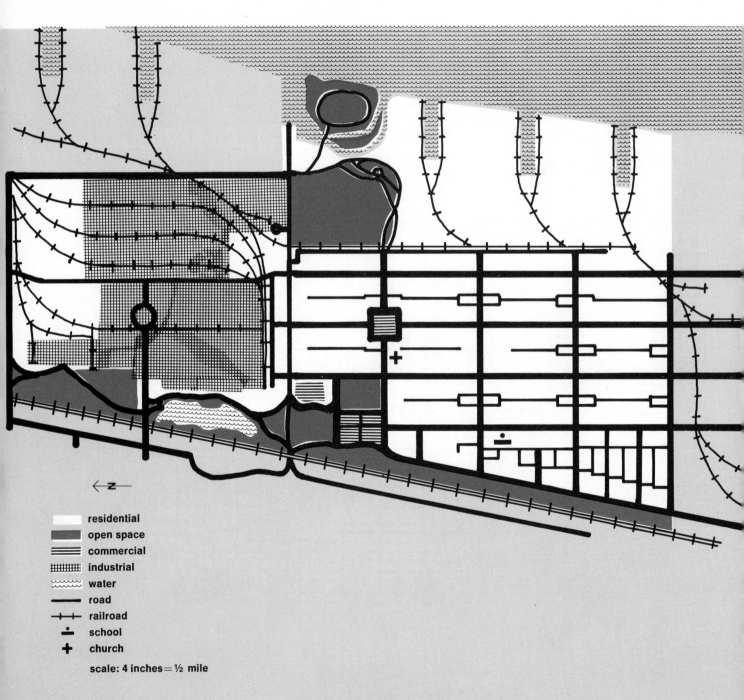

← N

	residential
	open space
	commercial
	industrial
	water
	road
	railroad
	school
	church

scale: 4 inches = ½ mile

CORAL GABLES, FLORIDA 1921

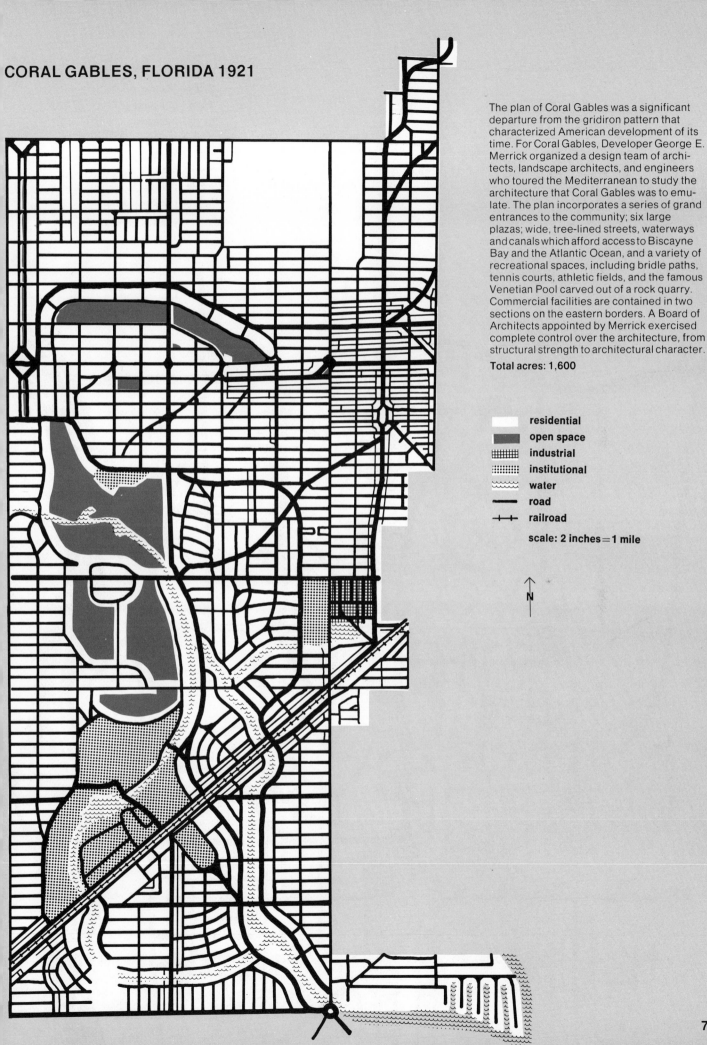

The plan of Coral Gables was a significant departure from the gridiron pattern that characterized American development of its time. For Coral Gables, Developer George E. Merrick organized a design team of architects, landscape architects, and engineers who toured the Mediterranean to study the architecture that Coral Gables was to emulate. The plan incorporates a series of grand entrances to the community; six large plazas; wide, tree-lined streets, waterways and canals which afford access to Biscayne Bay and the Atlantic Ocean, and a variety of recreational spaces, including bridle paths, tennis courts, athletic fields, and the famous Venetian Pool carved out of a rock quarry. Commercial facilities are contained in two sections on the eastern borders. A Board of Architects appointed by Merrick exercised complete control over the architecture, from structural strength to architectural character.

Total acres: 1,600

- residential
- open space
- industrial
- institutional
- water
- road
- railroad

scale: 2 inches = 1 mile

N

RADBURN, NEW JERSEY 1928

Radburn brought Ebenezer Howard's Garden City concepts to the U.S. and opened a new era in American planning. For Radburn, Architect/Planner Clarence Stein and Planner Henry Wright adapted Howard's ideas to a plan "in which people could live peacefully with the automobile—or rather in spite of it." The plan utilizes superblocks instead of the conventional rectangular block. The roads are planned for one use: service lanes for direct access to buildings, secondary collector roads around the superblocks, main through roads, and express highways. There is complete separation of pedestrians and automobiles. Large open spaces in the center of the superblocks, on which the houses face, are joined together by pathways to form a continuous park. Though the development ran into financial difficulties and could not be completed, it remains the most influential prototype of modern town planning.

Total acres: 640

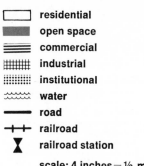

residential
open space
commercial
industrial
institutional
water
road
railroad
railroad station

scale: 4 inches = ½ mile

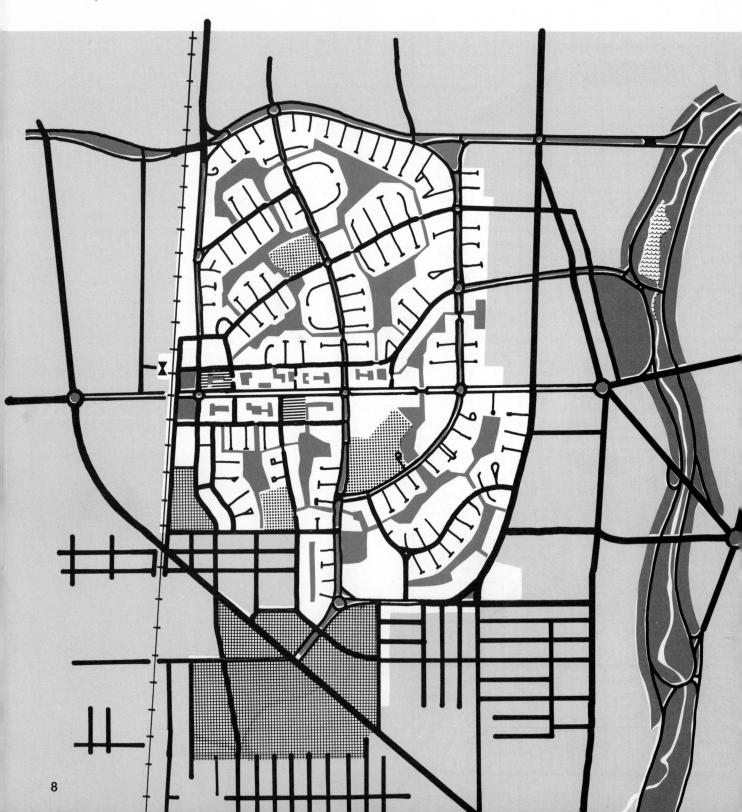

GREENBELT, MARYLAND 1935

Greenbelt was the first of three new towns built by the suburban resettlement division of the Federal Resettlement Administration under the direction of Rexford Guy Tugwell. They were the first to combine the three basic ideas of modern community planning: the Garden City, the Radburn concept, and the Neighborhood Unit. Hale Walker's plan for Greenbelt follows a natural, crescent-shaped plateau surrounded by woods. Two major roads, Crescent and Ridge Road, form the perimeter of the crescent. The area between is cut about every 1,000 feet by connecting streets which divide the site into residential superblocks. The inner crescent cups the community center, the focal point of the town. This is the seat of government and the location of the community's cultural, religious, educational, recreational, entertainment, and marketing activities. Though some of the woodlands have been sold for development, Greenbelt remains largely intact today.

Total acres: 3,370

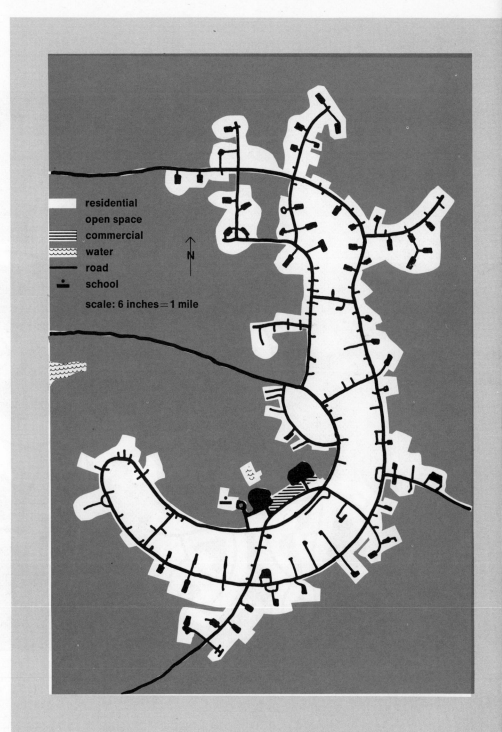

residential
open space
commercial
water
road
school

scale: 6 inches = 1 mile

N

GREENHILLS, OHIO 1936

The plan for Greenhills, executed by Justin R. Hartzog and William A. Strong, follows the natural contours of the undulating, wooded site. The many ravines of the site are preserved in the open space system. The plan generally follows the Radburn concept, though not as completely as that of Greenbelt. An interior path system is not included, thereby isolating the interior commons and negating the idea of a pedestrian communication system. In the center of the plan, fronting on an inner park, are a shopping center, common, community school and swimming pool. A large playfield is situated at the southeast edge of the site.

Total acres: 5,900

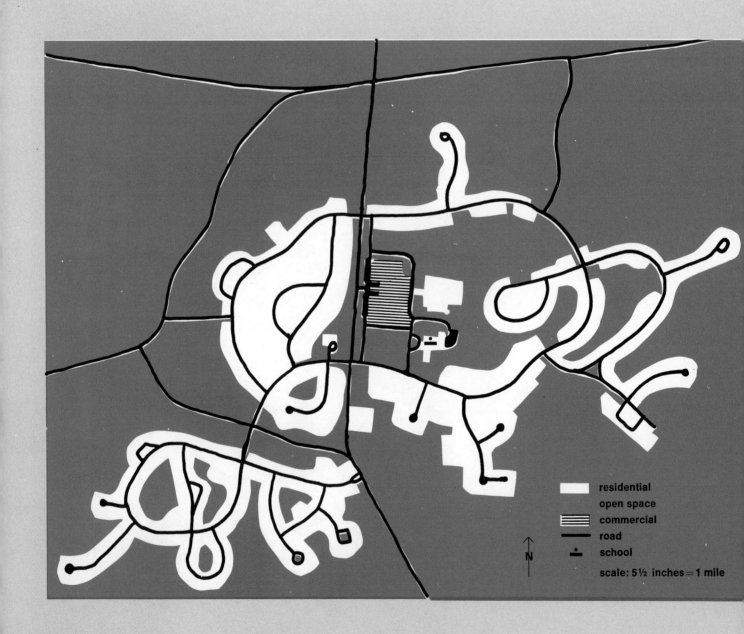

residential
open space
commercial
road
school

N

scale: 5½ inches = 1 mile

GREENDALE, WISCONSIN 1936

Greendale's plan, though based on the Radburn idea, takes a somewhat different approach. Planners Jacob Crane and Elbert Peets discarded a full system of superblocks in favor of row houses backing up to each other rather than fronting on a central open space. Nevertheless, the plan is well related to its natural site, preserving such features as a stream that flows into the center of the town. The plan also creates a system of internal greenways of various sizes, most of which are also natural drainage channels.

While there is no separation of pedestrians and vehicles, the system of roads, and the placement of housing in relation to the roads, creates an effectively safe environment.

Total acres: 3,400

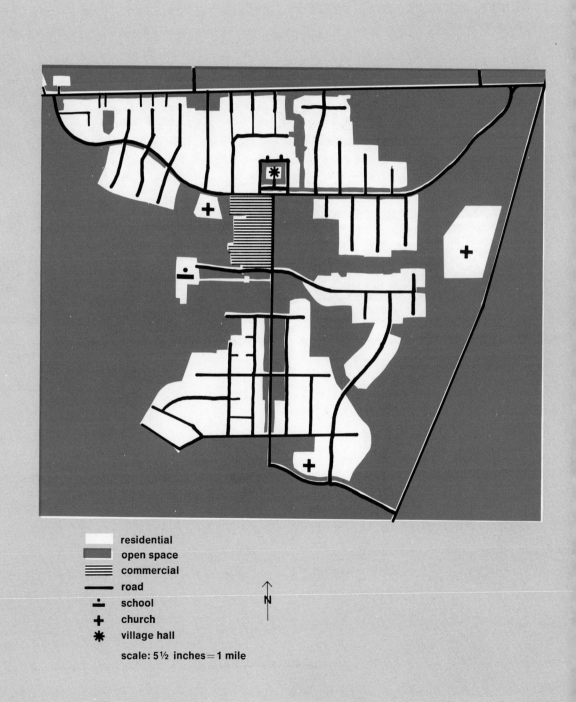

residential
open space
commercial
road
school
church
village hall

scale: 5½ inches = 1 mile

BALDWIN HILLS VILLAGE, LOS ANGELES, CALIFORNIA 1941

At Baldwin Hills Village, states Clarence S Stein in his book, *Toward New Towns for America,* "the Radburn Idea was given its most complete and most characteristic expression." Like Radburn's, its plan incorporates superblocks, houses facing central greens, and the separation of pedestrians and autos. There are no streets within the Village, and the dead-ends of the Radburn prototype have been replaced by garage courts. The planners and designers, Reginald D. Johnson and Wilson, Merrill & Alexander,

devoted a quarter of the site to green commons consisting of inner parks and garden courts. Walled patios for the private use of ground-floor tenants—and even some second-floor residents—are situated on the garage court side of the houses. Lewis Mumford has said of Baldwin Hills Village: "Here every part of the design speaks the same robust vernacular: simple, direct, intelligible. I know of no other recent community that lends itself so fully to strict scrutiny, simply because every aspect of its

physical development has been thought through.

Total acres: 80

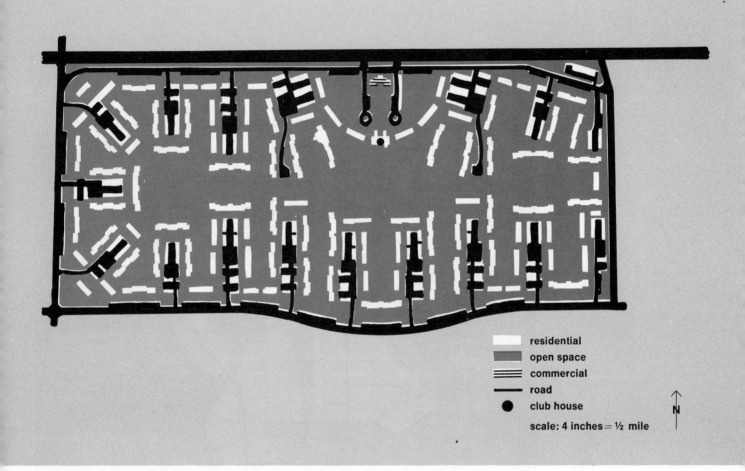

residential
open space
commercial
road
club house
scale: 4 inches = ½ mile
N

PARK FOREST, ILLINOIS 1947

The first of the post-World War II new communities, Park Forest is both a product of its time and a forerunner of later new-town developments. Though its single-family housing is executed in much the same fashion as thousands of subdivisions throughout the country, Park Forest's virtue is that it incorporates its housing into a larger scheme that preserves open space and controls the orderly development of commercial, industrial, institutional, and recreational facilities. The commercial center of the village joins the two major single-family and multifamily sections, both of which front on a large central park. An industrial park links the southern portion of the irregular site with a smaller single-family section to the north. Preparation of a new comprehensive plan for the village was begun in 1972.

Total acres: 2,700

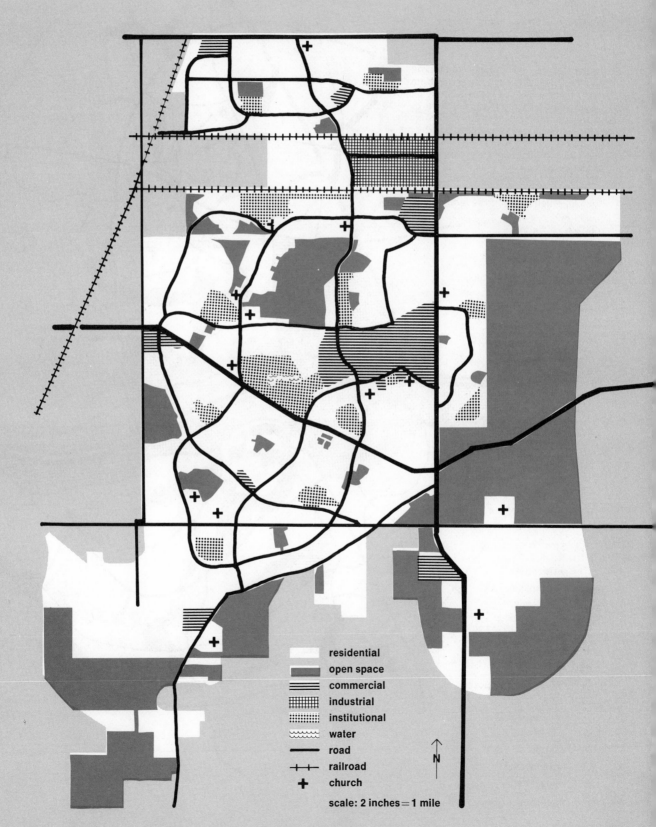

	residential
	open space
	commercial
	industrial
	institutional
	water
	road
	railroad
	church

N

scale: 2 inches = 1 mile

13

RESTON, VIRGINIA 1962

Reston shares with Columbia the distinction of having laid the groundwork for the now-burgeoning new-towns movement in America. Reston is the brainchild of developer Robert E. Simon, who envisioned the new town as a "serious experiment in urban planning undertaken on a city-wide scale, and an attempt to discover what should be done to create a quality environment." Projecting an ultimate population of 70,000, Reston's plan calls for two town centers and seven villages, each of the latter having a population of 10,000 and shopping, retail, educational, and recreational facilities, and each separated from others by open space. There is a wide mix of housing types, ranging from high-rise luxury apartments to townhouse clusters to single-family houses on large lots in the outlying villages. Some 1,300 acres are devoted to industrial uses, providing jobs for a projected 30,000 persons. In 1967, a tight money market forced Simon to surrender control to the principal investor, Gulf Oil, which has made several alterations in the plan.

Total acres: 7,400

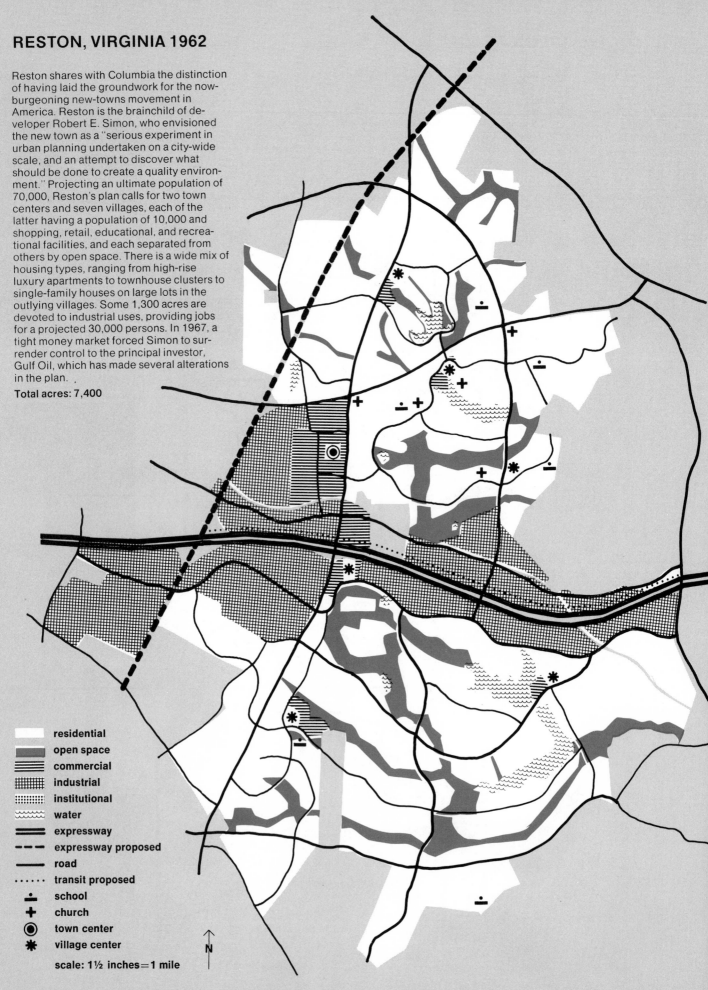

residential
open space
commercial
industrial
institutional
water
expressway
expressway proposed
road
transit proposed
 school
 church
 town center
 village center

scale: 1½ inches = 1 mile

N

14

HERITAGE VILLAGE, SOUTHBURY, CONNECTICUT 1966

Basically a retirement community, Heritage
Village occupies a beautifully wooded,
rolling site. All of its housing, which eventually will accommodate 4,200 to 4,700
persons, is grouped in cul-de-sac clusters
of townhouses joined by a system of pathways. All of the pathways culminate at the
Village Green, a 30-acre complex containing
a 22-store shopping center, a financial
building, a market building, and a professional building. The Pomperaug River forms
the eastern boundary of the site. (*See pp.111-113.*)

Total acres: 1,005

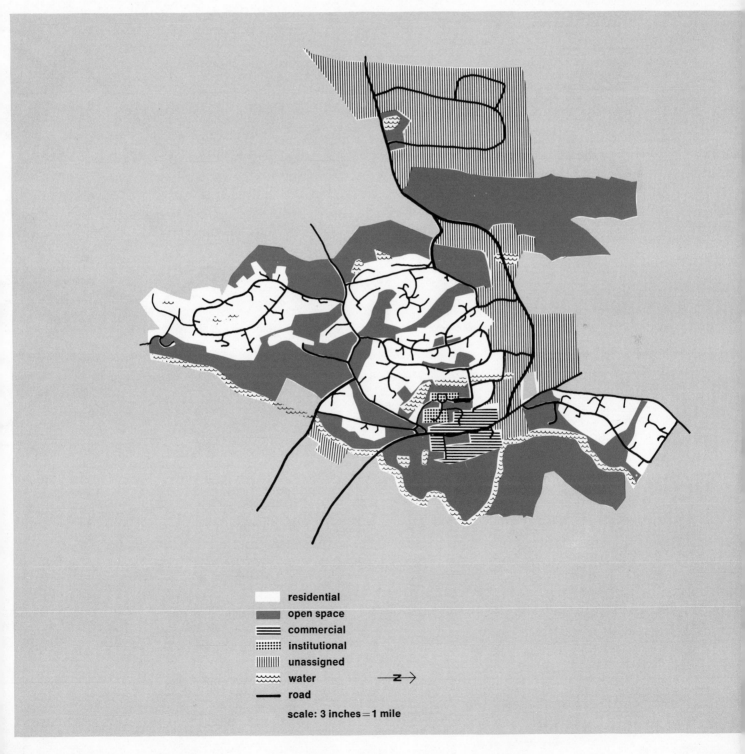

residential
open space
commercial
institutional
unassigned
water
road

scale: 3 inches = 1 mile

15

COLUMBIA, MARYLAND 1963

For Columbia, developer James Rouse set as his basic goals "to create a social and physical environment which works for people and nourishes human growth and to allow private venture capital to make a profit in land development and sale." Rouse initiated the multidisciplinary approach to planning and design—a process that has been followed in varying degrees by every major new town since Columbia. The plan is designed to accommodate some 110,000 residents when Columbia is completed in 1981. It contains seven villages clustered around a downtown core, each consisting of three or more distinctive neighborhoods and a village center for shopping and community activities. The 2,600 acres set aside for industrial use are expected to provide employment for some 13,500 persons in light manufacturing and research and development. The downtown is planned as a regional center serving a population of some 250,000 for shopping, educational, health, cultural, and recreational needs.

Total acres: 17,000

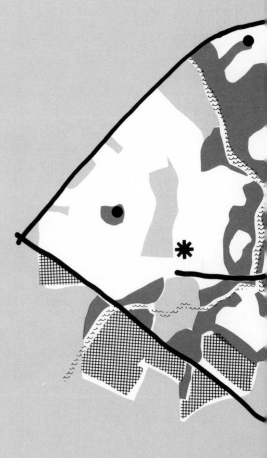

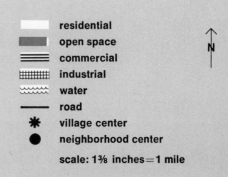

residential
open space
commercial
industrial
water
road
village center
neighborhood center

scale: 1⅜ inches = 1 mile

16

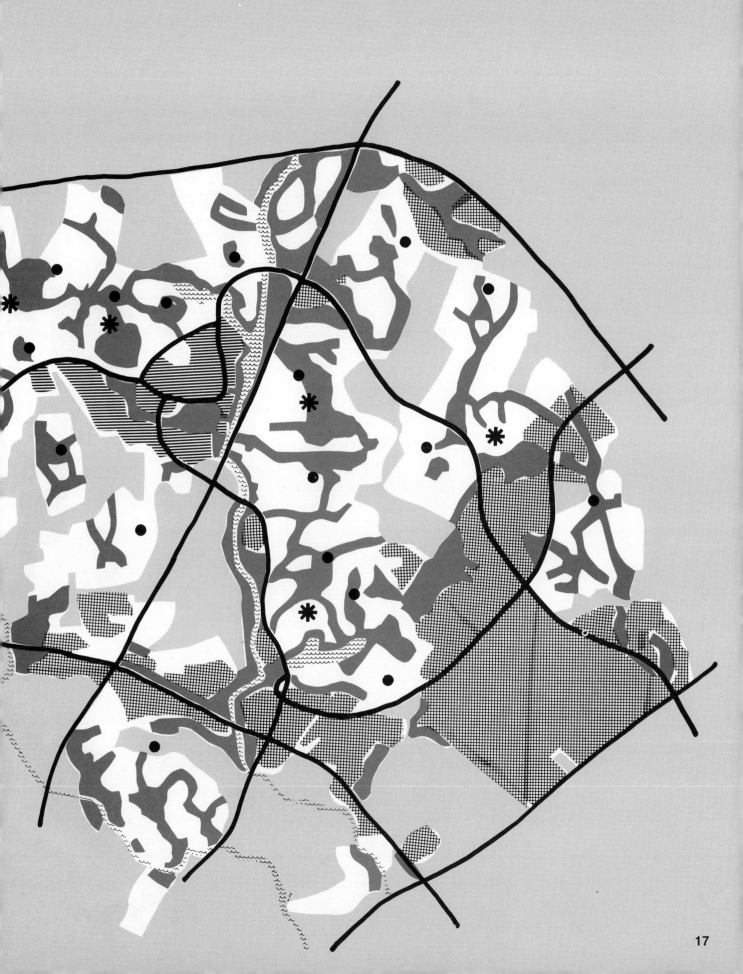

LAKE HAVASU CITY, ARIZONA 1964

Lake Havasu City occupies the most remote location of any of the new towns now under development. It lies in a thinly populated area 235 miles east of Los Angeles and 120 miles south of Las Vegas. Its founder and developer, Industrialist Robert P. McCulloch, envisions a "self-contained" city of 60,000 population when the development is completed. The plan calls for conventional single-family and multifamily housing developments centering on a linear core containing a civic center, shopping plaza, commercial area, medical park, and library. Dividing the core is the main street of the community, McCulloch Boulevard, which is connected to an island (formerly a peninsula) jutting into the Colorado River by the reassembled London Bridge. Most of the recreational facilities are situated along the 22 miles of shoreline at the edge of the city. (*See pp. 90-93.*)

Total acres: 16,630

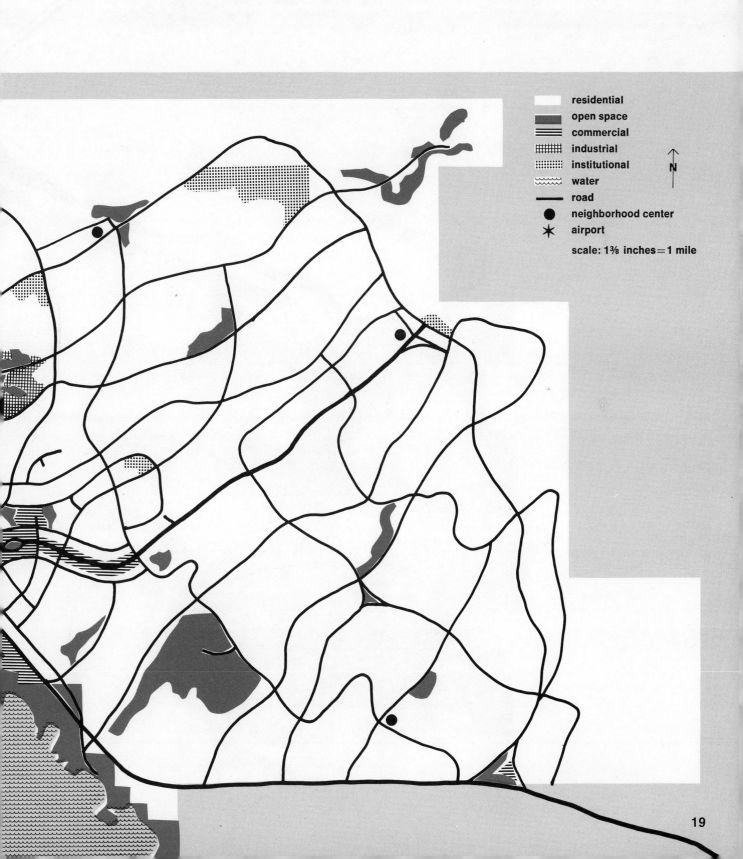

residential
open space
commercial
industrial
institutional
water
road
● neighborhood center
✳ airport

N

scale: 1⅜ inches = 1 mile

19

WALT DISNEY WORLD, FLORIDA 1968

Phase one of Walt Disney World was a 100-acre amusement park, completed in the fall of 1971. But its developer has much more in mind. One is EPCOT—Experimental Prototype Community of Tomorrow— scheduled for construction beginning in 1981. Envisioned as a laboratory for the testing of urban systems and urban concepts, EPCOT will contain a vertical core built atop a multilevel platform housing transportation nodes, shopping, and community services. Streets or other transportation lines will radiate from the core to serve clusters of residential communities housing 20,000 persons. Already under development is Lake Buena Vista, the first residential community. It is planned for 16,500 residents and 4,000 employees on a 4,000-acre site that also will contain a group of hotels and a commercial center. Almost a third of the site for Walt Disney World—7,500 acres— will be set aside as a wilderness preserve.

Total acres: 27,000

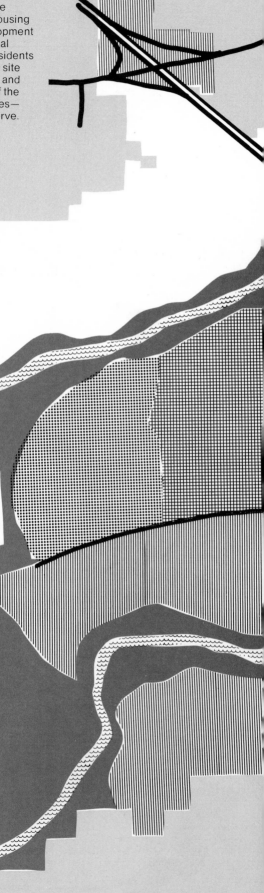

residential
open space
commercial
industrial
institutional epcot
unassigned
water
expressway
road
airport

← N →

scale: 1¼ inches = 1 mile

21

PARK FOREST SOUTH, ILLINOIS 1968

Park Forest South is being developed by the builder of Park Forest, which it adjoins on a site 30 miles south of Chicago. Planned for a total population of 110,000, the new town will contain more than 11,000 single-family and 24,000 multifamily units, including 4,500 units of subsidized housing for low- and moderate-income families. Its central element will be a linear, multilevel town center containing pedestrian malls and terraced plazas ringed by stores, restaurants, shops, and theaters. The center is connected to an internal transit system and rapid commuter lines to the Chicago loop, and the road network. Another major focal point is the 15,000-student Governors State University, a "senior college" for commuting students who have graduated from community and junior colleges. More than one in every four acres will be preserved as open space or recreation areas. Bicycle paths and walkways will join residential areas with shopping centers, 26 schools, and the university. (*See pp. 80-85.*)

Total acres: 8,291

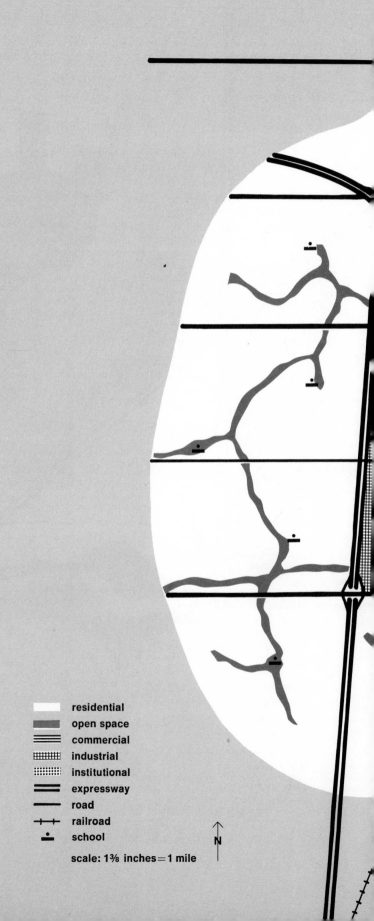

	residential
	open space
	commercial
	industrial
	institutional
	expressway
	road
	railroad
	school

scale: 1⅜ inches = 1 mile

N

JONATHAN, MINNESOTA 1969

Jonathan is situated in a farming area 20 miles southwest of Minneapolis. Its plan calls for an ultimate population of 50,000 in five villages linked by a system of pedestrianways. The villages and a sixth subcenter, an industrial park, surround a regional-scale town center containing major retail, office, medical, entertainment and apartment structures. Directly adjacent to the town center is a higher education complex planned to include a business and vocational school and colleges of liberal arts and physical sciences. This "learning center" will function as the basic core for the community's library/information storage and retrieval system, which will be tied into the communications network. Conceived as an essentially self-contained community, nearly a quarter of the site—1,989 acres—has been set aside for industrial use. Another 1,700 acres are devoted to open space, including a number of natural lakes that dot the site. (*See pp. 49-55.*)

Total acres: 8,193

- ☐ residential
- ◼ open space
- ▤ commercial
- ▦ industrial
- ▨ institutional
- 〰 water
- ── road
- ┼┼┼ railroad
- ✚ church

scale: 1³⁄₁₆ inches = 1 mile

ST. CHARLES, MARYLAND 1970

St. Charles is the first major new community in the nation to focus primarily on the housing needs of lower-income families. Eighty per cent of the project's 9,927 single-family homes will sell for $25,000 or less, and one out of four of the 9,195 apartment rental units will lease for $150 or less a month. To preserve a small-town atmosphere and the rural environment of the site, situated 30 miles south of Washington, D.C., the plan calls for 15 neighborhoods grouped into five villages of 4,000 to 4,500 families. Each village focuses on a parklike "square" around which schools and athletic fields, churches, community buildings, child-care centers, swimming pools, tennis courts, local shopping and other services will be located. Each of the 15 neighborhoods contains convenience shopping, recreation, and community meeting facilities. About 30 per cent of the site is planned as permanent open space and another 15 per cent is devoted to campus-style industrial parks, office buildings, and commercial facilities. The projected total population is 75,000.

Total acres: 7,900

residential
open space
commercial
industrial
water
expressway
road
railroad
* village center
● neighborhood center

scale: 1½ inches = 1 mile

N

25

MAUMELLE, ARKANSAS 1970

Maumelle is situated 12 miles north of Little Rock on a rolling site that has 3½ miles of frontage on the Arkansas River. It is planned for a population of 48,000 to 60,000 in five self-contained villages, each with its own shopping, recreation, and school facilities. Of the projected 14,350 dwelling units, 4,164 will be single-family detached homes; 6,020 duplexes, town houses, or garden apartments, and 4,166 mid-rise and high-rise apartment units. Maumelle's schools are proposed for year-round use as social, civic, and educational centers. Industrial use is planned for 1,071 acres, with rail and barge access. A town center fronting on a 55-acre lake at the center of the site will contain major department stores, specialty shops, apartments, office buildings, restaurants and nightclubs, a high school and community college, recreational facilities, and health centers. A health delivery system will provide health care in association with area hospitals and other health facilities.

Total acres: 5,319

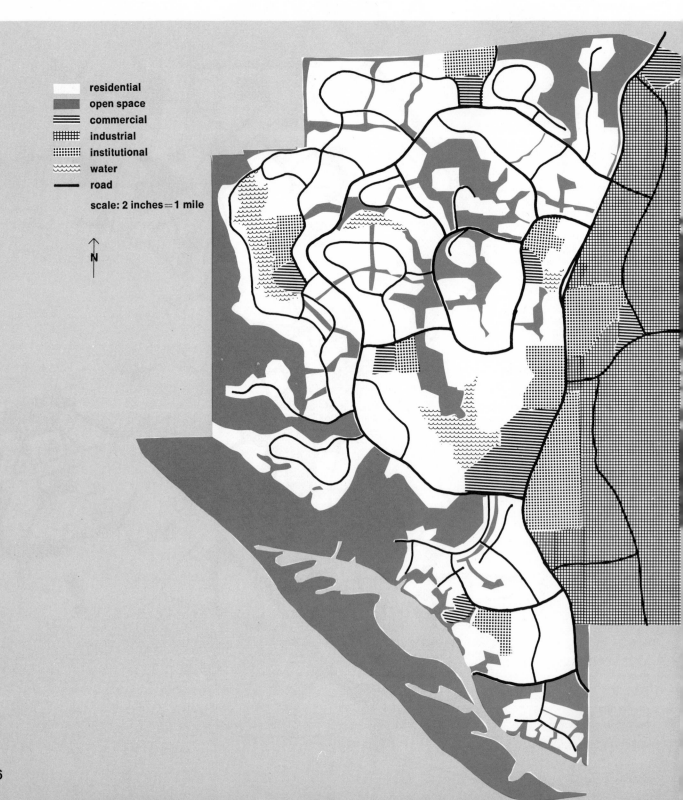

residential
open space
commercial
industrial
institutional
water
road

scale: 2 inches = 1 mile

N

LYSANDER NEW COMMUNITY, LYSANDER, NEW YORK 1971

A project of the New York State Urban Development Corporation, Lysander New Town is an attempt to introduce orderly growth and development within an area of urban sprawl near Syracuse. The major elements of the plan are a town center with adjacent major school facilities and industrial research and office facilities; a subcenter with minor commercial facilities in the northeast area of the site fronting on a golf course and marina, and 800 acres of industrial area on the western boundary. The proposed 5,000 dwelling units—30 per cent of them for low-income families—will be of high density near the town center, and of decreasing densities toward the boundaries of the site. When the development is completed in 1980, it will have an estimated population of 18,000 and provide employment for 12,000.

Total acres: 2,700

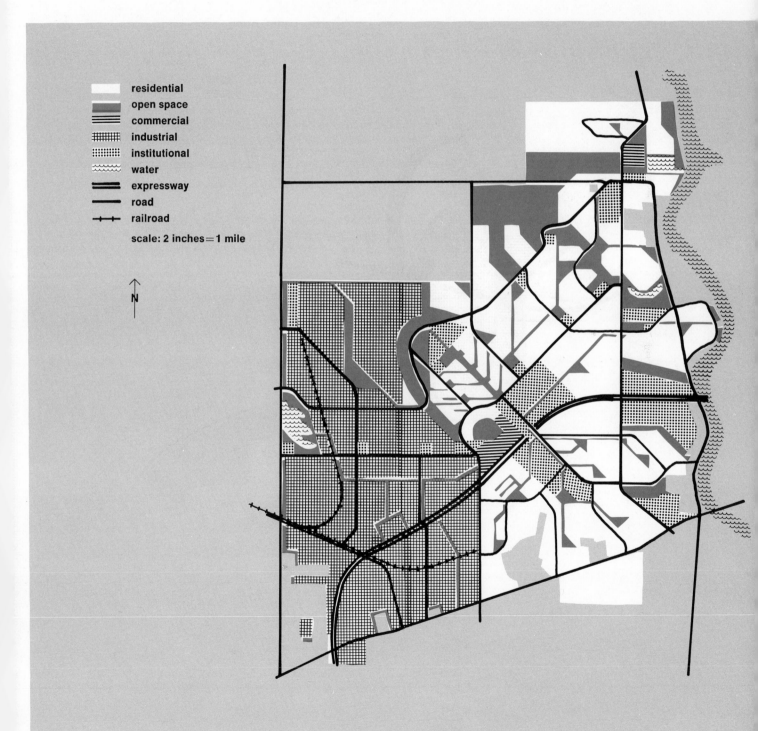

residential
open space
commercial
industrial
institutional
water
expressway
road
railroad

scale: 2 inches = 1 mile

N

CEDAR/RIVERSIDE, MINNEAPOLIS, MINNESOTA 1971

The nation's first new town in-town, Cedar/Riverside lies along the banks of the Mississippi 12 blocks from the heart of downtown Minneapolis. Its site is a largely deteriorated area of single-family homes and duplexes adjacent to a 240-acre area containing the University of Minnesota's West Bank campus, two colleges, and two major hospitals. The 15- to 20-year development plan calls for construction of 12,500 medium- and high-density, economically integrated dwelling units plus major commercial, hotel and office space in five individual neighborhoods clustered around a town "centrum." The projected population is 30,000, with the area serving a resident/visitor/working population of 75,000 daily. Approximately half of the housing units will receive some form of government subsidy. Pedestrian and vehicular traffic will be separated throughout the project. (*See pp. 49 and 54-55.*)

Total acres: 100

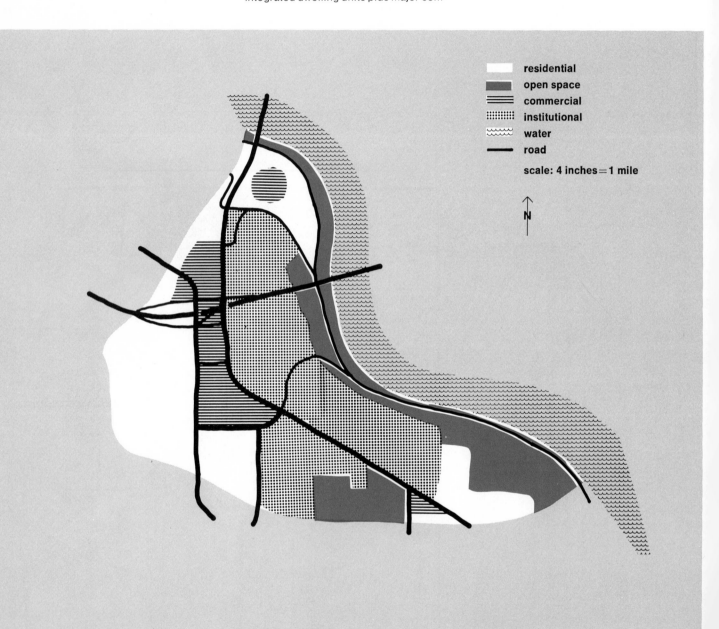

residential
open space
commercial
institutional
water
road

scale: 4 inches = 1 mile

N

AUDUBON, AMHERST, NEW YORK 1972

Audubon is being developed by the New York State Urban Development Corporation as a means of helping the town of Amherst absorb the impact of the new Buffalo campus of the State University of New York, which will have an estimated 26,000 students by 1977. The site, which incorporates the new campus at its southern edge, is pierced with existing subdivision developments that have been incorporated into the plan. The plan calls for the development of 9,000 residential units for an estimated 27,500 persons. The neighborhoods will be interspersed with commercial, office, and community facilities, as well as schools, playgrounds, and man-made lakes. Some 625 acres will be devoted to open space and recreational areas. A variety of housing types for a wide mix of income groups, including students and the elderly, will be dispersed throughout the site. Nearly 2,000 units will be subsidized.

Total acres: 2,000

□ residential
■ open space
≡ commercial
▓ institutional
∿ water
▬ expressway
— road

scale: 2 inches = 1 mile

N

29

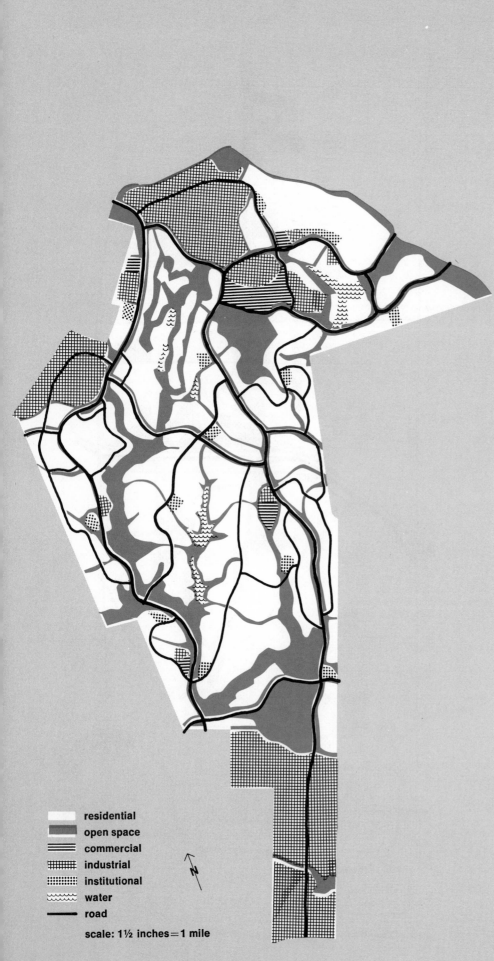

SAN ANTONIO RANCH, TEXAS 1972

Situated 16 miles northwest of downtown San Antonio, San Antonio Ranch is planned for an ultimate population of nearly 88,000 and a total of 28,676 dwelling units. Taking into consideration the economic and ethnic components of San Antonio's population, the plan calls for 29.2 per cent of the housing to be available to families with incomes under $7,500, and 76.6 per cent to those making under $10,500. Since San Antonio contains a large reservoir of unskilled labor, the plan allots 500 acres for a major vocational and technical training center. Residential areas on the largely hilly site are planned so that major streets need not be crossed to reach major activity areas, such as schools, shops, and parks. The plan includes two golf courses, three lakes, and three recreational centers containing swimming pools, tennis courts, and game fields.

Total acres: 9,318

residential
open space
commercial
industrial
institutional
water
road

scale: 1½ inches = 1 mile

RIVERTON, NEW YORK 1972

The Riverton site is about nine miles south of Rochester in the existing towns of Henrietta and Wheatland. A 400-acre industrial tract along the northern perimeter of the site will be bisected by the New York State Thruway, and the Genesee River defines the western boundary of the new town. Approximately 8,000 housing units, accommodating a total population of 27,000, will occupy 1,046 acres of the site. Of these, 2,790 will be garden apartments, 2,800 single-family houses, 1,520 sale and rental town houses, and 900 units in medium-high-rise apartments. The core of the community will be Riverton Center, the new community's downtown as well as a new regional center. The center will contain shops, theaters, restaurants, office towers, apartments, and a variety of social services fronting on a four-acre lake. (*See pp. 70-73.*)

Total acres: 2,350

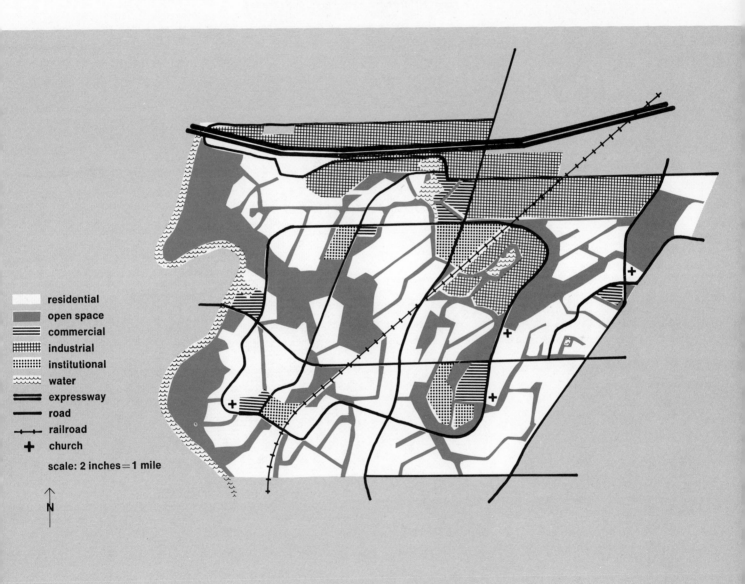

residential
open space
commercial
industrial
institutional
water
expressway
road
railroad
church

scale: 2 inches = 1 mile

N

FLOWER MOUND, TEXAS 1972

Flower Mound is being developed upon an existing small town situated among rolling grasslands some 20 miles northwest of Dallas. Its plan, to be developed over a period of 20 years for a total population of 64,000, calls for 14 neighborhoods grouped into four villages around the town center. Each village will have its own schools, shops, and parks and will be linked to other villages, the town center, and a 689-acre industrial park by a system of separated walkways and roads. A fourth of the site is reserved for open space, parks, golf courses, and neighborhood and village recreation areas, in addition to a parkland and marina development on the Grapevine Reservoir, which forms Flower Mound's southern boundary. Two major park systems will be developed through wooded areas and along stream beds. Complete health facilities, including a central hospital, outpatient clinic, laboratories, and professional offices also are planned. The 18,304 dwelling units will cover nearly half of the site.

Total acres: 6,156

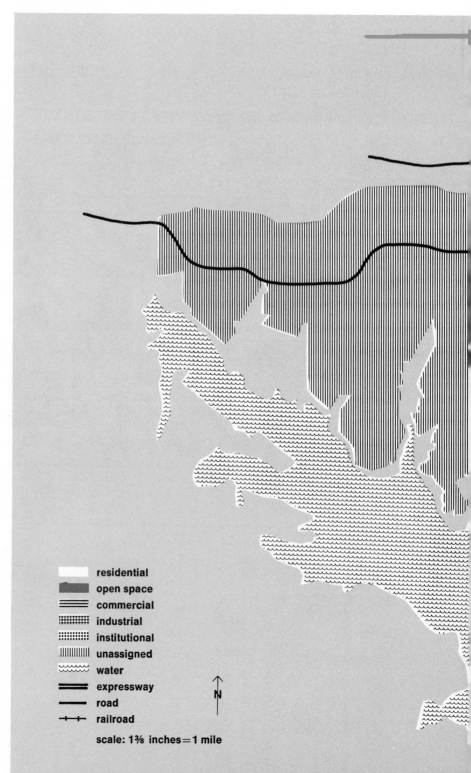

residential
open space
commercial
industrial
institutional
unassigned
water
expressway
road
railroad

scale: 1⅜ inches = 1 mile

GANANDA, NEW YORK 1972

Gananda's site 12 miles east of downtown Rochester is mostly rolling fields with occasional steep hills. The development will accommodate a total population of more than 80,000 over a 30-year period. Its smallest planning units are residential communities of approximately 1,500 dwelling units, each with a multiuse community center housing educational, cultural, and religious facilities and providing child-development activities for preschoolers and elementary students, community meeting rooms, recreational activity areas, and possibly consumer protection information. Four residential communities will constitute a residential district of about 6,000 dwelling units. The focal point of each district will be a program center offering a higher level of educational, cultural, religious and recreational facilities and a shopping center containing convenience commercial, office space, and possibly health and government facilities. The plan calls for four residential districts clustered around a regional center of major commercial, office, cultural, recreational and entertainment facilities.

Total acres: 9,800

□	residential
▓	open space
▤	commercial
▦	industrial
▒	institutional
〰	water
──	road
┼┼┼	railroad
●	neighborhood center

scale: 1½ inches = 1 mile

SOUL CITY, NORTH CAROLINA 1972

Developer Floyd B. McKissick envisions Soul City as a place where the poor, whites as well as blacks, will learn new job skills and participate in the ownership of the new town's industry. Soul City's site in Warren County, near Raleigh, is a depressed rural area from which McKissick hopes to draw many of the new residents of the community. In accordance with the social goals for Soul City, the plan places heavy emphasis on industrial development, devoting nearly 20 percent of the site to industrial uses.

The projected job base to support Soul City's total planned population of 50,000, is 24,000, including 8,200 manufacturing jobs. The plan essentially utilizes a network of roads defined by medium- to high-density residential development built around commercial/recreational/institutional activity centers situated at key intersections. Most of the single-family housing is tucked into interior areas adjacent to green spaces. A major town center at the northwestern edge of the site is adjacent to a proposed Afro-

Exposition Park. The town center is anchored at the south by a major educational park.

Total acres: 5,180

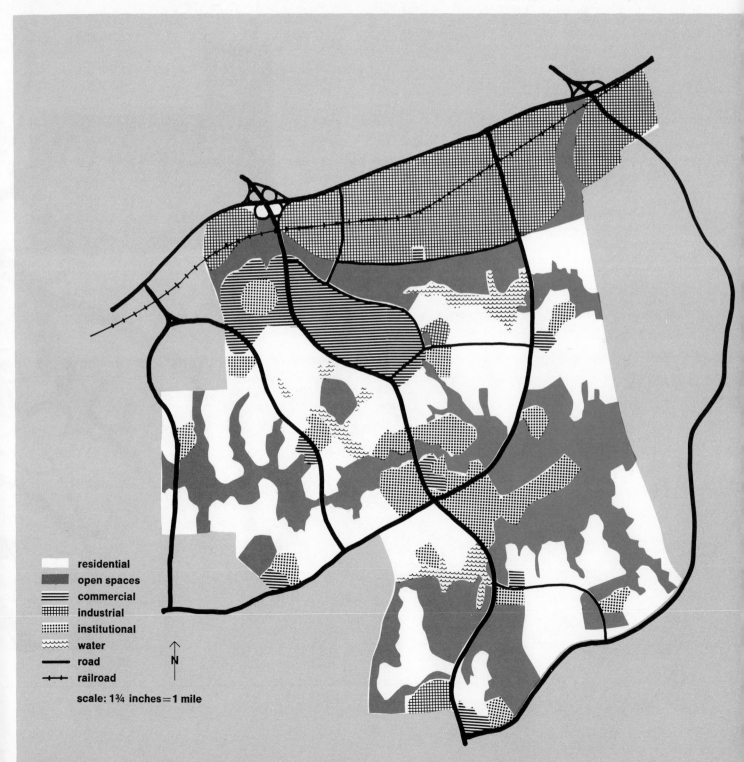

residential

open spaces

commercial

industrial

institutional

water

road

railroad

scale: 1¾ inches = 1 mile

N

35

THE WOODLANDS,
TEXAS 1972

The Woodlands is situated 30 miles north of Houston within that city's area of extra-territorial jurisdiction, paving the way for possible annexation at a later date. Planned for a total population of 150,000 over a 20-year period, the new town lies immediately west of Interstate 45 (Dallas Expressway) to which it will be connected at four inter-changes. The plan calls for seven villages and a town center containing 49,000 residential units, 26 neighborhood and village shopping areas, and a major regional shopping area of 1.5 million square feet. A 15,000-student branch of the University of Houston is proposed for a 400-acre site. The plan includes 2,000 acres for industrial use providing 30,000 jobs, and 3,359 acres of open space allocated for wildlife "corridors" through the development, parks, buffer zones between land uses, and pedestrian trails and pathways. Urban centers will encompass 1,265 acres, and a medical center is planned for the core area.

Total acres: 16,937

residential
open space
commercial
industrial
institutional
water
road
town center
village center
neighborhood center

scale: 1¼ inches = 1 mile

37

WELFARE ISLAND, NEW YORK CITY 1972

An auto-free new town in-town on an historic island in the East River is being created by a subsidiary of the New York State Urban Development Corporation. Covering 122 acres, all but 21 of Welfare Island's total land area, the development will accommodate some 17,000 residents in neighborhoods served only by free electric mini-buses. Private automobiles will not be allowed beyond a parking garage at the island's entrance. Apartment buildings ranging from four to 22 stories will contain

5,000 dwelling units—more than half of them for low- and moderate-income families. The buildings will be stepped down along the river frontage to open up the views, and will be U-shaped to create courts opening to the water. A walkway system will link buildings, parks, community facilities, and promenades along the riverfronts. The development of new public school spaces immediately adjacent to the apartment buildings is being carried out in partnership with the New York City Board of Education.

An underground pneumatic refuse collection system will eliminate the need for garbage trucks on the island. (*See pp. 99-102.*)

Total acres: 147 (including existing hospitals)

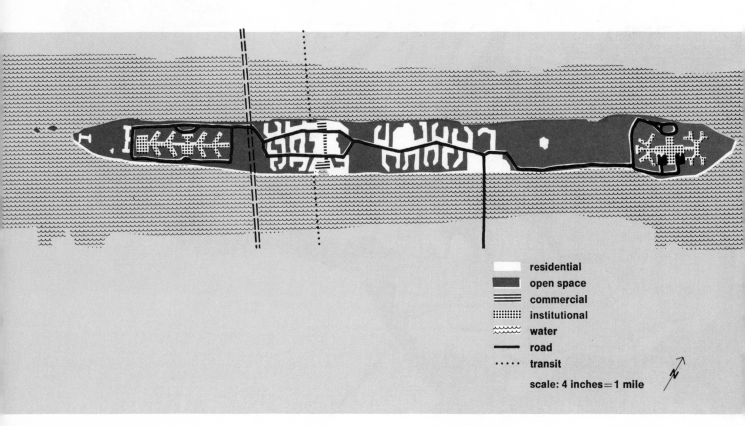

▢ residential
▨ open space
≡ commercial
▦ institutional
〜 water
▬ road
••• transit

scale: 4 inches = 1 mile

FORT LINCOLN, WASHINGTON, D.C. 1972

Though planning for Fort Lincoln began as early as 1968, it was not until late 1972 that it received HUD approval of a $28-million urban renewal grant for development of its streets, sewers, and parks. Fort Lincoln is a new town in-town situated just two miles from the U.S. Capitol in northeast Washington. It is planned for a population of 16,000 covering a wide range of incomes. The plan calls for a wide central open space in the middle of the community with a large lake and central green, from which malls and pedestrain walkways will radiate. Adjoining the green is an "upland woods," a 12-acre forest preserve which will have outdoor "environmental classrooms," picnic facilities, hiking trails, a nature study area, a miniature farm and zoo, and a children's adventure playground. Residential areas covering 155 acres (including schools) will be grouped in clusters around three community malls—landscaped corridors containing shops, clubs, taverns and other attractions. A town center will contain shopping, entertainment, cultural and educational facilities.

Total acres: 342

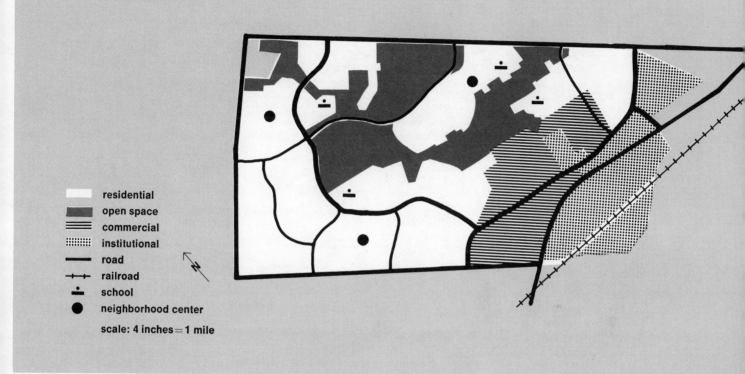

residential
open space
commercial
institutional
road
railroad
school
neighborhood center

scale: 4 inches = 1 mile

II. THE STATE OF THE ART

THE CURRENT STATE OF THE ART of new-town design and development can be summed up in a word: *systems.* The word, of course, describes a process, not a result. Yet systems design, by attempting to include and interrelate all the social, physical, economic, political, and even psychological factors that make up human existence, offers a vital new hope for producing new towns that truly serve the needs and aspirations of people.

Virtually all of the essays that follow concern themselves with systems—the first two with total systems design, the others with one or more of the various subsystems that form the total. Taken as a whole, they present a compelling argument for the value of systems design. Yet, as some of the authors point out — especially Ralph Rapson in his essay — there is always the danger that, by being too preoccupied with and enamored of the process, the designers and developers of new towns can lose sight of the result. Often, says Rapson, "The result is compromise, dilution, and homogenization."

For all of its promise—most of which has not yet been realized—systems design must be recognized as only a means to an end, not the end itself. While the systems approach may be able to prevent mistakes and oversights in new-town design and development, it cannot assure excellence. It is as true today as it ever was that excellence results from insight and inspiration which transcend the process. Systems design can be a valuable aid to inspiration, but it is not a substitute.

SYSTEMS DESIGN: AN OVERVIEW

Archibald C. Rogers

FOR THE NEW TOWN there are three basic kinds of system: the new town as a physical artifact, the design and decision-making process required to put this artifact in place, and the management mechanisms and processes required to operate the artifact after it is in place.

All three systems must be designed. The design of all three must proceed together from the very beginning because concepts at the level of the design process, the physical form, and its operation all interact to alter the other two systems.

The medium is problem-solving: To solve the problem requires first that the problem be described and a correct description in turn requires a thorough understanding of the problem.

For systems affecting the environment (the built environment, the natural environment, the social environment—and it is hard to conceive of a system today without such an effect) there are three mechanisms through which the design and decision-making process functions to the end of solving the problem correctly. This is a team of three teams, a three-legged stool in which each leg is coequal in strength and length lest the stool teeter or collapse. These are the design team, the decision-making team, and the community team.

THE DESIGN TEAM

The design team is a multidisciplined group of peers whose component members are identified and mixed to fit the initial, gross description of the problem. This team is the new architect-artist charged with "praying" over the problem, with intuiting alternative concepts, with imagining the futures of these concepts as seeds of art, with realistically evaluating these alternatives against each other and against external factors, with describing the chosen alternatives not only

in the symbols of words and numbers but also graphically, for the symbolism of graphics is a universal language that alone can express all elements of extremely complex concepts simultaneously instead of sequentially.

The design team is the initiator.

THE DECISION-MAKING TEAM

The decision-making team is composed of potentates—individuals who command resources by virtue of their public and private positions. Their resources may be economic, legal, or political. This team too is specially tailored to fit the gross description of the problem identifying "resourceful" programs and agencies that are affected by the problem and therefore influential in its solution.

This team also functions as a group of peers. It reacts to alternatives posed by the design team at each sequential node in the system. It renders responsible and "whole" decisions based not only on abstract preference but on increasingly firm commitments to implement the decisions taken—decisions that are not logrolling lip-service to a dominant agency or agencies but are proportionate commitments by each agency represented. The decision-making team must therefore have plenipotentiaries from each affected agency, rather than the current ritual of liaison observers.

The decision-making team's function is the incremental allocation of resources at every node in the decision-making process and the insurance thereby of feasibility.

THE COMMUNITY TEAM

The community team is the third leg of the stool. It is of supreme importance yet the most difficult of the three to integrate into the process. It is powerful for it retains the ultimate authority to accept or veto decisions. It is today a cynical and highly sophisticated "enemy" of both the designer and his traditional client, the potentate.

Yet for both the design team and the decision-making team, it is the community that is the true client. The trick is to so identify and incorporate the community into the design and decision-making process that its negativism is converted into a positive, participatory role in posing and testing solutions to its very real problems.

The size and structure of the community team are determined by the description of the problem. For a transportation system the community is probably at the scale of a region. It probably cannot be organized but it can be introduced into the process by properly educated and positive newspapers, television stations, and other media.

For a public facility in a neighborhood, the affected community can and should be organized as a true team, participating in a structured way with the design and decision-making teams.

For a new town, while there may not be a resident community at the beginning, there generally will be a surrounding community that must be involved. In any case, development will soon create a resident community that will force its way into the process unless it is invited in as early as possible.

The function of the community team, however scaled and structured, is to enlighten the process by articulating the community's needs and aspirations. Its articulation probably will require sensitive translation into the jargon of the designers and potentates.

The three teams are ad hoc and presumably dischargeable on completion of their task. Yet they also are new and democratic institutions emerging at a time when our democracy and its old institutions seem not to be working well. They

are experimental and hopeful for they address the question of whether a powerful and generally successful democracy—the leader of Western society—can build a beautiful environment. The answer is not to be found in current efforts to create powerful entities charged with rebuilding our cities and demanding in return, as a condition for fulfilling their charge, that they be freed from democratic constraints.

AN OPEN TRIALOGUE

The essential objective is not just to overcome the adversary position of most communities by incorporating them into the process, but also to restore our democratic processes and release our latent national creativity—a creativity that is muted today but once was the very hallmark of our revolution.

This requires that the process no longer be isolated in the architect's ivory tower or the guarded boardrooms of the architect's public and private clientele. It requires an open trialogue among the three teams, open at the level of initiating and evaluating alternative solutions and at the level of deciding among them. And this openness requires a going-in acceptance of the discomforts and risks involved in public disclosure—a risk to the designer that his tender and tentative concepts may be ridiculed publicly, a risk to the potentate that his carefully polished image may be damaged by overt controversy.

But the community must also accept the risks inherent in an open trialogue. It must accept that it cannot have its cake and eat it—that while it is easy enough to agree on a problem that needs correction, any real solution will involve tradeoffs that will harm some of its constituents and benefit others. It must understand that process and product are indivisible—that it cannot stay aloof from the

difficulties and mysteries of the process while reserving its reaction until a solution is reached.

The community must accept the currently unfashionable proposition that society and its physical environment are inseparable—that there is no future for human renewal without physical renewal and that physical renewal that does not support human renewal by the honest involvement of the affected community is equally irrational. It must be prepared to publicly expose its private and fragile aspirations and to accept the difficulty of articulating them.

The community's physical and economic needs are simple enough to identify and express—and hardly subject to public ridicule in a materialistic society. But what of man's silent hunger for beauty and art, for life eternal and the symbols of ultimacy, for privacy and contemplation, for congregation, for creative release, for self-identity? These aspirations must be voiced. They must become qualitative elements in the hitherto quantitative cost-benefit matrix against which the problem and its alternative solutions are evaluated. And these unquantifiable elements of the matrix must then be quantified, even though based on arbitrary and intuitive decisions.

THE PHYSICAL ARTIFACT

In exploring the tri-system design of the new town, the most convenient starting point is the physical artifact. This is a closed system in the sense that each new town is described geographically, socially, and economically as an identifiable entity. Each new town can and should have its own unique personality, but there are attributes common to all of them within the physical system that is the new community.

The first of these is the question of size. New "towns" have been proposed theoretically from the scale of very modest neighborhoods to grandiose, self-sufficient new cities embracing perhaps as many as 500,000 citizens. The maximum scale probably will be determined not by an abstract exercise in arithmetic but by the forces that create the opportunity for a new community.

The community cannot be so large as to be indigestible in terms of required resources—the availability of talent, funds, and, perhaps of greatest importance, land. The talent required is currently in short supply because it involves not only new attitudes and expertise within the established design professions but also the newly emerging ability to manage the development process itself.

The larger the community, however, the more likely it is to break through the current network of constraints that so seriously inhibits large-scale, intelligent development. Perhaps the most probable limit at the maximum end of the spectrum would be a community of 100,000 to 200,000 persons developed over several decades.

CRITICAL MASS

At the minimum end of the spectrum the most important issue is that of "critical mass." The community must be big enough to be a real profile of the social and economic life of our society. It must be capable of supporting most of the physical and nonphysical facilities required for a rich community life, even though many of these needs sometimes can be provided by a larger community nearby.

One advantage of the smaller scale is obviously its digestibility. Another is its flexibility. It could be plugged into existing sites within and around metropolitan areas and smaller cities far more easily than the larger community. Such a community might be no larger than 5,000

dwelling units, or approximately 15,000 citizens.

THE LOCATION

The second area of common concern is the matter of location. This will to a certain extent be influenced by the scale selected, but smaller communities can be used in these differing kinds of locations:

1. *As additions to small cities outside metropolitan areas.* Elements can be added to the edges of existing small cities, often in a wedge-shaped pattern, which could double or triple the size of the older city when the final increment is completed. An example of this is the development of Montgomery Village as the first such wedge extending the old town of Gaithersburg in Montgomery County, Md., under the county's experimental town-sector zoning.

2. *As additions to metropolitan areas.* This option would use the new community to add to the edges of a metropolitan area or, better, to infill vacant areas within the metropolis. These vacant areas occur not only in the suburbs (as in the location of Reston, Va.) but also within the inner city (Fort Lincoln in Washington, D.C.). While mapmakers show metropolitan areas as though they have no developable segments, there are many such segments within all metropolitan areas that would benefit from the insertion of well-designed new communities of a small scale.

3. *As remodeled older areas.* While the idea of totally clearing and rebuilding many existing dilapidated communities is out of fashion—and for good reason—it is possible though difficult to apply the new-towns concept to such developed areas. The technique involves the discriminating selection of new-town elements and fitting them sensitively into the existing community (for example by slot housing or the rehabilitation of existing stock). While this application will be re-

quired primarily in the slum areas of the older inner cities, it already is evident that a great many of the early postwar suburbs will require the same kind of treatment—without necessarily increasing their overall densities.

4. *As increments of large new cities.* This application of the smaller new town recognizes the difficulty inherent in the large community: its drain on available resources. It might therefore be wise to use the smaller new towns on a preplanned and scheduled basis as increments for building large new cities. There is, however, a myth involved in these large-scale new towns—the myth of self-sufficiency. The fact is that no matter where these communities are situated and no matter what their size, they inevitably are connected to the larger external system, whether this be the industrial economic system or the physical transportation skeleton at the national scale. Thus, the idea of self-sufficient new towns should be somewhat downgraded, although it has considerable merit and a great appeal to the American mind. As Winston Churchill somewhat acidly commented during the war, "The American is inclined to follow the large idea, and the larger the idea the more quick is he to accept it without question."

LOCATIONAL MAGNETS

In the location of all new towns, small or large, there is the factor of locational magnetism. In the past this has related primarily to the opportunity for industrial employment, which in turn was generally related to certain geographic features. Thus most of the older cities of the United States are situated on waterways so that the raw material for industry can be imported and the finished products exported. Water also was important in powering the industrial plants themselves.

A more recent phenomenon has been the location of industrial plants—and therefore the creation of employment magnets for new communities—in areas having a stable and trainable employment base, such as the Southern Piedmont. The premise behind this locational decision was the presumed cheapness of Piedmont labor compared with that of older industrialized areas, such as New England, which were heavily unionized and therefore commanded higher per-unit wage rates. This probably is no longer a compelling reason for relocating industry because even the Piedmont is beginning to experience the effects of unionization and higher labor costs. Nevertheless, the *opportunity* to make this kind of locational decision is new because our new systems of transportation and power generation have divorced industrial locations from the waterways.

The latest phenomenon is simply the response of industry and its potential labor force to amenity. The beneficent climate of the Gulf Coast, Florida, the Southwest, and the Pacific Coast has encouraged the development of an industrial base and the population to support it. The wealth of cultural activities, as well as the wide variety of employment opportunities and consumer purchases, also has led to a concentration of industry and labor in metropolitan areas (although industry is tending to move to the suburban periphery of these areas).

Amenity is an important new factor to be recognized in the development of new towns, and it can be provided artificially as part of the built environment despite the advantages inherent in the natural amenities of climate, foliage, terrain, etc.

TRANSACTIONAL CENTERS

A final factor in analyzing the effect of magnets on location are the glimmerings

we now see of a postindustrial economy. These imply a reduction in the importance of the traditional manufacturing employment base and an acceleration in the importance of the service area of the gross national product. These new kinds of opportunities can be magnified by restructuring the older downtown cores of our existing cities, and the cores of large-scale new communities, to perform a new mission as *the* transactional centers of the postindustrial economy. Similarly, the magnetism of research and development as part of the service sector also can be reinforced—though probably in outlying areas rather than the cores.

OPTIONS OF FORM

In addition to the generic concerns of size and location there are the available options for the form of the new town. This form can to a certain extent be determined independently of size and location. Ideally there should be a sort of deliberate competition among new communities for the tremendous market that awaits them. Each community should establish its own personality, and therefore its own approach to form, so that the consuming public will have a full spectrum of environmental options available on its shopping shelf.

Today, in both the suburbs and the older cities, this spectrum exists hardly at all. The shopping public is buying only one kind of environment, for that is all that's available. It is assumed that this environment is what the public wants because the public buys it. The same argument could be made for the Model T if it were the only product on the automotive shopping shelf.

THE GARDEN CITY

The most common form of new town grows out of the Garden City movement of 19th-century England. This is the genesis

of the new town of Tapiola near Helsinki and of the better new developments in the United States, such as Columbia and Reston. It is also the genesis for much of the suburban sprawl that has marked our postwar environmental expansion. At its best it provides a low-density residential environment well set within the natural environment and penetrated sensitively by it. Because of the romantic nature of its origins, the architectural treatment within this form tends to be romantic—a sort of anachronistic recollection of the preurban society of the early and middle Renaissance.

THE URBANE MODEL

At the other end of the form spectrum is the high-density urban new town with its emphasis on artificial environment and on the values of urban life as a direct contradiction of nature and the rural life. This is by no means as prevalent as the garden city.

It perhaps is best illustrated by the new town of Cumbernauld near Glasgow. Cumbernauld does not ignore nature. It is a high-density, highly urbane built environment set crisply into a marvelous natural terrain. The edges between the built and the natural are quite clear and are guaranteed by a greenbelt surrounding the city. Because of Cumbernauld's tight design and the greenbelt, the natural amenities surrounding the city are within walking distance for all citizens.

This form also can be quite romantic in its recollection of the Italian hilltowns and a nostalgic restatement of the prerural society of medieval times.

THE MACHINE FOR LIVING

The Machine for Living is perhaps uniquely American in its belief in high technology and mechanical systems to provide amenity. No such city or parts of such cities have yet been built, but the best known example of this form is the Experimental City in Minnesota. Also, some elements of core-city development, such as the Post Oak project near Houston, are exploring this kind of form.

ORGANIC INCREMENTALISM

While the three form options described above imply a sort of monolithic, all-designed-at-once community, there is a fourth alternative which may be both more feasible and more appropriate to the real world of U.S. urban development. This implies incrementalism and a kind of organized chaos containing both high-density and low-density areas and a rich variety of environments appropriate to different individual or community lifestyles. It could have elements of all the other three alternatives, including the Garden City in outlying areas, Urbane concentrations within the inner city, and a highly technological and mechanized core.

In any case, this form could provide *internally* for a high variety of environmental choices as other new communities provide these *externally* in competition with one another. The chaos that might result from this form could be redeemed and translated into a rich kaleidoscope by the design strength of the public armature that organizes the whole.

EXTERNAL LINKAGES

The system that is the physical new town is inevitably linked externally to other systems. There are two fundamental links: that between the built environment and its natural setting, and that between the built environment and its indwelling society.

The ideal of the first link should be equilibrium, even though this ideal cannot be achieved under the iron laws of physics. The new town should be designed so that it can put back into nature's

bank as much as possible of what it withdraws. It should contain self-cycling systems that throw off the least amount of emissions to pollute the air, water, and earth—and indeed the eye and ear. It should be economical in the withdrawal of raw materials from both its immediate area and others. It should work with nature—with the climate and the prevailing winds and the terrain—both above grade and below. By these means such high-consumption products as air conditioning may be minimized, even though an educational program may be necessary to reinforce the marketability of a community without air conditioning.

The second link is of equal importance. The indwelling society must be nurtured by the environment of the new town. There should be opportunities for the expression of its creativity as corporate groups and as individuals. There should be elements in which the pride of the community is expressed and which demonstrate the unique personality of the community and its neighborhoods. The external ties must also be recognized in terms of the indwelling society's relationship to the economic and social activities and amenities in the surrounding community.

There also are a number of functional external linkages which may not be as important as the two cited above. The new town's functional systems inevitably will be linked to external systems such as transportation, welfare, education, and medical care. In some cases, the community's internal security system will be linked to manned or mechanical external security systems. The entire communications system, with all its untapped potential in the fields of health, education, and culture, is linked to the larger systems on a metropolitan and national scale.

In many ways the most underrated ex-

ternal linkage is that between the new community and the stream of history. Each new increment of today's built environment is an expression of this stream. This is not an excuse for nostalgic romanticism, even though there are ennobling elements of the past that can be reinterpreted for the present. Nor is it an excuse for a brutal futurism that can alienate the indwelling society. Rather, it is an opportunity for honest experimentation with new forms and systems in which the community itself can participate.

INTERNAL LINKAGES

The most important internal linkage is the public armature—the system of transportation, utilities, and communications involving the movement of people, ideas, goods, wastes, and power. This is the fundamental link to the architectural flesh that fills out the new community. The nonphysical linkages involve the need to nourish the indwelling society and to create, through public and private opportunities, the economic magnets necessary for its success.

There will be nodes of differing functions knit together by the public armature—some involving employment, others of a cultural nature. There is merit in considering these nodes multipurpose, so that the idea of segregated uses, which has been so important in creating today's sterile environment, is not carried over to the next generation.

THE DESIGN AND DECISION-MAKING PROCESS

The second system is a derivative of the physical system, but it is also the creator of this system and therefore inseparable from it. The design and decision-making process, the trialogue that flows among the three teams, is the beginning point of the systematic approach to developing new towns. It can be described in sequen tial steps although these steps do not occur in the real world as separate elements following one on the other.

INITIATION

The first step is the initiation of the project in advance of any formal organization of the three teams or the trialogue. The initiator of a new town will probably be either a private entrepreneur or a government official who administers new-towns programs. The first effort of the initiator will be to "sell" his ideas. And this selling can be enhanced greatly if he begins to create immediately, on an informal basis, the three-legged stool. He should bring in one or more representatives of the affected community, the affected agencies, and the potential design team. The architect will be invaluable in this effort if he is permitted to start with the design of the three teams and the procedural system from the gross description of the problem.

THE PLAN FOR PLANNING

The end product of this embryonic team should be a "plan for planning." This charge requires a new kind of service that is emerging in the architectural profession. The team must analyze the problem and from its analysis design the three teams and the trialogue. The plan for planning will be schematic to the extent that the analysis of the problem must be broad until the three teams are established.

ORGANIZATION

The third step is implementation of the plan for planning—the establishment, by the appointment of highly qualified individuals, of the design team, the decision-making team, and the community team (if not as an organized entity, at least as a set of procedures to be used to involve the community).

RECONNAISSANCE

The first step to be taken by the three teams is to charge the design team to conduct an intensive examination of the problem and its milieu—the identification of positive and negative factors and forces that must be harnessed. From such a reconnaissance will come an identification of the available resources and the ranking of problems and opportunities in order of their importance. Then alternative strategic objectives can be described—graphically in many cases—and evaluated in terms of their fit, their attainability, and their balance between negative and positive forces. The decision-making team's first decision, in partnership with the affected community, is to select from the surviving alternatives *the* strategic objective to govern the balance of the process.

CONCEPTUAL STRATEGIES

The next step requires the design team, in dialogue with the community and in coordination with the decision-making team, to develop alternative conceptual strategies that form the basis for the physical design of the new town. These strategies will tend to represent a spectrum of alternatives, all theoretically capable of accomplishment within the objective agreed upon. An optimum alternative can be identified, documented, and described (verbally and graphically) as the design team's recommendations for the next node of decision. But all selected alternatives must be similarly presented. Of course the decision-making team is not bound by the design team's recommendations and customarily develops, for its own practical reasons, other recommendations.

If the three teams work together creatively, the end result of this decision-making node is probably an entirely new

conceptual alternative composed of parts of those originally posed by the design team. In any case, a conceptual strategy is now agreed upon to govern the last step in the process.

THE TACTICS OF IMPLEMENTATION

The final step in the procedural system is the development of detailed planning, engineering, and architectural documents and the incremental building of the new town. Here the principle is clear: The conceptual strategy must be rigidly adhered to throughout the life of the development process. It must be expressed visibly in the public armature. And because this armature is where most of the public tax moneys are invested, it becomes the most important tool for ordering the development of the surrounding flesh—provided the public investment is made in a coherent way and in advance of the development.

To assure coherence and the beneficial evolution of the surrounding environment, the strategy must have integrity and cannot be shifted in midstream. But because a large-scale new town may require several decades to develop, there must be flexibility in the tactics. Unpredictable changes will occur in technology, social attitudes, and economics. These changes must be recognized and adapted to if the overall design is to be successful.

An important tactic of implementation is the inclusion of the community as the third team in the process. If the community is treated honestly and is respected for its views—which means having its views incorporated where feasible—it becomes a proponent of the new town, thus removing many political constraints. This is "political design" in its highest sense.

Another important tactic is a clear schedule of stepping-stones up to final completion. The first stepping-stone need not be the most important in terms of its impact on the final form, but it must be the most easily attainable.

THE OPERATIONAL SYSTEM

The third system involves the design of the operational mechanisms and processes that will become the managing entities for the new town. Virtually every new town has the opportunity to experiment with new kinds of public/private institutions to perform its physical and non-physical operations. These mechanisms must be designed at the same time as the physical facilities, and they must be "put in place" incrementally as the new town develops and its population begins to grow.

While the total cost and benefit of the design for the operational system and its component institutions must be measured in a conventional economic sense, the definition should be expanded greatly. For example, the cost and benefit of raising tax revenues should not be limited narrowly to the most income at the least cost of collection. There are additional costs and benefits peripheral to the fundamental task of revenue collection, and these should be put into the equation. The most glaring example is the dependence by communities, new and old, on the real property tax. Within the operational system a great opportunity exists for new approaches to raising public funds and new mechanisms for administering this phase of the operation of the new town.

Although smaller communities will be linked to the larger external public school systems of the cities in which they are situated, there is an opportunity for experimenting with the public education system within the new town—particularly in terms of capitalizing on the potential of our television technology as it moves into its next phase of two-way telecommunication.

While the physical form of the new town will be "completed" at some point in time, the operational design must recognize that the flesh around the armature will be in a constant state of change. It therefore should include mechanisms and processes to minimize the demoralizing, visible effects of change. The dynamic forces behind change should be used to constantly upgrade the architectural flesh. Moreover, the public armature, as a great work of civic art, should have the highest priority on maintenance and improvement funds, for this skeleton is the visible symbol of the social life of the town.

The operational system, in its design, offers perhaps the greatest challenge and is the most important of the three systems in terms of creating significant models that can be exported to benefit older cities. The real breakdown within municipal government today is not so much caused by a lack of funds, racial tensions, and other such problems. It is due to the stultification of the public institutions that manage these cities—institutions that have developed into great bureaucracies preoccupied with technical competence and (presumably) the honesty of their civil servants. But these institutions have become so aloof and so self-protective in their desire to maintain their powers that they will not adapt to the radical changes that mark contemporary society. To address this problem through new institutions appropriate to the operation of new towns is perhaps the greatest of all design challenges.

SYNTHESIS AND COMPROMISE

The three basic systems must be designed independently, but in the end their final design must be synthesized as *the* concept for the new town. And there will be compromises affecting the original concepts of each system. A school system re-

lying on new communications technology, for example, may alter radically the form of the physical spaces for schools. If the tax resources are limited, there will be a need to make the most of every tax dollar. Where these dollars are invested in physical facilities, it would seem rational that public structures be designed for multipurpose use and 24-hour operation. Again, this will have a radical effect on the form of certain facilities proposed in the design of the physical artifact.

Each new town should become the opportunity for deliberate experimentation with both physical and nonphysical forms. Its armature must be a great work of civic architecture and not, as in our current view, the meanest and least funded of civic works. It should incorporate the symbols of permanency for which we hunger and the symbols of the pride and personality of each community.

We should design the architectural flesh around this armature so that it accepts gracefully the key fact of our time: unpredictable change at an unprecedented scale and speed. For the architect this means de-programming. It means designing spaces that are easily adaptable from, say, a school use to a housing or manufacturing use. It means that the great art of architecture must be expressed in the overall skeleton of a community rather than the transient flesh of its buildings.

Finally we must recognize the fundamental importance of art and try to give it expression in the design of the whole community and its components. For art is not an optional item to be consumed by an affluent society when it has consumed all else it needs or desires. Art, in the words of Maritain, is part of the daily bread of each individual. And if this is so, the art of architecture is the most important of all the arts.

JONATHAN AND CEDAR/RIVERSIDE

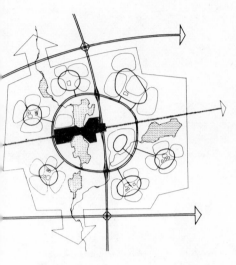

Jonathan's urban design concept calls for a regional town center and higher education complex surrounded by five villages and an industrial area. An eighth of Jonathan's 8,000 acres will be devoted to industrial use, providing employment for 40 per cent of the area's working population.

It would be hard to imagine two new towns more different than Jonathan and Cedar/Riverside. Jonathan is a satellite new town being built on farmland at the fringes of the Twin Cities metropolitan area. It ultimately will contain 50,000 persons on 8,000 acres. Cedar/Riverside is a new town in-town (the nation's first, in fact) being carved out of a dense, decaying urban site 12 blocks from the heart of downtown Minneapolis. It will contain 30,000 persons on 100 acres.

Yet Jonathan and Cedar/Riverside have much in common. First, they are "paired" new towns, each part of an experiment in intercommunity relations that is getting its first test here. Second, they are both being developed under the leadership of Henry T. McKnight, one of the nation's leading conservationists who, as a Minnesota state senator, authored the landmark Minnesota Omnibus Natural Resources and Recreation Act of 1963. And third, they are both being planned under the umbrella of the Twin Cities Metropolitan Council, one of the country's most effective regional governments.

The goal of Jonathan's developers is to duplicate the complete income profile of the metropolitan area, thus offering a wide variety of choices to prospective residents. The first of its five villages, begun in 1967, is well under way, containing some 1,500 residents in a broad mix of housing types and prices, a village center, and a booming industrial center—all interconnected by a network of pedestrian pathways.

Cedar/Riverside is the outgrowth of a painstaking eight-year process of property acquisition on a willing buyer-willing seller basis. It is being developed without the use of condemnation powers and without massive bulldozing.

The development site is a 100-acre tract owned by Cedar/Riverside Associates within a 340-acre triangular area that began its decline as early as 1900. The community is bounded by the Mississippi River on one side and on the other two sides by two major interstate freeways, which provide linkages to the entire metropolitan area, including Jonathan. Occupying roughly three-fourths of the land area is part of the Midwest's largest health and educational complex. It includes the University of Minnesota's West Bank Campus, two colleges, and two major hospitals.

Almost half of Cedar/Riverside's planned 12,500 dwelling units will be for low- and moderate-income families and will be integrated with a communitywide architectural design that will not distinguish between income levels. Its diverse community facilities will include a flexible "activity centrum" designed to encourage residents to bring in ideas for shaping and molding its functions. Pedestrian and vehicular traffic will be separated throughout the community.

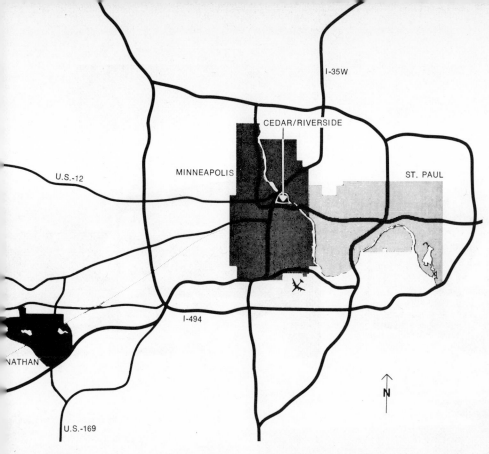

Interstate 35W provides a direct physical link between the sister new towns of Cedar/Riverside, near downtown Minneapolis, and Jonathan, situated 22 miles away.

The first ten years of Jonathan's development (shown in model form opposite) envisions a regional-scale downtown encircled by residential villages and industrial parks. The first village, now under construction (below), has single-family houses, town houses and medium-rise apartments served by a village center (upper left in photo).

Top left: A "pirate ship" tot-lot along the pedestrian system. Top right: A different kind of tot-lot for the children of a townhouse cluster. Above: The Village One shopping center, containing convenience shops, a medical/dental clinic, and professional offices to serve the village's 8,500 residents. Right: The International Time Sharing Building, one of more than a dozen plants to have located in Jonathan.

Top, center left, and above: Three of Jonathan's housing types—single-family, low-rise apartments, and town houses, the latter using a mailbox cluster as a gathering spot for residents. Left: A recreation pavilion at Lake Grace, one of the three natural lakes on Jonathan's farmland site.

Over the next 20 years, the blighted
Cedar/Riverside area will be replaced by
a dense complex of housing for all income levels, commercial developments,
and community facilities serving 30,000
persons (below). In the meantime, many of
the existing structures are being converted
to community uses. Right: Cedar Square
West, the community's first new housing
development. Its first stage, containing
1,299 apartments, plazas, neighborhood
facilities, and underground parking, was
recently completed.

New construction at Cedar/Riverside is being staged so that the social fabric of the community can be maintained during development. Cedar Square West (above) is being built with a minimum of disruption to its neighbors. The mini-park pictured at left was created out of a vacant lot by residents of the community, who also designed and executed the wall mural.

The Design Process: Step by Step

George J. Pillorgé

Daniel R. Brents

AN ATTITUDE OF PROFESSIONAL MODESTY and mutual respect lies at the heart of systems design for new towns. As architects, we are one of a team of professionals usually organized and directed by a public or private developer. The degree of our leadership role varies with each project depending on the personality and knowledge of the developer, his personal relations and relative confidence in other professional team members, and the phase of the project. It is not useful to worry about who is leading, but more important to interact well with one's teammates in the orderly solution of problems. In that way, all lines of communication remain open, and the critical insights that each team member needs from the others can result in a better, more innovative design.

We seek to draw systems design solutions from the problem itself. The design is a result of carefully considered economic and social objectives constrained by the nature of the site and available resources. Our approach is a systematic analysis of all program elements and their relationships through a series of planning and decision-making steps. The design attitude is one of exploration.

TYPES OF NEW TOWNS

In our work we recognize five types of new towns, categorized by size and location:

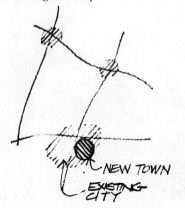

1. *New towns in-town* is a term invented by Harvey Perloff to describe communities developed within the urbanized limits of existing cities. Being within a highly urbanized setting, one usually can expect high-density, high-intensity development—perhaps 70 or more persons per acre. Social concerns and participation by the surrounding community will be strong considerations, often in direct confrontation with the economic objectives and resources of the developer.

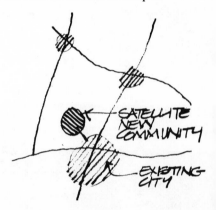

2. *Satellites* are the most common type of new town. They range from large subdivisions of 1,000 acres to so-called new towns of 15,000 acres or more. In form, density, and life-style the satellites basically are continuations of the suburban fabric. Typical densities range from five to 15 persons per gross acre. To the architect familiar with the design of large subdivisions or large apartment/townhouse complexes, the satellite could look superficially similar. To some extent this is true, but when more than 3,000 persons or 500 acres are involved, new design issues arise. These often are systems design issues.

3. *New cities* differ from satellites by being functionally independent of a nearby metropolis, and relatively self-sufficient with a full range of activities. There are no new cities in the United

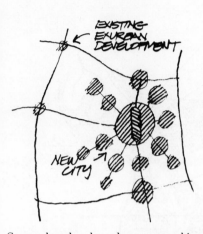

States, but they have been created in other countries as tools of a deliberate national policy of urban and industrial decentralization. Brasilia, Cumbernauld, and the British and Russian new towns are examples.

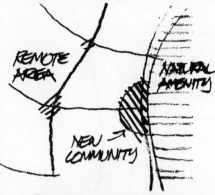

4. *Recreation new towns* are springing up all over the United States. They usually involve 1,000 to 15,000 acres in remote locations on naturally beautiful, often magnificent properties. Because of a combination of marketing and ecological considerations, they often demand more of their designers and developers than conventional new towns.

5. *The Planned Unit Development (PUD)* is not a new town in the usual definition, but it is extremely important as a concept and a key component of any new town. The PUD is a natural design area

for architects. Usually covering 20 to 500 acres, it can be part of the framework of a larger new town or a traditional suburban development.

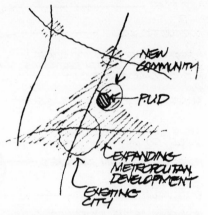

At a site-planning scale, the PUD is the fundamental building block of a new town. If all suburban growth were carried out in the PUD pattern of 50- to 100-acre sites and a high level of community services, the results would look like the new towns being built in the United States today.

MAJOR VARIABLES

The five types of new towns have many factors in common. It is the ways in which they vary that will determine their unique character.

The most basic variable is the nature of the developer. Until recently the developer typically has been a private firm with a strong individual at the helm. But now the developer is becoming less dominated by a single man of vision and is more often a corporate firm with substantial experience in real estate development. With growing frequency, major industrial corporations are entering the field as a means of diversification.

Since the Greenbelt new towns, the public sector has not taken an active developer role, but this is changing. At the federal level, Title VII of the 1970 Hous-

ing Act provides the private developer with a mixed bag of carrots and sticks for new-town building. At the state level, the New York Urban Development Corporation is acting as a public developer capable of combining public powers and private entrepreneurial drive to achieve rapid action in the public interest. Other states are following the lead.

The developer's primary objective is to make a "reasonable" profit on his (and others') investment while keeping the risk within "acceptable" bounds. The developer's definition of a reasonable profit, typically measured as an internal rate of return (IRR) of 20 per cent or more, may have a direct bearing on the ultimate quality of the project, its scope, and the design budget. Acceptable risk may affect the use of innovative solutions and the pursuit of secondary objectives that might increase capital risk.

To the extent the public sector enters the picture, the priority of socioeconomic objectives may change. But profit is still number one because it is the private sector's fundamental incentive. Title VII will not change this priority.

THE CONTEXT

Another major variable among types of new towns is the natural and man-made condition of the site and its surrounding area—the context. The *natural* context is the location and size of the property and its related climate, vegetation, terrain, geology, and hydrology.

If the location is urbanized, the total context is altered by the level of community services in place, previous responses to natural conditions, and the legal and regulatory complexities affecting the project. In a new town in-town, for example, the existing utility and community-service network could outweigh, in design significance, the natural conditions that would be of paramount importance to a recreation community built in a rural area. And urban projects usually encounter much stronger political and regulative controls than do rural projects, though increasing concern for the natural environment is changing this.

PRESSURES AND FORM

All of these contextual elements, the developer's nature and objectives, and many other factors interact to create pressures that ultimately affect the community's structural form. A direct response to any single pressure affects the options for response to others. In a rational, systematic design process the pressures are assigned priorities, and responses are chosen to balance cost against effectiveness.

The process of evaluating and selecting responses becomes more demanding as the pressures become more urgent and complex. The systems designer, as a subordinate decision-maker to the developer, has the task of intelligently perceiving the key data and assisting his client in making rational decisions.

Social considerations aside, the first set of pressures are the natural conditions: land form and location, hydrology, geology, vegetation, and climate. By mapping existing conditions, a pattern of development opportunities will begin to emerge. It will indicate alternative "least cost/highest return" locations and possible locations for land uses, pedestrian and vehicular transportation, and utility systems.

TRANSPORTATION AND OPEN SPACE

Of all the infrastructure channels, transportation and open-space systems are likely to be the most important in structuring the plan. They are fundamental to the usefulness and quality—and therefore the value—of the locations they border on. Transportation systems endure

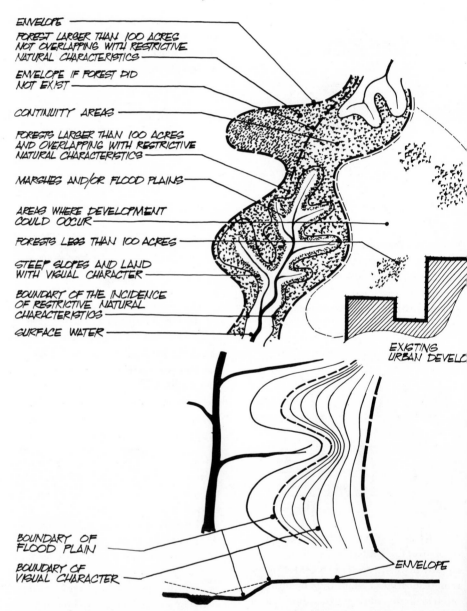

ENVELOPE

FOREST LARGER THAN 100 ACRES NOT OVERLAPPING WITH RESTRICTIVE NATURAL CHARACTERISTICS

ENVELOPE IF FOREST DID NOT EXIST

CONTINUITY AREAS

FORESTS LARGER THAN 100 ACRES AND OVERLAPPING WITH RESTRICTIVE NATURAL CHARACTERISTICS

MARSHES AND/OR FLOOD PLAINS

AREAS WHERE DEVELOPMENT COULD OCCUR

FORESTS LESS THAN 100 ACRES

STEEP SLOPES AND LAND WITH VISUAL CHARACTER

BOUNDARY OF THE INCIDENCE OF RESTRICTIVE NATURAL CHARACTERISTICS

SURFACE WATER

EXISTING URBAN DEVELO

BOUNDARY OF FLOOD PLAIN

BOUNDARY OF VISUAL CHARACTER

ENVELOPE

and are high in cost, demanding of space, and sensitive to alignment.

Taken together, the transportation and open-space systems will establish the skeleton for all other systems. Most new-town plans separate pedestrian and vehicular circulation *à la* the Radburn prototype. This frequently suggests pedestrians (and bicycles, carriages, and

horses) in the open-space system and vehicles, of course, on the roads. The open-space system often will follow valleys (where the most attractive vegetation usually is found) and roads will follow the high ground. This permits a series of pedestrian underpasses where the two systems intersect.

The transportation and open-space systems also will determine the location of gravity-fed utilities. Storm and sanitary sewers may be located in the open-space system (valleys and swales) with development on higher land, or the gravity system may be designed in parallel with the road system. There are other alternatives, but this example does indicate how decisions about locating one or two key systems affect the location and operation of the others.

At the scale of site planning and small PUDs, sanitary and storm sewers join transportation as major influencing utility systems. These are rigid, joined systems, and they must be consistent with slopes. On the other hand, water, gas, electric, and telephone systems usually are nets which do not significantly influence the structure of the community.

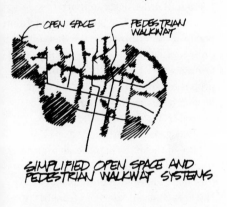

SIMPLIFIED OPEN SPACE AND PEDESTRIAN WALKWAY SYSTEMS

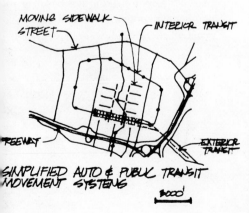

SIMPLIFIED AUTO & PUBLIC TRANSIT MOVEMENT SYSTEMS

In all cases the elements already in place are of paramount importance. The design of the new town always will respond in layout and phasing to the location of an existing highway interchange, a sewerage lift station, or a water main. There is always intense pressure to keep the front-end costs as low as possible so that if a utility exists it will be used as long as possible before another is built.

ARCHETYPES OF COMMUNITY STRUCTURE

In the initial stages of planning, the systems designer must reduce masses of information to manageable form. He needs tools that help him condense data intelligently into key determinants. Studies of urbanization patterns suggest several archetypes of community structure which organize the infrastructure and focal points into cohesive systems that provide alternative responses to varying pressures.

Few if any new towns are literal representations of a single archetypal form. Usually many forces interact to warp one type or produce an amalgam of several in reaching an ultimate systems design. But the use of pure archetypes as working hypotheses early in the design process can be an extremely helpful design tool to study and propose linkages between systems and activities, and to relate the proposals to objectives.

There are four basic archetypal systems patterns, each of which has endless variations that allow it to adapt to local conditions, as well as particular advantages, disadvantages, requirements, and performance characteristics:

1. *The grid system.* Advantages: high accessibility; minimum disruption of flow; expansion flexibility; excellent psychological orientation; adaptability to level or moderately rolling terrain. Disadvantages: requires flow hierarchies; lim-

ited in its adaptability to the terrain; potentially monotonous. Examples: New York City; Milton Keynes New Town.

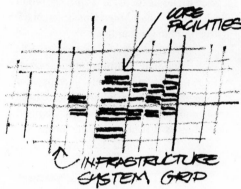

2. *The radial/concentric system.* Advantages: a direct line of travel for centrally directed flows; economics of a single centralized terminal or origin point. Disadvantages: subject to central

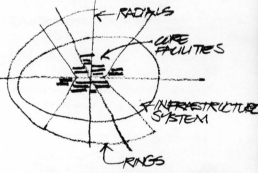

congestion; local flow problems; difficult building sites. Examples: Washington, D.C.; Gruen's "New Urban Pattern."

3. *The linear system.* Advantages: high accessibility; adaptability to linear

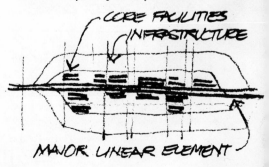

MAJOR LINEAR ELEMENT

59

growth; useful along the limiting edge (water, ridge line). Disadvantages: very sensitive to blockage; requires control of growth; lacks focus. Examples: Ciudad Lineal by Sona y Mata; Chamblis; MARS Group Plan for London.

4. *The multicentered system.* Advantages: optional locations for focal activities and system terminals; good psychological orientation; adaptability to existing conditions. Disadvantages: depends on the stability of key points; potential accessibility problems; tendency to dilute focal activities. Example: Rome.

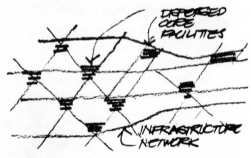

Each of the archetypes links systems to focal activities, which we refer to as core facilities. Principal determinants of the community structure, they may include

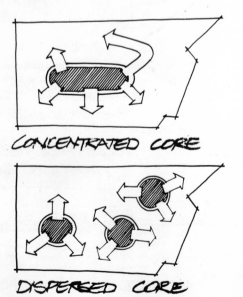

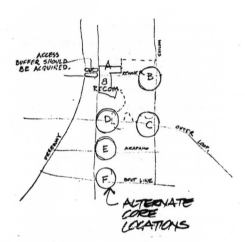

retail, employment, recreational, and cultural activities that can be concentrated or dispersed. The choice mostly depends on the socioeconomic objectives.

The locations of core facilities, whether concentrated or not, depend on such other contextual variables as the availability of suitable land, the impact on their surroundings, access, market conditions, and cost.

As the design analysis proceeds, the study of these options grows more and more complex. One tool, the matrix, allows the designer to graphically display key objectives, variables, systems, and facilities; to establish alternate relationships, and to evaluate consequences. Like any manual tool, the matrix can digest only a limited amount of information, but its value to the designer is its simultaneous presentation of variables and relationships.

The designer must select the matrix elements carefully to match his clearly identified needs. It will not be useful if the designer does not formulate his objectives clearly. Our firm has experimented with computer graphic techniques of matrix analysis and has found that they contribute little more than a manual analysis can offer.

NEIGHBORHOOD CONCEPTS

In 1929 Clarence A. Perry proposed the "neighborhood concept" as the smallest significant planning unit. He saw it as a means to organize and distribute public facilities. Since then the neighborhood has persisted as the basic residential planning unit.

Perry's neighborhood concept took as a guide the institution requiring the smallest population for its support: the elementary school. The size of the neighborhood was determined by the distance children could walk to school—usually a 10-minute walk or a quarter of a mile. The proposed population for such a unit, termed here the "investment unit," ranged from 275 to 3,000 families, depending on density.

One of the many significant alternatives to the neighborhood planning unit is the "social intensive unit" proposed by Herbert Gans and derived from his research in Levittown, Pa. It is based on the number of people who can maintain a constant, working, face-to-face relation-

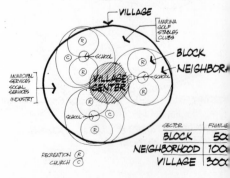

ship, ranging from 10 to 12 families. This unit has its greatest significance at the scale of site planning and small PUDs.

The "social extensive unit" is an area where residents have choices among different social groups, and ranges from 50 to 100 families. In many small, privately initiated communities, this unit is not often important because the population is relatively homogeneous, but it can be important in publicly sponsored new towns where a diverse population is programmed.

These concepts overlap considerably, but they are convenient as yardsticks in planning the community facilities and allocating land areas during the first programming stage of small PUDs.

LOCAL NEIGHBORHOODS

The designer's two most important considerations in planning local neighborhoods are the social and market objectives and the systems design objectives. Recent studies of local neighborhood groupings in existing new towns have shown that casual social interaction and satisfaction are much higher in single-family cul-de-sacs than in traditional linear arrangements. The findings also indicate that dissatisfaction increases significantly in neighborhoods where densities are 12.5 to 25 dwelling units per acre, because of increased noise and a lack of privacy. The closer proximity also is accom-

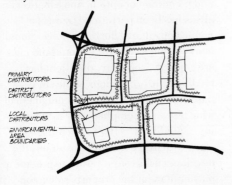

panied by decreased social interaction and an apparent desire for more usable open space.

These findings support the growing popularity of the limited-access system and similar concepts of clustering. The limited-access system makes use of specified traffic hierarchies, with perimeter streets carrying through traffic and neighborhood streets carrying only local traffic.

Usually, residential clusters, loop streets, and cul-de-sacs are used in this system, thus shortening utility connections, increasing safety, and freeing more central open space from traffic. The prototype is Radburn, N.J.

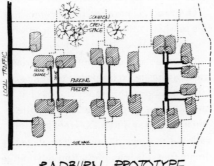

RADBURN PROTOTYPE

In modern terms, a prototype for the single-family cluster might contain 10 units on lots of 4,000 sq. ft., with a parking ratio of 1.75 and a net density of five dwelling units per acre. Although this lot size is considerably smaller than Radburn's average of 7,500 sq. ft., the density is lower than Radburn's six dwelling units per acre because parking, roads, and common open space are increased.

The Radburn prototype has several advantages: Vehicles and pedestrians are separated; larger amounts of common open space are released; low noise levels are maintained, and infrastructure costs per unit usually are reduced. Its problems include the concentration of conflicting vehicular activities in the cul-de-

sac, no provision for service vehicles, and dangerous traffic in the central parking area.

In another prototype proposed recently by British architects and town planners, all vehicles enter a feeder cul-de-sac containing visitor and service parking. Short

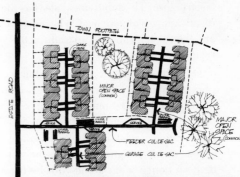

BRITISH PROTOTYPE

garage cul-de-sacs link up with the feeder, thus localizing traffic and reducing it near the residences. The garage cul-de-sacs accommodate residential parking and service and refuse collection vehicles. Visitors, however, approach the units on the opposite side of the residences, which front on a secondary open-space system. The disadvantages compared with Radburn are higher land coverage caused by the garage cul-de-sacs and slightly higher infrastructure costs.

In the typical suburban subdivision the infrastructure is a grid or curvilinear system that is highly efficient and flexible for limited traffic flows. It often allows free

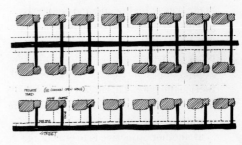

TRADITIONAL PROTOTYPE

access to all areas and does not inhibit through traffic. The subdivision distributes all land to individual lots and street systems, with little or no open space. Lot yields, which may be higher than those in cluster developments, usually are more than offset by the increased cost of the infrastructure. The subdivision also has the disadvantages of poor usable lot areas and the concentration of all traffic at the residential entrance.

One of the hallmarks of the Radburn plan and of many recent new towns is an internal walkway system separated from the vehicular system. Usually the pedestrian system is related to the green-space system and is designed to reduce the resident's reliance on the automobile for trips within the community. The study of new towns cited above, however, indicates that internal walkway systems may attract more buyers but they may not reduce internal traffic and parking loads. Surprisingly, walking was found to be infrequent in new towns in-town.

Other studies have shown that, for specific trips other than casual walking, most residents won't walk to a facility that is more than 200 to 400 feet away. The implications for the numbers and locations of playgrounds, tot lots, and other open spaces are clear. The indirect implications bear on the location and relationships of specific housing types and community facilities.

If an important design objective is to make it easy for low-income or elderly groups to reach local retail, cultural, and employment facilities without benefit of public transportation, housing for these groups should be placed very close (400 feet) to the core. This means high-density housing that is consistent with market demand.

If another objective is to encourage children to walk to school, lower-density

housing should be placed around the school. Other objectives and strategies can be matched in a similar way: high-income housing close to retail activities; middle-density housing close to major open space. Every case requires carefully designed relationships among objectives, prototypes, context, and systems.

PUBLIC TRANSPORTATION

Public transportation systems are an alternative or supplementary method for linking neighborhoods and facilities, and may have important effects on local community organization. They often are proposed to solve specific problems of terrain, marketing, remoteness, or access.

Our firm has planned three communities in which innovative transportation systems are used. In one, a large mountain recreational community, an aerial tramway has been proposed to link two villages, one on the upper slopes of a mountainous ridge and another a mile and a half away and 3,200 feet below in a valley. Engineering and cost analyses indicate that it is feasible, although it might not have been considered had the need to unite the villages been less pressing. The environmental benefits would be substantial—and in this case would have a tangible market value.

In a resort community in Puerto Rico, access to much of the site will be limited to pedestrians and electric carts. This is largely a response to the market and the availability of land, for it allows a higher gross density and a unique "Mediterranean" village atmosphere in the restricted areas.

At Fort Lincoln New Town (Washington, D.C.) a rail transit system is proposed to link the community with the metro system and to enhance internal circulation. The system was designed to alleviate parking needs (allowing a higher

gross residential density) and to create greater local office and retail demand. To provide a safe fallback position, however, the designers must show that the community is feasible without the transit system. This requires a fully developed road system which may compete with the transit system.

Because of the high costs of installing systems, such as rail and cable transit, the needs and benefits must be compelling if they are to be possible. For less expensive systems, such as buses or electric carts, requirements are less stringent but may prove equally difficult to meet.

The potential effects of any of these systems on a community's structure may be great or relatively insignificant. The systems designer and his team members will have to balance the structural impact, costs, benefits, and needs for such systems thoroughly and realistically.

SYSTEMS DESIGN METHODOLOGY

The methodology described below may help establish work steps and anticipate events. Obviously the process must be adjusted for each project, and the relative importance of issues may vary.

It is assumed that the most likely project for an architect's first "new town" is a small Planned Unit Development of 100 acres or so. Usually, before the architect is involved, the property has been selected by the client, who has the land under contract or option, and a market analysis has been performed by an economic consultant, during which regional markets and trends for various land uses are studied. Normally, the client has modified the projections of the study based on his experience, his judgment of what he can accomplish, and his marketing capabilities. After further discussions with his economic consultant, the developer asks for proposals to provide a master plan for the property's development, and selects his architect.

The client provides the architect with a U.S. Geological Survey (USGS) map of the region showing contour intervals of 20 feet. The property has recently been photographed from the air and a new map with two-foot contour intervals is being prepared. The architect should receive a copy of a recent survey of the property, a copy of local zoning and subdivision ordinances, and a list of target deadlines. The deadlines always fall in the very near future.

The preliminary program worked out by the client and economist may project a certain number of housing units of varying density, and other uses such as a retail center or regional office or industrial space. The program for development is to be carried out over a specified timespan, and annual figures are listed for the number of units or square feet to be built (absorption), the sale price of each housing type, and the unit densities.

The client is a private developer and carefully attuned to his reading of the market. His land may vary in cost from $200 to $40,000 an acre depending on location, natural amenities, the size of the holding, and the anticipated land uses. Construction costs may be fairly high in the area and the market primarily disposed towards single-family detached housing. If so, high-density and especially high-rise residential development may be considered a risk, particularly if the location is suburban. The cost of the land, the program, and community receptiveness to the project are the most basic issues at the start of the planning process.

The previous scenario accurately portrays the normal situation for most projects of 100 to 3,000 acres, but on some the predesign phase may be quite different. Our firm was engaged to begin planning for a 15,000-acre mountain property on which some initial physical feasibility studies had already been done. No definite market analysis had been conducted, however, and we were required to hypothesize a program for use in early studies. Market studies were then done. This change in the usual order permitted an added design cycle.

PROJECT ORGANIZATION

During preparation of the proposal, initial steps are taken to organize the project by outlining the scope of work. At our firm, we normally describe the overall task and identify each contributor's subtask, making a note of the relationships during this phase. We use this information to construct a diagram, similar to a PERT network, which displays tasks, who is to perform them, and at what times. This network helps the project move smoothly and provides a basis for accurately estimating time and costs.

It should be kept in mind that this schedule will change—perhaps drastically. Projects of this type are subject to long and intermittent "holds," as well as changes of direction. This often causes severe difficulties in staffing and total workload projection. The design team must be prepared to make the best of it, and to respond quickly when needed.

In carefully examining the tasks and objectives, the architect may find that other team members are needed besides the economist. It may be advisable to recommend engineers, traffic analysts, sociologists, or natural scientists for the design team. For typical smaller projects, such as a 100-acre PUD, civil engineering and traffic consultants may be enough.

For one of our firm's projects, a 100-acre PUD near Boston, the natural conditions were studied by our planning staff, which includes landscape architects. In the mountain community project our studies were supplemented by natural scientists, including geologists, an ecologist, and a meteorologist. We also consulted golf course architects, planners and operators of ski facilities, hotel specialists, and several others. For our work on a Wilmington, Del., Operation Breakthrough project, we used the services of a consulting sociologist. We believe that consulting services should be matched to specific project requirements and need not be from the architect's own shop.

At this time, the architect should review all available material to determine what else he may need. Gaps in the information on zoning requirements, soil borings, a two-foot contour map of the site, and a county soils survey from the local U.S. Department of Agriculture are typical data that should be requested at an early date. A base map at an appropriate scale should be prepared. The economic program also should be checked to make sure that the projected uses and densities will fit on the site. If they won't, the architect should develop a hypothetical program and sketch concept to serve as a preliminary illustration of why the program does not fit and what can be done about it.

RECONNAISSANCE

Reconnaissance begins with a site visit at the earliest time. Photographs and slides of the site should be taken and keyed to a map or aerial photograph. A base map can be prepared at a scale of $1'' = 100'$, using the USGS map, and the architect's on-site observations recorded on it. These notes will prove important later. Eventually they should be recorded in a finished graphic format for use in zoning presentations.

Existing conditions surrounding the site (local context) should be noted on a map of the area. They should include land uses near the property, natural phys-

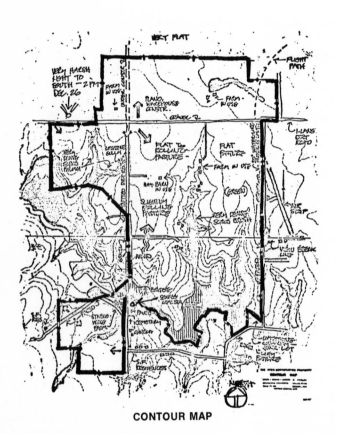

CONTOUR MAP

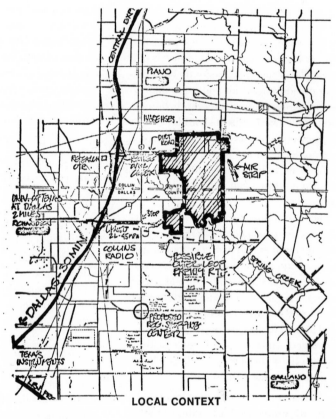

LOCAL CONTEXT

ical characteristics, the locations and capacities of utilities, local traffic data, and visual observations.

During this visit the architect should meet with the client and other team members to discuss constraints on development, plans for future utilities and transportation routes, and similar inputs. Together they should develop a list of agencies that have power of review, including the U.S. Department of Housing and Urban Development (if Title VII), and municipal, county, and state agencies, as well as school districts, utilities, conservation bodies, and others.

The architect also should review local zoning and subdivision ordinances, building codes, and school requirements. Meeting with local officials is advisable in most cases. An exception is a project for

which additional land acquisition is contemplated or local political conditions are so sensitive that information should not be disclosed publicly.

The lid has been on one of our projects for nearly three years. This works a hardship on the design process, but it must be adhered to strictly. In every project, the limits on disclosure should be discussed thoroughly with the client before any public groups are contacted.

The first site visit is a unique opportunity to gather a great deal of important information and to establish close rapport with the client, other team members, and review officials. No serious planning problems have emerged yet, and everyone is enthusiastic.

A vital part of the reconnaissance is full exploration of the client's objectives

and thoughts, additionally gaining a thorough understanding of the market forces that have shaped the preliminary program. It is also the time to explore alternative general concepts and suggest corrections in the program.

Back at the office, all of the data that the architect has gathered or generated up to this point should be collected and recorded, and a copy of this report sent to all participants.

ANALYSIS

The next step is to determine how much and specifically what areas of the site are usable for the major land uses. A certain amount of crude information can be obtained from the USGS maps, but at this point mapping with two- to five-foot contour intervals is necessary. If the project involves a large amount of land, detailed mapping may be postponed until specific development areas are located.

Aerial photographs used for mapping should be studied. Besides providing accurate locations for various landmarks, an analysis of stereo pairs can give information on soils and bedrock conditions, vegetation, and site drainage.

The USDA county soils report shows soil types for all properties in the county and gives recommendations for various land uses that can be accommodated. This information can help the designer identify the parts of the site that should remain undisturbed and other areas where development is feasible.

Where environmental conditions are highly complex or the effect of development on the natural systems must be predicted with great accuracy, additional

studies should be made by natural scientists. In the mountain recreation project, natural science studies identified areas where bedrock conditions were unstable and those where conditions were optimal. Water recharge areas (aquifers) were located, and distances from the aquifers and streambeds to developed areas were recommended. The effects of tree removal were studied, as were the effects of development on wildlife. These constraints were followed carefully in the design process to conserve the magnificent natural resources of the site and to protect the region from a negative impact.

If the property is situated near a creek or river, the 50-year floodline should be identified. This can only be located definitively if the architect has two- or five-foot contour interval mapping. This area is suitable for open space and some recrea-

tional uses, such as playing fields, pathways, or other nonstructural facilities.

On two projects we have seen premature design without flood information cause complete redesign late in the process. It is startling how much land can be taken by a 50- or 100-year flood.

The topographic relief of the property can be plotted on a base map without two-foot contours so that the high and low points are easily identified, together with the extent of grade changes. A slope classification diagram should be prepared from a base map, showing these incremental changes in percentages of slope: 0-5 per cent, 5-10 per cent, 10-20 per cent, 20-30 per cent, and 30 per cent and above. This information is important in accurately locating areas of constraint on development, and the two-foot contour map is again essential for accurate information.

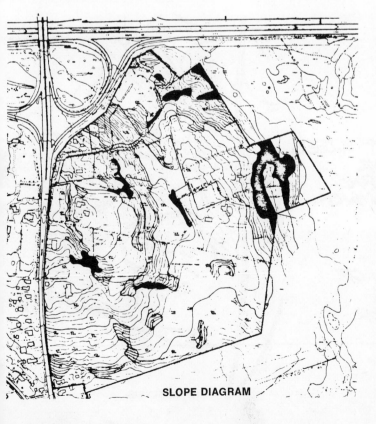

SLOPE DIAGRAM

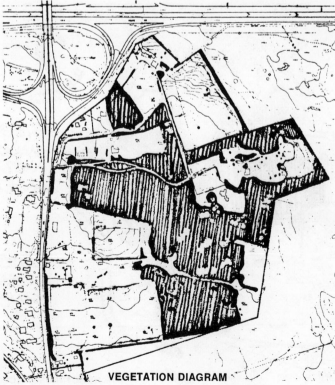

VEGETATION DIAGRAM

Accuracy of analysis is vital at this stage because other factors often act to limit the amount of land available for development. Other maps should be prepared showing the extent and quality of tree cover in various locations, prevailing winds, microclimate, and other environmental factors.

In a project of 200 acres on the ocean near Boston, the subsoil and related foundation costs were the prime determinant of land-use planning. Maps relating these two factors were used as the bases for evaluating alternate plans and finally for a financial analysis. The project was found to be economically unfeasible in spite of its extraordinary location and almost unlimited market for apartments.

SYNTHESIS

All the critical information is now at hand for anlysis of a small project. The mate-rial can be synthesized on a separate base map to show areas of constraint on development. Using the data from the slope classification map, we ordinarily outline the areas of over 20-per-cent grade and generally prohibit development there. The 50-year flood plain is located on the map, adding another constraint. High-quality tree cover, rock outcrops, and other natural landmarks are located. Areas of subsurface drainage or poor soil conditions are plotted. The locations of existing utilities, roads, and similar elements are noted along with the site reconnaissance observations. The result is a composite drawing that locates the constraints and opportunities for the property's development. There usually is some overlap in the constraint areas.

If the site is large enough or the scope of the project causes highly complex con-straints or requirements, a great deal of information must be gathered. Information related specifically to location can be presented and analyzed graphically, using a series of clear, reproducible maps called screens. By superimposing screens, a composite is produced to locate areas of constraint. Computer graphic programs can accomplish this, and include the weighting of priorities among constraints, should the project require such sophistication.

The final step in land analysis is determining the suitability of the land for development. We have found it convenient to divide a property into sectors, using the information from the reconnaissance and analysis maps. The sectors identify areas that have similar characteristics, such as flat/open/good soil to sloping/densely covered/poor soil. For each sector we list

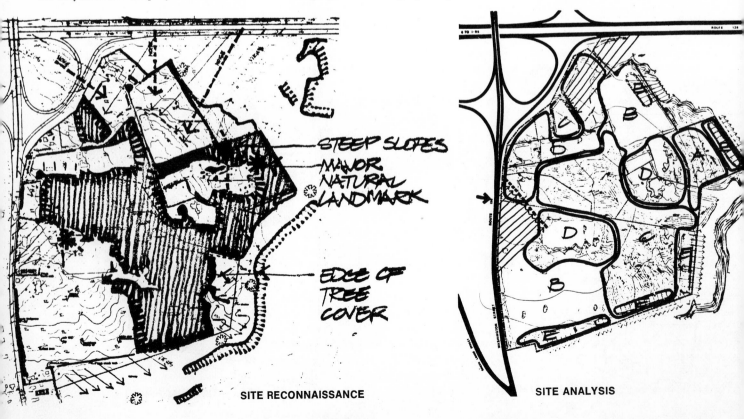

SITE RECONNAISSANCE

SITE ANALYSIS

the suitable land uses and measure the sizes, in acres, with a planimeter. Now we know how much of the site is usable for development.

If needed, matrices should be developed at this stage. For smaller projects these might compare land-use requirements to various site conditions or formal characteristics to objectives. For more complex projects the comparisons may be more finite and elaborate. The designer may reach a point where the critical variables are so many and the vital information so interrelated that the matrix becomes completely overburdened. At this point, and not before, computer analysis may become practical.

ALTERNATIVES

Now the designer can start developing alternate plan concepts. The key determinants in the alternates are infrastructure routing and the locations of core facilities.

The point or points of desirable site access are located and several possible traffic and pedestrian routes are identified, making use of ridge lines, slopes, and locational criteria. The engineer and traffic analyst should be consulted during this stage.

Optimal road alignments are located to permit good access to various sectors within the site. The effect of these alignments on parallel sanitary and storm drainage systems should also be considered. Problems with these systems can be overcome at some expense with force mains and pumping stations.

Next the designer should indicate the alternate locations for the core facilities—the central community facilities (retail, recreational, cultural) that provide community identification. Alternatives might include a core that is outwardly oriented near the main access point to achieve high visibility from the

road, or one that is internal. A third alternative may propose dispersing the core elements. These alternatives may be evaluated by a matrix comparison with objectives.

Several alternate concepts for the overall organization of the site will begin to emerge. The next set of alternatives involves the location of higher-density housing. Each infrastructure route and core alternative suggests related alternatives for high-density housing locations, including those near the core, along the major open space or amenity areas, or scattered through the site. The alternatives will relate to the sector data, which specifies land uses, and to the objectives.

As a designer develops four or five of the best alternates, he is mindful of the overall strategy for developing and marketing the components. Schemes are selected that can be built in a logical, orderly sequence of phases. Because it's to the developer's advantage to limit front-end costs for the infrastructure, at least one scheme may begin with development near the point of major access. From the economists' absorption schedule, the designer knows how much low-density sale and rental housing is to be developed in the first years, so the sectors and infrastructure are phased to take this into account.

The designer may also try to make sure that the initial development occurs in a way that takes advantage of the site's natural amenities. In this way, the image of the new town can be attractive and significant from the beginning.

Now the designer has several alternate concept diagrams which illustrate the diversity of possible development. Each major program element has been located. The size of each element should be calculated or estimated to know whether the program fits the site.

If the program must be modified, the designer should discuss how this might be done with the economic consultant. The economist can recommend alterations in housing types, densities, or phasing likely to have the least detrimental effect on the financial analysis. This illustrates the give-and-take among the systems designer, other team members, and the client. The continuing process of cross-checking provides a simultaneous, interrelated approach to all the aspects of the work.

The role of managing and assigning priorities in this fluid situation may fall to the systems designer. Sometimes the developer assumes this role along with his ultimate decision-making authority. If so, the designer is more free to act as an advocate, but he must still be responsive to other points of view.

ALTERNATIVES ANALYSIS

Now each of the alternate diagrams contains (in theory) the same program yields. They can be refined into sketch plans so that the road and pedestrian systems and other elements are known to be workable. Again, team members are consulted. Later steps will rely on the practicality and level of detail of the alternate plans. The plan elements are measured again, and program yields are noted.

Preliminary cost analysis is possible at this point. Lengths of roadways, areas of parking, extent of site grading and landscaping, building areas, and all other measurements are made and related to unit-cost data. The preliminary cost estimate is sent to the economist for a preliminary financial evaluation.

The feasibility and potential return for developing any of the alternates may be evaluated in several ways. Usually the annual costs of development and operations are compared with annual revenues. The result is the annual cash flow, which

67

changes from a negative figure in the first years (reflecting high initial costs and low returns) to a positive figure at some point in the development period.

Other factors may contribute: the amount of initial equity needed, the risk, or the required pace of absorption. Any of these may put a project in a "go," "no go," or "hold" situation. If none of the alternates yields an acceptable return, the program may be run again using a constant return and varying the land cost downward. The developer probably will hold all work until he can negotiate a new land price. On the other hand, the project may stop while the client goes to his investors for more funding, or to convince them that the pace is realistic.

This is a good time to discuss the alternates with local officials. Their comments can be useful in refining the plan and the zoning strategies in the next step. The discussions also give the designer the chance to gain their support and goodwill by involving them in the planning process.

DESIGN

Once an alternate has been selected and critiqued, the work moves into the final design stage. For a project of 100 acres or so, we have found it useful to go immediately into detailed site planning, so that we can be sure the program and all systems work properly and that otherwise unexpected issues are resolved. On larger projects, such a level of detail often is not possible until a later stage.

The plan is revised and refined to incorporate new data: evaluations of the infrastructure functions and cost; adjustments in the size or location of plan elements; evolving market and sales strategies, and zoning objectives. At this level of detail, actual configurations of clusters and the building footprints and lot areas are designed, pathway systems are lo-

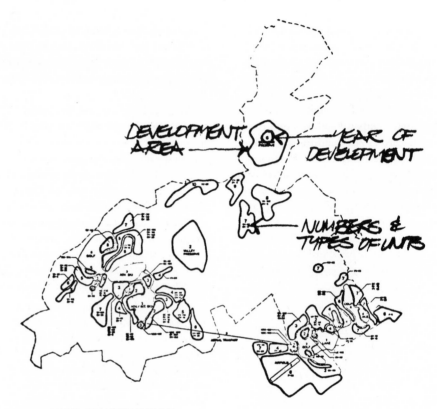

DEVELOPMENT SEQUENCE PLAN

cated, parking spaces drawn, and utilities sized.

The concept has been planned in phases. Each phase is designed to meet specific growth objectives for program elements and is measured precisely in terms of the land areas required. Sale and rental units are located and enumerated, density figures tabulated, and quantities taken off. The infrastructure phasing is planned to permit a logical growth of the systems, which may require further adjustments in the program. Cost estimates are prepared again, in corresponding detail.

The resulting documentation is important in three ways: The planning work and projected costs are as accurate as possible; the plan is demonstrably workable,

and the concept is clearly understandable to review officials.

EVALUATION

The projected yields and development costs are subjected to a new financial analysis. If satisfactory, results are used by the developer to obtain permanent financing. If this is a federally financed project the analysis will be reviewed by HUD. During this phase, the designer may start preparing the materials to be used for zoning presentations.

PUBLIC REVIEW

In Title VII projects HUD will review the plan to make sure it meets federal criteria and standards. The plan must provide a balance of activities and facilities; an attractive, efficient, economical, and functional entity; a contribution to local social and economic welfare; substantial new employment opportunities; a viable alternative to disorderly urban growth, and increased residential and employment choices for a population with diverse socioeconomic characteristics.

Previous discussions and reviews of local zoning and subdivision ordinances will have indicated whether the project can be realized under existing regulations or whether new ones must be proposed.

The limited-access system with clustered residential groups has ignited one of the most critical issues in new-towns planning today. Inherent in the scheme are large open spaces, used as buffers between roads and residences and as neighborhood recreation areas and footpath systems. The increased open space is produced by decreasing the size of individual lots and by reducing setbacks, sideyards, and other standards set by traditional zoning ordinances. The typical planned new town is not compatible with existing requirements because of higher net residential densities; atypical neighborhood resident configurations; smaller lot sizes; setbacks, sideyards, and building positions; building heights; smaller streets; a lack of rear refuse collection, and much more planning flexibility for future changes.

The designer and developer who propose a PUD alternative have a tough, uphill battle before them. To the developer it is vital that he achieve the projected return. His land costs are fixed and construction costs are rising. He must develop at densities above the norm. He knows the market and recognizes the urgent demand for quality housing. And he is confident he can sell higher-density housing if it is attractively done in an appealing environment.

To provide environmental appeal he wants to create as much visible and useful open space as possible, and perhaps to augment it with such expensive features as community centers, recreational facilities, and excellent landscaping.

Retail and office uses may be necessary to make the project viable financially, because these are strong profit generators. He also hopes to keep planning flexible over the entire area so that he can respond if market conditions change. For these and other reasons, he usually is willing to risk a struggle for the zoning he needs.

To the designer there may be other compelling reasons for the PUD alternative: Current studies indicate strongly that the traditional subdivision is not conducive to safety or contemporary lifestyles. He has specific design objectives which he hopes to meet in the most direct, practical way. He is concerned about the impact of development on the environment.

The developer and designer therefore collaborate to establish zoning objectives and strategies. Frequent meetings with local officials should be held throughout the planning process to be sure they understand the plan and its concepts. Local attitudes are likely to be expressed: the preservation of open space, the effects on schools and taxes, the appearance of the high-density housing, the possible failure of the project, the competition of the retail and office facilities with existing business, and refuse collection—among many others. The client and design team should prepare their case as thoroughly as possible, and remain ready to act swiftly as new events unfold.

The client may set up the legal framework for a homeowners' association which will maintain the open space and recreation facilities. He and the team members may also collect documentation and evidence on the market strength of apartments and town houses among upper-middle-income groups, potential tax revenues, the number of anticipated schoolchildren, and loads on the local utilities systems.

Several presentations should be given to officials to demonstrate the high quality of the developer's past projects and of the housing types and configurations proposed. The planning group may stress the advantages of the officials' being able to predict growth needs for streets, utilities, and schools for a large area.

The proposed PUD zoning ordinance for the new town will be discussed in exhaustive detail with officials. It should be designed not to exceed the changes required by the concept. At some point the planning team may want to investigate a more traditional zoning concept that would define the uses allowed in specific locations but permit cluster development and extensive open space.

WORKING WITHIN CONSTRAINTS
Clearly, several constraints act to limit the success of contemporary new towns. Critical among these for systems designers are land costs affecting the range of planning options; traditional zoning and subdivision controls restricting the opportunities for designing innovative communities; financing that affects the types of systems to be used, the depth and breadth of planning studies, the creativity of systems design, the quality of the built environment, the success of meeting social objectives, and the market interpretation, tending to limit development to a range of options within the status quo.

For the time being the systems designer will work within these constraints. By improving and streamlining his work, and by understanding the nature of the variables involved, we hope he can successfully improve the expanding urban fabric.

RIVERTON

Riverton is the second new town to be developed under the guiding hand of Robert E. Simon Jr. After relinquishing control of his first new town, Reston, Simon became president of Riverton Properties, Inc.

Riverton lies about nine miles south of Rochester in the existing town of Henrietta, N.Y., which had largely been engulfed by urban sprawl over the past 20 years. The town has enthusiastically welcomed the developers of Riverton, seeing the new development as an opportunity for more intelligent growth and more community facilities.

With initial construction getting under way in 1973, Riverton is planned for an ultimate population of 27,000 persons in 8,000 residential units when it is completed in 15 years. The initial development will contain 500 units of mixed rental and sale housing.

Also scheduled for construction in 1973 is an office building that will be the first increment of Riverton Center, the new community's downtown. Here, on a densely developed site that will be more "metropolitan" than most new-town centers, residents of Riverton as well as the surrounding region will find shops, theaters, and restaurants. Office towers and apartments will also be included, and the center will front on a private four-acre lake.

A number of social services will be housed in Riverton Center and elsewhere in the new town. These will include health, higher education, recreation, elementary and secondary education, day care and religious programs. Many of them will be created by the Riverton Foundation, a nonprofit umbrella organization through which Rochester institutions will be able to extend service programs and locate some facilities in Riverton. Social services, says Simon, "are not just frills that would be nice to have if someone would only pay for them. These are the kind of programs which will help make the difference between cities of apathetic masses and communities of concerned human beings."

Also scheduled for completion in 1973 is Riverton's first community building, the first nine holes of an 18-hole golf course, a swimming pool, four lighted tennis courts, a ball field, and portions of Riverton's walkway network. The housing will be organized around the walkway system, which will connect with a 25-acre public park and the Riverton Center.

Riverton Center will serve as a regional magnet for shopping and services. It will contain high-rise office and apartment buildings, a variety of retail shops, and a number of service facilities. A four-acre lake will separate the center from Riverton's main residential areas.

A central plaza designed for public gatherings will be the major focal point of Riverton Center. The pedestrian streets of the new downtown will lead to several squares and to a park on the shore of a man-made lake.

Riverton is situated in a booming development corridor just nine miles south of Rochester. It straddles the Genesee River and the New York State Thruway. A planned interchange with the Thruway and the forthcoming Genesee Interstate Highway will give Riverton excellent auto access in all directions.

PLANNED UNIT DEVELOPMENT: THE BUILDING BLOCK OF NEW TOWNS

Malcolm D. Rivkin

When Moliere's Bourgeois Gentilhomme learned the definition of prose he remarked, "Why that's what I've been speaking all my life!" To many sensitive designers, Planned Unit Development (PUD) is what they have been trained to do with land and buildings—even though the marketplace has not provided much opportunity thus far.

There is no real magic in the concept. The Urban Land Institute defines a PUD as "a project, predominantly of housing, with the following elements: dwelling units grouped into clusters, allowing an appreciable amount of land for open space; much or all of its housing in town houses or apartments or both; most economical and efficient use of land, making possible higher densities without overcrowding; where desired, part of the land is used for nonresidential purposes, such as shopping and employment centers."

One of the most important features of PUD, the common open space and common community facilities, has been made more feasible by the extraordinary growth of condominium ownership systems over the past decade. Now all states have laws enabling the creation of condominiums; few were extant in 1960. Common areas and facilities are maintained by home associations to which each family pays a fixed fee or annual dues.

It is important to note that while PUD is the basis for most new-town planning it is more commonly employed in suburban subdivisions for individual projects ranging from 50 to 1,000 acres. Indeed, the design flexibility principles are being employed increasingly in high-density, core-city office and residential complexes, so that the term PUD (as well as its approach to zoning) is applied to many types of projects where construction and public agency approvals are based on the quality of site and bulk design—even down to projects of a few acres.

PUD is quite similar to other innovations that catch on. Its acceptance is the result of diverse pressures and interests that have coalesced. That PUD is not yet generally adopted by developers and communities is a sign that both the pressures and the coalescence have a long way to go. But the pressures for quality and for more efficient utilization of land have borne some results, and the hard economic facts about land costs have added a practical dimension to this search for quality and efficiency.

FINANCIAL INSTITUTIONS

Many of the constraints against innovation have been caused by the conservatism of lending institutions. FHA and the mortgage bankers created the tract subdivision, and for many years their rigidity prevented anything else. But now financial institutions are beginning to accept PUD. This acceptance has been aided by the passage of Title VII and the lesser known Title X, which provides federal assistance for comprehensively planned subdivisions that fall short of full-scale new towns.

SAVINGS IN CAPITAL COSTS

Many PUDs have demonstrated considerable savings in capital costs over sprawl patterns to accommodate a given level of population. One of the most directly realizable benefits has been a saving in the cost of land per unit. As land values continue to rise, the only way to provide housing that most families can afford is to increase densities. The usable common open space that does not have to be excavated or otherwise developed for structures is a means to compensate for density with amenity at a relatively modest cost compared with finished lot prices.

The capital costs of water, sewer, roads, other utilities and their maintenance often are reduced dramatically by clustering and PUD. This was demonstrated in an April, 1967 report of the Howard County Planning Board, estimating the costs of development in that Maryland county if future growth took place according to one of three patterns. Model I projected a future based on sprawl—a continuation of the pattern that prevailed before the appearance of Columbia. Model II assumed that Columbia would be completed as planned but the remainder of the county would succumb to sprawl. Model III was based on the assumption that almost all of Howard County's anticipated growth would take place along the PUD principles demonstrated in Columbia. The report concluded that:

1. The cost of land for all uses except parks and open space is considerably less under PUD, and the added increment for amenity is only a small portion of the total savings.

2. The land absorption requirements for the anticipated level of growth are considerably smaller with PUD than with sprawl.

3. The cost of water and sewer installations is less than half with full-scale PUD than with sprawl. Assuming a similar number of dwelling units under all alternatives, PUD demonstrates considerable savings, due to the shorter length of pipe required under clustering and the ability to plan and stage large-scale installations efficiently through the use of utility corridors.

4. There are considerable savings in road construction, maintenance, and other services. (The roads cited in the survey are only local in nature and do not represent major expressway systems.)

PROFESSIONAL SKILLS

With all its savings, PUD is a far more complex and demanding approach than conventional subdivision layout where land surveyors or civil engineers simply set houses and streets on a grid with little attention to the natural forms of the environment. The complexities of relating settlement to landscape require—and local regulations normally demand—that design professionals be employed for PUDs. This offers significant hope that the quality of America's future urban environment can be improved.

THE CORPORATE BUILDER

The costs of PUDs and larger new towns have stimulated the emergence of the well-capitalized, efficient "corporate builder." The small builder or developer cannot operate at the new-town scale and can work with PUDs generally only under some subcontractural arrangement with a development entrepreneur. While the per-unit land and utility costs are less, the scale of acreage and the front-end professional costs for architects, planners, etc., is such that only the corporate builder can compete.

PUD AS A REGULATORY DEVICE

PUDs can be applied only when local zoning ordinances expressly allow for this form of flexibility. Normally local zoning codes establish exclusive-use districts, separating residential from commercial areas and allowing only a narrow range of densities within a given residential zone. In the suburban parts of most metropolitan areas, the predominant form of zoning is for single-family houses and rigidly described lot dimensions.

Many communities have begun to adopt special PUD provisions that are exceptions to traditional procedures and require special efforts from the developer and designer. A Douglas Commission survey of 1969 revealed that some 1,200 communities had instituted forms of PUD ordinances—about two-thirds of them in metropolitan areas.

USES AND DENSITIES

The form of ordinance varies greatly. Some still deal with strictly residential uses, allowing the developer to cluster the same number and types of dwellings he could build under conventional zoning on smaller individual lots, leaving the balance in open space. Others allow mixtures of dwelling types within the conventional densities, and many permit commercial and office units as well.

An increasing amount of interest is focusing on "bonus" provisions through which a community will specify that a developer can build more dwelling units or more uses if he provides more than the required open space or community facilities and amenities such as school sites, water features, plazas, etc. The PUD ordinance for New Castle County, Del., for example, will allow a PUD to have medium-density residential levels in a low-density zone if it provides a certain amount of open space and community facilities.

PUD is also being used as a carrot to attract low- and moderate-income housing in communities where it is needed but land and construction costs make it prohibitive. By offering developers a density bonus, officials reason, mixed income housing will become palatable. Fairfax County, Va., now requires that 15 per cent of the housing in its PUD and medium-density zones be for low- and moderate-income families, and provides a bonus for developers who exceed that amount.

The use and density provisions of PUD ordinances vary greatly, as does the minimum size of tract allowable. As with many other aspects of regulatory procedure, the designer must learn to operate within a different system in each area where he works.

APPROVAL PROCEDURES

There is far more standardization about the approval procedures for a PUD than for the substance of the ordinance itself. The "burden of proof" is placed on the developer and his designer, and a complex and often time-consuming process involving considerable public exposure is prescribed.

The process normally begins with the submission of a preliminary sketch plan to the local planning agency. The sketch plan identifies the basic site-planning concepts, the density levels and uses involved, and some measure of the impact on surrounding areas.

After initial discussions with the planning agency, and if the project appears to meet the community's general specifications, a detailed preliminary plan is prepared and presented to a public hearing. In this respect PUD differs from many conventional zoning techniques where the public agency makes its decisions-on compatibility and performance without public debate.

If the project survives the public hearing and the planning agency's subsequent review, it then goes before elected local public officials who make the final determination. Modifications requested by the authorities can occur at these various checkpoints. The final development plan, often at a fine level of detail, also goes through a similar procedure.

PUD approvals frequently require the developer to specify his construction schedule. If the project is delayed or a period of one to five years passes with no activity, local authorities can revoke the permit.

Because PUD is an exception to normal procedures, this method of public exposure can be essential in protecting the local public interest. But because PUD standards are rarely spelled out with pre-

cision, the developer undergoes the considerable risk that public prejudice can harm or block his program. This, plus the lengthy time span often involved for approvals, reinforces our contention that only the best-capitalized developer can undertake PUD.

THE DESIGNER'S ROLE

Under PUD procedures, the designer becomes the agent of the developer and the persuader of both the public and the public agencies. His involvement in both time and function goes far beyond the traditional professional/client relationship. He becomes the spokesman for the project, and is often the principal participant in public hearings. He has to work with the local regulatory agencies and to sense when and how to modify and compromise. He has to bear the impatience of his employer and the intransigence of officials and citizens. He has to learn local procedure and understand the attitudes, prejudices, and extent of receptivity of a citizenry that more often than not regards the PUD as a giveaway to developer interests.

Above all, the designer has to emerge with a product that meets the needs of both the market and the community.

THE TRANSPORTATION SYSTEM

Alan M. Voorhees

THE FIRST REQUIREMENT IN PLANNING a new town's transportation system is to develop a design that encourages more walking. It is quite clear from the many interviews we have conducted in Reston, Va. that the need for other transportation facilities can be cut in half or more by providing pedestrianways that conveniently link residential areas with social, cultural, and recreational areas.

Although it is difficult to get people to walk for groceries or for the normal shopping trip, certainly trips to the bank and many other personal service trips can be converted to walking if there is a good link between the residential areas and such activities. There is a limited amount one can do about the work trip, but perhaps five to 10 per cent of the people would walk to work if residential and employment areas were linked by pedestrianways.

After some concept of the land uses has been established and the activities that generate pedestrian movement have been defined, one should study the pedestrian links involved and then forecast the pedestrian travel that might develop. After this forecast is made, it should be determined if there are ways to increase pedestrian flow by adjusting or modifying land-use arrangements to get people to walk to service activities, jobs, and cultural and recreational facilities and to get people closer to people.

The pedestrian system in Farsta, the new town in Sweden, for example, has pedestrianways that link the subway with the downtown center and then continue under the arterial street to tie in with the residential areas.

It might even be worthwhile to think of people-mover systems as a way of encouraging people to walk more. This was the concept of the minirail system in the original plan for Fort Lincoln, which tied to-

gether the various educational, commercial, and residential systems. People-mover systems can be used to stretch the lengths people will walk.

The lengths people are willing to walk also depend on how pleasant the pedestrianways are and how segregated they are from traffic. But from the work we have done, it appears that time is more important than amenities.

PUBLIC TRANSPORT

After the pedestrian system has been developed, the first concern should be public transport: how to get public transportation into the community and linked with the pedestrian system. There should be a wide range of public transport systems, from trailways for golf carts and other small vehicles, like those in Litchfield Park, to special bus service, like that in Columbia.

The Fort Lincoln minirail system was

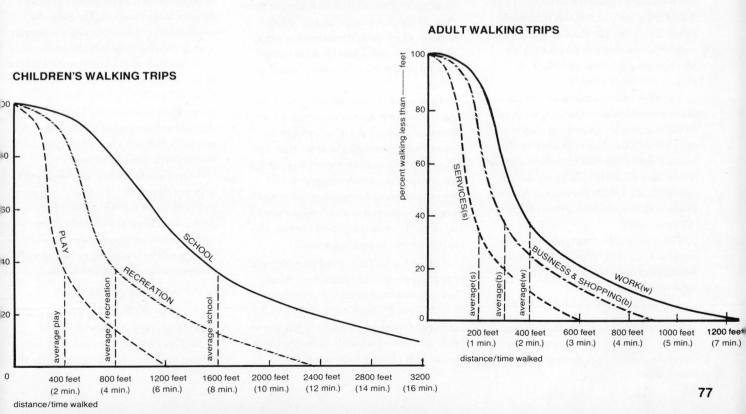

CHILDREN'S WALKING TRIPS

PLAY · RECREATION · SCHOOL
average play · average recreation · average school

400 feet (2 min.) · 800 feet (4 min.) · 1200 feet (6 min.) · 1600 feet (8 min.) · 2000 feet (10 min.) · 2400 feet (12 min.) · 2800 feet (14 min.) · 3200 (16 min.)

distance/time walked

ADULT WALKING TRIPS

percent walking less than ——— feet

SERVICES(s) · BUSINESS & SHOPPING(b) · WORK(w)
average(s) · average(b) · average(w)

200 feet (1 min.) · 400 feet (2 min.) · 600 feet (3 min.) · 800 feet (4 min.) · 1000 feet (5 min.) · 1200 feet (7 min.)

distance/time walked

planned to meet two requirements. First, it would act as a circulation device so that schoolchildren could move from classrooms to specialized learning centers without having to be chauffeured. Second, because many of the community's poor and elderly residents might not have automobiles, the system would allow them to move throughout the new town quickly and safely and to participate fully in the life of the community.

In Reston, an association was formed to provide bus service to downtown Washington and back during the peak hours. The association rents buses from local bus companies and collects the fares. Each bus has a captain and picks up passengers at stops in Reston.

Until the end of 1970, the local bus service in Columbia consisted of two large loops served at one-hour intervals throughout the day. The next step was the operation of buses during the peak weekday hours on a subscription basis. A Call-A-Ride Service (CARS) was then instituted. Every day but Sunday it provided service to those who called the CARS office, stating the time and place of pickup and the destination.

The most recent innovation in Columbia is a combination of several services. In the morning buses pick up passengers on a subscription basis. During the day buses follow a fixed route to the downtown area where most trips are going. In the evening Call-A-Ride Service is provided because the needs during these hours are the most varied.

Thus, the public transport system in any new town should reflect not only the town's density but also the specific objectives related to it.

HIGHWAYS AND TRAFFIC

Next in order of priority is the highway network. It should be recognized that streets that serve both through traffic and access to the adjoining land are generally inefficient. Each street should be primarily for either access or through traffic. Streets can be grouped into three classes: traffic, service, and connector.

Traffic streets are further grouped into three classes: freeways, to which no commercial or residential property has access, and which generally carry over 40,000 trips per day; major arterials, which have very little commercial or residential property facing on them, are served from side streets, and carry 25,000 to 40,000 trips per day; and arterials, which have commercial but not generally residential development along them and which generally carry traffic in the 10,000- to 25,000-trip range.

There are four types of service streets: major collectors, which serve more than 150 dwelling units; minor collectors, which serve less than 150 dwelling units; loop streets, which connect single streets or adjoining streets that do not serve more than 25 dwelling units; and cul-de-sac streets, which provide outlet at one end only, have special provision for a turn-around, and serve less than 25 dwelling units.

Connector streets fall into three categories: major connectors, which do not serve adjoining land development but serve traffic generated by more than 150 dwelling units; minor connectors, which have adjacent land development and serve less than 150 dwelling units; and parking connectors, which do not have adjacent land development but provide direct access to parking areas.

On the basis of observed parking practices and probability estimates, it has been determined that on those streets which serve 25 dwelling units or less the chance of meeting another car where two cars are parked opposite each other will occur only about once a month for an average driver. Thus two parking lanes and one moving lane should be sufficient on such streets.

When a street serves more than 25 dwelling units, two moving lanes should be provided. When the traffic is generated by less than 150 dwelling units (1,500 trips per day), the probability of traffic meeting is slight. Where volume is over 1,500, the chances of traffic meeting are much greater, and the design characteristics of the street should be improved to provide better operational conditions. In this case, a 12-foot lane is recommended.

As traffic builds up in urban areas, two major things happen: commercial development and noise increase. A study in Broward County has indicated that commercial property develops only on streets that carry 10,000 or more vehicles per day, although commercial development sometimes will occur on streets below these volumes if these streets intersect those of larger volume. The noise on streets carrying 10,000 vehicles per day is about 65 decibels, which can increase to 80 decibels or more as commercial traffic builds up. From a residential point of view, 70 decibels is considered maximum. Thus new residential development should be discouraged along streets that reach 10,000 vehicles per day, and 100-foot setbacks should be required.

As traffic volume approaches 25,000 trips per day, more and more access controls should be applied. Most of the access should be prohibited on streets over this volume except where traffic conditions will be improved by taking traffic away from the nearest intersection.

FUNCTIONAL REQUIREMENTS

We have developed the following standards for the various types of streets:

1. *Freeways:* 12-foot moving lanes, 40-foot medians, and design speeds of 60

mph. They should fit in with the urban development, and careful attention should be given to all the details of their design and of the surrounding land.

2. *Major Arterials:* At least four 12-foot moving lanes, two 12-foot breakdown lanes, a 20-foot divider, and a design speed of 50 mph. Access should be carefully controlled. Residential development should be served from side streets and a detailed traffic analysis should be made to determine how best to serve the commercial property—whether from service roads, special entrances, or side streets.

3. *Arterials:* four 12-foot moving lanes, two storage lanes for breakdowns, and a design speed of 40 mph. Residential development should be discouraged from abutting arterials. Commercial property can have direct access.

4. *Major Collector Streets:* two 12-foot moving lanes, two eight-foot parking lanes, and a design speed of 35 mph. If the adjoining development requires parking on only one side, one parking lane is enough.

5. *Minor Collector Streets:* two 10-foot moving lanes, two eight-foot parking lanes, and a design speed of 30 mph. Only one parking lane is needed if there is development along only one side.

6. *Loops and Cul-de-sacs:* one 10-foot moving lane, two eight-foot parking lanes, and a design speed of 25 mph. In apartment house areas, two moving lanes should be provided.

7. *Major Connector Streets:* two 12-foot moving lanes, no parking lanes, and a design speed of 35 mph.

8. *Minor Connector Streets:* two 10-foot moving lanes, no parking lanes, and a design speed of 30 mph.

9. *Parking Connector Streets.* Two 10-foot lanes, and a design speed of 25 mph.

Besides these street standards, we

too much traffic. Roads should have no more than four lanes and should appear to have a minimum amount of pavement surface. Although we have cut down on the miles of streets per inhabitant in most new communities, we have ended up with a lot of roadway surface, particularly concentrated in a few roads.

We must also develop a roadway system that provides good, safe transportation without too wide a variation in the level of service among its various elements. But I must state again that the planning of new towns must start with the pedestrian, from the point of view of both transportation and livability. All other transportation elements must conform to that framework.

PARK FOREST SOUTH

Park Forest South is the only American new town that can claim the distinction of having its own local government even before construction began. That came about in 1967 when the residents of a bankrupt 225-unit housing development on the future site of Park Forest South joined with the developers, the late Nathan Manilow and his son Lewis, to incorporate the new town. The developer/citizen partnership hasn't always worked smoothly, but it has worked well enough to offer proof to skeptical developers that it can be done.

Park Forest South is also the only new town to take its name from an earlier example of enlightened planning: Park Forest, situated adjacent to the new town on the outer fringes of the Chicago metropolitan area.

Planned for a total population of 110,000 on a 14-square-mile, gently rolling site 30 miles south of Chicago, Park Forest South already has a population approaching 5,000, as well as a booming industrial park and an innovative new university that is attracting students from miles around.

The Governors Gateway Industrial Park, which has excellent rail and highway connections, has enticed so many light and medium industries that its original 800 acres have been expanded to 1,200. Only some 25 per cent of the industrial land will be occupied by buildings. The rest will be given over to landscaped parking areas and open space. New Community Enterprises, the firm set up by the Manilows to develop Park Forest South, owns its own sewer and water system and is providing tertiary sewage treatment and separate sewerage and storm runoff systems.

The industrial park is temporarily the site of Governors State University, which is being housed in an industrial building until its $20-million campus is completed in late 1973. One of two experiments in higher education established by the Illinois Legislature, Governors State concentrates on advanced education for the growing number of students who now go to junior college. It will admit, on a first-come basis, anyone holding a junior college degree or its equivalent with a C average. There are no grades or set academic requirements, and no one can flunk out. All students are expected to have outside jobs or be actively engaged in efforts to help meet the needs of the people in their home communities.

The town plan, developed by Arcop Associates of Montreal and Carl Gardner & Associates of Chicago, departs from the form that most current satellite new towns are taking. Instead of local subcenters dispersed around a central core, Park Forest South will have a three-mile linear "Main Drag" with a commercial/recreational/municipal center on its east end, the university and a medical/health complex in the center, and a small residential area and subcenter on the west leg.

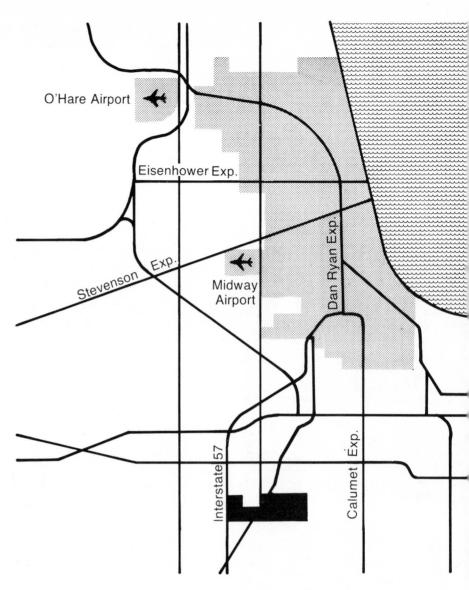

Park Forest South's location (right) gives it excellent access to Chicago 30 miles to the north. A commuter railroad line already serves the town, and Interstate Highway 57 forms its Western boundary. One of the town's first public structures (below) doubles as a fire station and a village hall.

O'Hare Airport

Eisenhower Exp.

Stevenson Exp.

Dan Ryan Exp.

Midway Airport

Interstate 57

Calumet Exp.

Of the ultimate 35,000 housing units called for in the town plan, 70 per cent are to be multifamily medium-and low-rise apartments and condominiums, and 30 per cent single-family houses and town houses. The Brooksbend garden apartments (upper left) and Burnham Oak apartments (left) are two of the town's early residential developments. As a Title VII community, Park Forest South will commit 12 to 15 per cent of its total units to low- and moderate-income housing scattered throughout the residential areas. Above: An arched footbridge is part of the pedestrian circulation system.

A year-round ice rink (below) is the first structure to be completed in Park Forest South's linear downtown, called the "Main Drag." Its vaulted roof is a series of pyramidal fiberglass units that were lifted into place. Pine Lake, near the center of the town, serves both as a gathering place for community events (bottom left) and a secluded fishing spot (bottom right).

Left: One of the town's bicycle paths crosses under a roadway in a residential area. Below: One of the numerous citizen meetings where issues about development, planning and other aspects of community life get aired and resolved. Bottom: The Burnham Oaks condominium garden apartments.

THE MASTER PLAN FOR MANAGEMENT AND DECISION-MAKING

Knowlton Fernald Jr.

THE KEY TO SUCCESSFUL DEVELOPMENT of a new town is carefully organized management that includes the ability to make quick, sure, practical, and efficient decisions throughout the life of the project. Thus a master plan for management and decision-making is perhaps more critical than the master plan for development because it provides the format for continuing accomplishment.

The management master plan must be created during the earliest stages of the project and continually tested and refined.

This chart is a guide to that process, indicating key management and decision-making benchmarks and milestones in the evolution of the new community.

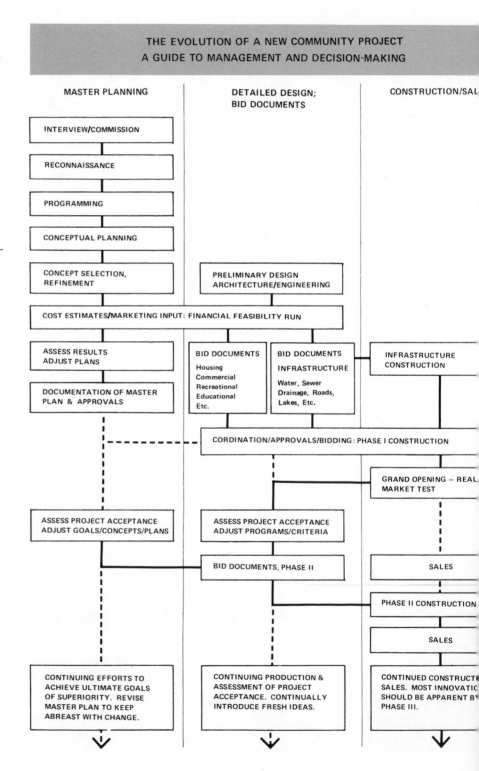

THE EVOLUTION OF A NEW COMMUNITY PROJECT
A GUIDE TO MANAGEMENT AND DECISION-MAKING

PHASING GROWTH: HOW FAST? WHERE NEXT?

Raymond L. Watson

THERE ARE TWO MAJOR ASPECTS to planning the phased development of a new town: "How fast?" and "Where next?" "How fast?" relates to the overall question of absorption, of how much of each land use that ultimately will exist in the new town should be developed each year. "Where next?" relates to the pattern that growth will follow, where each year's additions are to be placed and what the "interim composition" will look like.

It is useful to consider these questions one at a time, but they definitely are not independent of each other, and they are very much interrelated with virtually all of the planning questions that must be answered before development starts. Any particular "How fast?" option tends to have associated with it only a limited number of "Where next?" options, and vice versa.

An early high rate of absorption for single-family, low- to moderate-income housing, for example, would require early development of the flattest land, and an early high absorption of housing in the highest price ranges would require early development of the hillsides, lake frontage, and other desirable sites.

On the other hand, a decision not to develop the flattest land early would reduce the potential early residential absorption in the lower price ranges, and likewise for hillsides/lakes and higher price ranges.

Similarly, the "How fast?" decision for one land use will tend to restrict the options available for the rate of absorption of other uses. A decision for low early absorption of industrial acreage, for example, greatly restricts the potential early absorption of residential acreage, which in turn greatly restricts the potential early absorption of commercial acreage, and so on.

It is between the phasing questions and planning questions that some of the most interesting and (if overlooked) most critical relationships occur. Scheme A may be considered the ideal juxtaposition of land uses for a small area (say an admixture of residential types and price ranges with local shopping facilities), while Scheme B is considered less than ideal (say its residential is segregated by type and price range and isolated from local shopping). If serious phasing problems are anticipated with Scheme A, while Scheme B is easy to phase, the "ideal" scheme may have to be sacrificed.

The two principal types of phasing problems that typically cause the less-than-ideal scheme to be adopted (or the adopted ideal scheme to be abandoned in the middle of implementation) are the excessive costs of roads and utilities, and the political opposition of the early population. In our Scheme A/B example the desired admixture of residential types may be impractical if phasing decisions call for the early residential absorption of one type and the ideal scheme calls for wide dispersion of that type. Or if early absorption is to be predominantly higher cost single-family housing, it may be politically impossible later to develop pockets of high-density or low-cost residential.

REGIONAL GROWTH TRENDS

The most important single constraint on the phasing options of any developer is the rate at which the region surrounding the new town is growing. The amount of growth that will occur in the region as a whole places an absolute upper limit on potential absorption.

Unless he has political influence above the regional level, the unaided private developer on the periphery of a built-up area has to take regional growth trends as exogenous and just hope he can predict them with some degree of accuracy. All he can do is try to increase his share of the growth, but in the long run he can assume his efforts will be offset by others who are trying to do the same.

The unaided private developer in an isolated area—a rare bird—may try to increase the rate of absorption by giving away land to industries that locate there. But he would be competing with established industrial centers that offer closer proximity to existing labor pools and customers. So the effect on his phasing could be negligible.

A subsidized private developer can have a little more effect on his share of regional growth. With a public agency fronting for him, he can increase the amount of public investment in the infrastructure, which generally will make it easier for industry to locate there sooner. But the more subsidized private developments there are in a region, the less is the ability of each to influence its share of growth.

In practice, the public developer, even when it is a national government, has only limited power to influence regional growth trends. It has not happened in England, despite more than half a century of national commitment to a policy of building new towns and decentralizing growth. Even in the Soviet Union, where the state theoretically has the power to redistribute population by fiat, it has not been able to do so. The absolute final limit on the population of Moscow has to be raised every five years or so, and the settlement of lands east of the Urals has been much slower than planned.

CULTURAL BIASES

In the long run, the cultural environment of the new town will have a pronounced effect on the cultural attitudes of its residents. If the developer can somehow create opportunities for individuals to experience situations that contradict their preconceived attitudes, then it is likely

that with the passage of time attitudes will change. In the short run, cultural biases are nearly impossible for the developer to influence, and therefore are powerful constraints on his choice of phasing options.

COMPETITION

The maximum absorption obtainable by a new community in a given time period will be influenced heavily by the amount of other land in the region that would be at least as easy to develop in the same time period. An unaided private developer cannot significantly alter his long-run share of the regional market, but he can change it dramatically in the short run— if he wants to pay the price and has the resources to do so. By reducing his improved land value even to zero, the rate of absorption can be boosted substantially for short periods. If his competition is unwilling to match him, he may be able to capture 100 per cent of one or more segments of regional growth for a year or two.

Because he can increase public investment in the area, thus making the land he is giving away more valuable, the subsidized private developer should be able to sustain an excessively high share of the regional growth for a longer period. Of course if several subsidized private developers are pursuing this new strategy at once, their individual efforts will be less effective.

Like regional growth trends, the degree of competition that the new town will face is determined largely by impersonal forces over which—except in the short run—the developer can exercise very little influence.

FINANCIAL RESOURCES

The final factor determining what the new town's rate of absorption will be is the developer's willingness to commit the resources that are available. The developer

can exercise a fair amount of control over this, but the willingness to commit resources is at least in part a function of how successful the new town is expected to be in terms of attracting people and employment.

The greater the risk, the less inclined the private developer will be to commit his resources. A subsidizing authority can assume this risk, but that agency may not be much more adventurous than the developer. The financial risk is merely translated into a political risk. In case of failure, political heads will roll, funds will be cut back, authority will be curtailed, and special commissions will be appointed to investigate. A public developer faces the same political risk.

A private developer may have no doubt that his new town will be successful, yet may still be restrained from committing all available resources because alternative uses of part of his capital would yield greater returns. And a public developer is always subject to the threat of its allocation being revised downward.

FORMULATION OF A PHASING STRATEGY

Given the goals he hopes to achieve in building the new town and the constraints within which he has to work, the developer should be able to narrow down the feasible phasing alternatives to one or two strategies that hold the most promise of success.

Like the new town's land-use plan, the optimum phasing strategy will be the result of many tradeoffs. Any strategy that maximizes any one goal will almost certainly fall far short in attaining many others. Because of the great number of variables (or goals) he is concerned with, the developer can best consider the component options of his strategy one at a time, then make the tradeoffs between the strategies that seem best for each variable.

A balanced socioeconomic mix is one of the more difficult goals to achieve. Economics and cultural prejudices both operate to exclude the poor—especially the nonwhite poor—from the ranks of the first-generation settlers. Industry that employs lower-income groups can locate only where access to this labor pool is already available.

For satellite new towns, this means providing transportation to bring nonresident workers into the community or to take residents from the community to jobs closer in. Or the developer might try to absorb low-income housing units and jobs immediately and provide local buses and "transportation cars" to service the group's transportation needs.

An alternative strategy would be to ignore the lower-income groups for the first few years and concentrate on absorption of higher-income residential acreage. The danger is that land values may climb so rapidly before the low-income housing can be introduced that it is permanently excluded from the community.

Another type of balance sought is that between the various types of land uses. Ideally, employment centers and commercial facilities should be centrally located within a convenient distance of the populations served. This is nearly impossible in the short run because there are not enough people to support some facilities, and others may not be convenient to everybody.

The major economic factor working against land-use balance in the early phases is the fact that residential absorption is a positive contribution to cash flow, and commercial centers yield a negative net income. The developer can either sell the development rights on the first centers or he can let the first residents be inconvenienced until the positive cash flow from the residential development is big enough to carry the first commercial centers.

The tradeoffs between financial goals of the developer and the level of esthetic design he wishes to achieve have probably been discussed at greater length than any other aspect of land development. In a phased development, heavy investment in esthetics in the initial stages will increase the value of the land to be developed later, thus giving the developer an incentive to pay for a higher quality physical environment.

Some costs, such as development of open space and landscaping parkways, can be deferred until the cash flow is not so critical. Other amenities, such as community recreation facilities, may well sell themselves. When the prospective resident compares the cost per month of having the amenities with the cost of comparable housing without them, he may be willing to pay the premium. Otherwise the developer has to decide how much of his own gain he is willing to forego in order to achieve each marginal increase in the quality of design.

Independent of esthetics, the developer has to make tradeoffs between short-run and long-run financial gains at every turn. If he holds down his rate of absorption in the early years he can theoretically develop at higher densities later, with higher land values. But holding costs limit his options in this direction.

MONITORING AND REVISING STRATEGY

The phasing strategy and the land-use plan have to be developed almost as a single entity. The phasing plan is just another aspect of the ultimate development that the land-use plan represents. If either the phasing strategy or the land-use pattern have to be altered, then both will probably have to be altered.

The biggest mistake one can make is to consider phasing an after-the-fact input and, once prepared, a finished plan. It is a before-the-fact consideration that plays an inimitable and continual role in the *process* of community development.

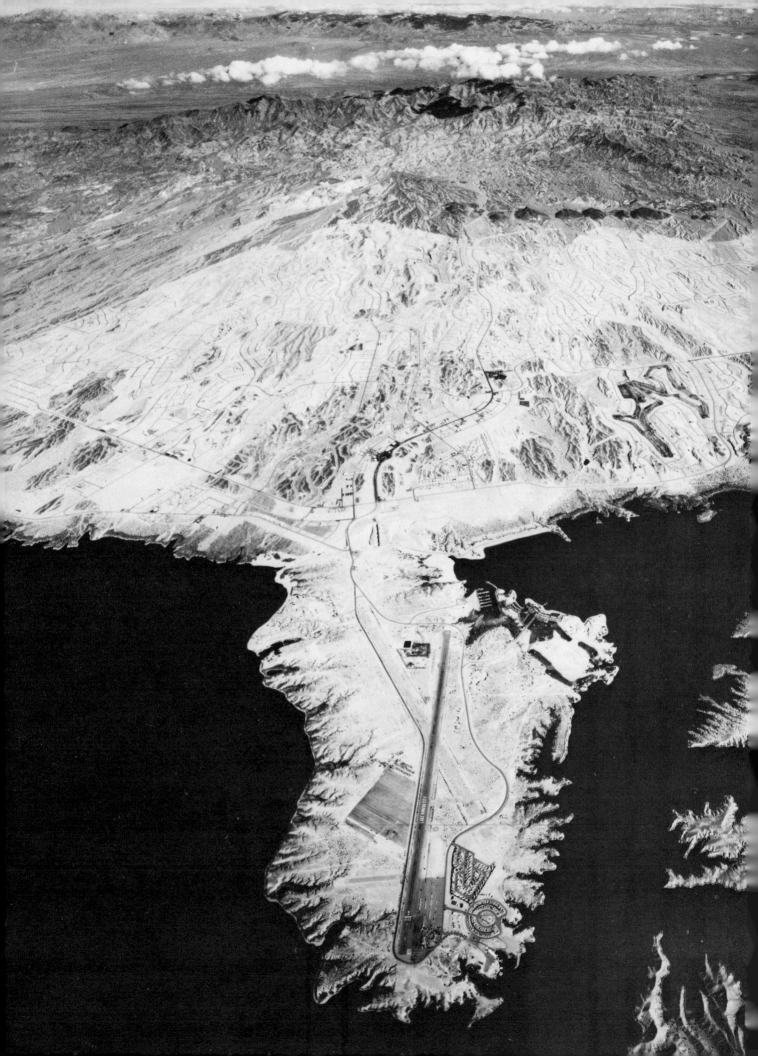

LAKE HAVASU CITY

Though Lake Havasu City is described by its developer, McCulloch Properties Inc., as a year-round resort community, it is a full-fledged new town in virtually every sense of the word. In fact, because of its remote location, it has the potential of being the most self-contained of the American new towns being developed today.

Begun in 1964, Lake Havasu City is planned for a total population of 75,-000 at a maximum density of six persons per acre. Its economy is envisioned as a balance of 40 per cent tourism, 20 per cent service businesses, and 40 per cent light industry. Tourism and industry both have been given a major boost by Robert P. McCulloch, head of the development firm. In 1968, McCulloch bought London Bridge and transplanted it to Lake Havasu City, where it is expected to draw 10 million visitors annually. In 1965, McCulloch opened an assembly plant for his chain-saw company, then announced in 1970 that all of his diversified manufacturing operations would be moved there by 1975.

To lure residents, virtually all of whom will live in single-family detached houses, the developer initiated a "see before you buy" program through which prospective buyers were flown in to inspect the new town. Property was sold only after the prospective owner had stood on it. The merchandising technique has since been adopted widely by resort developers.

In keeping with its image as a resort community, Lake Havasu City has a wealth of recreational amenities. Its 22 miles of shoreline, which have been made part of the Arizona State Parks system, contains long stretches of public beach. Water skiing, boating, and fishing are readily available. Campgrounds and hiking trails lie within the town limits. And four hotels are already in operation, with others in the planning stage.

The 1971 aerial photo at left shows the extent of development and land preparation at Lake Havasu City after seven years of existence. The two-square-mile peninsula in the foreground is now an island connected to the "mainland" of Arizona by London Bridge (then under construction). The peninsula is also the site of an airstrip, an inn, golf course, and a marina. Directly above the bridge, McCulloch Boulevard curves past the circular park of the civic center to the main shopping district. The Mohave Mountains rise in the background.

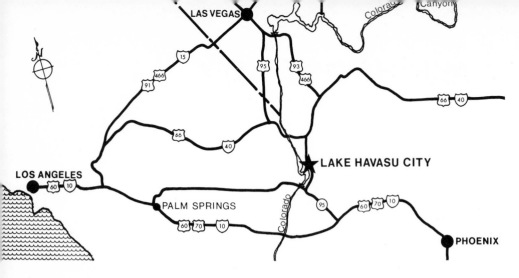

Left: Lake Havasu City's remote location is 235 air miles east of Los Angeles, 150 air miles northwest of Phoenix, and 120 air miles south of Las Vegas. Below left: Nautical Inn and beach looks north toward London Bridge and beyond to a shopping center, an industrial park, and the northern portion of the new town.

Below: A professional office building faces a public park near the civic center. Bottom: The first of the city's four present elementary schools. Right: London Bridge, which was erected on its new site before a channel was dredged separating the peninsula from the "mainland."

THE DEVELOPMENT PROCESS

Philip David

I WILL ATTEMPT TO ISOLATE the elements —mainly financial—that must be considered in the real-life creation of a new town. The economics of new towns should first be viewed in the perspective of more conventional development so that we can better understand their unique aspects and special problems.

THE LAND

The *sine qua non* in real estate development, without which a project cannot be created, is land. The value of the land may be 10 to 20 per cent of the total project cost and substantially less if the raw land cost is separated from land development costs. But its relative cost hardly reflects land's importance in the total project.

There is an abundance of land in the United States. The 50 states contain about 2.3 billion acres of land, of which nearly 58 per cent is used for crops and livestock, more than 22 per cent is ungrazed forest, and less than three per cent is in urban and transportation use (although this is increasing). The problem confronting the developer is not the total land supply, but land in areas where demand for housing or office space exists.

The developer ultimately finds himself in a most complex situation. He has to perform many acts simultaneously, and yet all of the outcomes are interrelated and affect the action he can or will ultimately take. Before acquiring the land, for example, he has to have assurances that he can obtain the required zoning. Yet before he can apply for a zoning change he must own or control the property. Before he acquires the property and applies for a zoning change, he must have made an economic analysis and market study of the project's potential. In doing an economic analysis he must make assumptions about what to build and get estimates of construction and other development costs.

Often before he acquires the land the developer will want to determine whether he can get mortgage financing, for what portion of the project cost, at what interest rate, and for what term. To determine whether the project is financeable the developer will have to get architectural renderings made of the proposed buildings and some estimate of their cost. The developer also will have to provide the prospective lender with a cash income statement of the project to demonstrate that the property will generate enough to pay off the loan.

The developer also has to arrange for interim funds to finance the project during construction. The construction lender normally makes the construction loan when there is a permanent mortgage loan commitment that will be available to pay the construction loan once the building is completed.

The developer may acquire the land before he has obtained assurances on financing, zoning, the cost of construction and development, market conditions, the demand for space, and other uncertainties, and upon his estimate of his ability to deal with the risks involved in the project.

RISK AND INNOVATION

Having acquired the land and arranged the appropriate zoning, the developer will employ an architect to prepare plans consistent with the estimated costs and net usable space assumed in his economic analysis of the project. Considering all the risks involved in the project to begin with, he is reluctant or feels unable to be innovative or imaginative in design. Just as he will build in a proved area to reduce risks, so will the speculative developer use well-proved designs. (In a subdivision development, the builder comes up with a site plan and has four or five different models of houses designed or borrowed from another project—his or a competitive builder's.)

He then arranges permanent mortgage financing on his own or through a mortgage broker. The lender is looking to the income to be generated by the property for the repayment of his loan. The amount loaned is not necessarily related to the cost of building the project. The lender is less concerned about costs than about the value of the property based on the income it will generate and the amount of net cash income available to service and secure the loan.

While the project is being built, the developer will rent or sell space or houses through his own organization or outside brokers. Once having completed the rental project, the developer will either manage it through his own organization or hire an outside management company—usually a real estate brokerage firm.

The developer's activities generally parallel those a new-town developer will have to perform, but there are important differences. The biggest and perhaps most significant difference is the longer development time span. Time becomes one of the most significant factors in the economics of development. Construction costs, land costs, costs of improvement, land sales prices and density of uses are meaningless in the absence of a time framework. Values and costs can be assessed only in terms of time. How one determines present value can be left to the academicians; that present value has to be determined is the second fundamental fact of life.

The significance can be illustrated by this example: If a developer puts a $1-million cash investment in land and improvements and does not begin sales for seven years, and his cost of money is 10

per cent, his investment in these improvements, including financing costs, will be about $2 million, or double the original cost. While profits before financing costs may be substantial, the interest cost may consume them all and in fact produce a loss.

The balance that will have to be achieved in new-town development will be between inflows of cash from sales of land and rents and outflows of cash for land acquisition, land improvements, and other costs of operation. If there were no cost for money, the developer would not have to be concerned with the point in time when he installs the improvements in order to show the project in its most impressive state, thereby encouraging people to move there.

But time is of the essence in terms of meeting the required cash outflow with cash inflow, in terms of meeting interest and principal payments on debt, and in terms of the effective return realized on the equity investment. In this simplified model the investor finances the entire project with all invested capital or equity funds for $10 million for 2,000 acres of land, land improvement, and other costs ($5,000 per acre). Assuming he intended to sell all the land in the fifth year to developers and users for $8,000 per acre, or $16 million, the developer would realize an effective rate of return of 10 per cent. ($10 million invested at a 10-per-cent rate compounded annually would grow to $16 million by the end of the fifth year.)

An investor might feel that this is an adequate return, but if the sale did not occur until the tenth year because the demand did not materialize or because of other delays, then the effective rate of return would fall to about 4¾ per cent— well below an acceptable return. The sale price, the investment, and the timing of the investment are the same, yet the proj-

ect becomes economically unfeasible only because of the timing of the sale.

The longer term of the investment has other implications for a new-town developer. It is much more difficult to estimate construction costs, interest rates, the availability of financing, costs of public facilities, land sale prices, and the demand for various land uses when dealing with a 20-year horizon for a new community than for a subdivision or office building that will be completed in two to three years.

THE CASH FLOW STATEMENT

How can we manage the uncertainties and risks related to a new town? The cash flow statement is the central control board through which we plan all of our assumptions about organization, marketing, sale prices, land use, timing of sales, timing of improvements and expenditures, advances for public facilities and services, income level of residents, the commercial/residential/industrial mix.

When one assumption in the cash flow model is changed, the implications have to be worked through to see how the change affects other parts of the project and what action must be taken and policy changes made. For example, if it costs $1 million more than estimated to build a lake, the developer has to (1) obtain a million more in cash, (2) raise the price of the lots or industrial/commercial land, or both, by that amount or a greater amount to cover the financing costs, (3) reduce other facilities by that amount, or (4) accept a lower return on investment.

The cash flow forces the developer to state explicitly his assumptions about each of the following types of inputs:
• Land allocation for residential, commercial, and office/industrial purposes.
• Residential land use in sale and rental single-family houses, town houses, and apartments.

- The pace of residential development.
- Land acquisition, planning, and development costs.
- Summary of the land sale proceeds.
- Breakdown of these units into an annual cash flow showing the cash required yearly to make up the deficits between cash receipts and expenses.
- Summary of annual cash flow of the park and recreation association.
- Breakdown of cash flow for the development company and the park and recreation association for the first 18 months.

A table will be prepared to show the assumptions underlying these factors, including land allocation, residential land use, pace of residential development, residential sale prices by dwelling unit and acre, commercial/industrial development pace and price, summary of consolidated land sale proceeds by year, communitywide development and administrative costs, capital budget, operating budget, summary cash accounting, residential lot and industrial development costs, summary cash expenditures to develop the new community, land disposition, and proposed staff organization.

The importance of when the funds are received, as well as the ability to realize the higher prices projected for land sales in the later years and the risk of higher carrying costs and development expense, has led an executive of the Rouse Company, developer of Columbia, to state: "Even at this late date, despite our successful progress thus far, there are reasonable changes in the assumptions . . . that have a good chance of occurring that would make Columbia a nonprofit-making project."

THE ECONOMIC SUCCESS OF NEW TOWNS

Robert Gladstone

THE PLANNING FRAMEWORK for a new town is founded on the economic, social, and physical environment in which it is to be built. The social and economic transcend the bricks-and-mortar or "hardware" aspects of the new community. They help define the characteristics of individual residents, institutions, and local government—the "software" of the community.

The starting point and single most important ingredient for the economic success of a new town is support in the marketplace at a level adequate to sustain large-scale, multiuse development. In specific cases this translates into the presence of sufficient regional demand for land and a strategic site location so that the new town can attract its share of the regionwide market.

A vigorous economic environment and development pace directly benefit the new town's financial viability. Because of the substantial front-end financial requirements, rapid returns are essential. The adequacy of these returns is measured directly by the rate at which land can be absorbed into the development marketplace.

METROPOLITAN MARKETS

Two factors are critical: markets that are large in relation to the size of the community, and the prospect of significant penetration into these markets. Our experience indicates that market penetrations in the five- to 10-per-cent range are possible, although ambitious. To achieve this, strongly competitive, attractively designed, and effectively merchandised housing that offers a high value and a unique environment must be created.

This is why new towns in-town and suburban satellites seem to offer the most consistently viable settings for new towns. It is in and near the major metropolitan areas that the two tests of major market and significant penetration can be met most effectively.

Metropolitan markets that carry overall housing demands of 10,000 or more units a year can provide new towns with markets ranging from 500 to 1,000 units a year against five- to 10-per-cent market penetration. This is action, and action is what new towns require for success under the pressure of their financial needs.

Making overall volume targets for new towns more difficult is the fact that the start-up pace is often lower than the rates achievable at later, more mature development stages. Thus an average pace over a period of years represents a combination of the lower-than-average performance levels at the outset and the above-average levels at peak years in the typical 15- to 20-year development period.

Easing the competitive aspects of new towns in relation to typical suburban subdivisions is the fact that they uniquely can, and indeed must, offer improved environmental arrangements for their residents and workers. The marketplace today is especially responsive to environmental factors.

WORKERS AND RESIDENTS

The meaning of the new-town economic structure goes beyond marketing factors, however. It extends to the underlying objective of creating them as diversified, multiuse, and at least partially self-contained urban units. Two important goals are, first, to provide a diversity of jobs within the community, thereby offering an ample range of employment opportunities to residents with a minimum work-to-home journey and, second, to provide a range of housing choices, at appropriate price and rent levels, large enough to accommodate all those who work within the community.

The relationship between workers/residents and the marketing of residential and commercial sites is mutually reinforcing. Key employers provide jobs initially, thereby generating housing demand from their employees. The workers and residents will in turn require services, thus generating support for more employees who will need housing in or near the new town. This cycle is basic to all types of new-town development.

For both new towns in-town and suburban satellite communities the metropolitanwide market provides underlying demand and economic support that is not only a critical but principal source of marketing strength. Not all residents in Columbia, for example, work there. Nor do all who work in Columbia live there. This pattern is to be expected because of the range of housing choices available and because some who choose to live in a new town may not be able to find jobs there.

It may also be by choice, however. Indeed, choice is the key value to be served, and it is made possible by adequate, convenient transportation between the new community and other locations in the area. We have found that between 50 and 60 per cent of a new town's residents will commute to outside jobs and a similar proportion of its workers will commute from homes elsewhere in the area.

But for one group—low-income families—the choice is severely constricted. Not less than 20 per cent of the population, and in some areas as much as 25 to 30 per cent, are excluded from the range of housing choices—even where these choices include such federally assisted housing as that built under the Sections 235 and 236 programs.

NEW-TOWN FINANCING

We often have said that "jack" is the giant-killer in new towns. The homicidal danger is too much "jack" going out too early and not enough coming back later on. The essential financial measure for

97

success in new-town development is the time elapsed between the investment of money at the outset and in the early years of development, and the return of funds in the later stages. The larger the front-end investment, the longer the developer must wait for net cash-flow returns, and the smaller relative size of those eventual returns, the less likely it is that the project will be economically justifiable.

"Patient" capital and long-term investments are not unusual, however. The construction of a steel mill or oil refinery involves "patient" and in some cases extraordinarily high-risk money. Just as in a new town, each of these investments is created to form the basis of later cash flows and each must be evaluated in terms of its time-discounted rate of return on the initial investment.

We usually establish pre-tax rates of return on investment over the development period in the range of 15 to 20 per cent (higher in some cases) as a threshold for economic feasibility. Pre-tax yields at this level, especially if they are combined with the tax shelters available in capital-intensive real estate development, can produce post-tax returns attractive enough to compete reasonably well in today's money marketplace.

LAND ACQUISITION

The most prominent among the first costs in new-town development is land. Although it varies widely, the supportable price for undeveloped land in a strong location would be in the order of $1,500 per acre. Like most rules of thumb, however, this one is subject to such critical factors as the scale of the regional market, the extent and cost of offsite work and land preparation, the site location in relation to its target markets, projected rates of land absorption, and others. By contrast, in new towns in-town supportable values in the dollars-per-square-foot range are

feasible, depending on the density of development, the market scale, and related cost factors. But farther out in remote locations, figures even at the level of hundreds of dollars per acre may not be supportable.

The scale of land acquisition also must be gauged by market, development cost, and return. By definition a new town must be large in relation to its market and economy, but it should not be so large that it cannot be absorbed and developed in a 10- to 20-year period.

FISCAL INTERDEPENDENCE

A new town must generate adequate tax revenues and service charges to support the full array of services and facilities provided by the public agencies serving it. Included are not only such items as schools and protection services, but also intangibles such as general administration.

And local government not only needs the fiscal strength derived from the new town in the form of taxes and service charges, but also must develop the capacity to perform the various, often sharply escalating, tasks needed to make the new town function effectively. These include the timely delivery of an adequate school system, major thoroughfares, police and fire protection, recreation programs, health services, and a full array of regulatory measures.

New towns usually are sited in rural or modestly urbanized locations where governments are not only unable but frequently unwilling to accommodate significant urban growth. Sympathetic cooperation if not active support by the host government is essential for success.

Another key fiscal matter relates to the infrastructure costs, which usually are sizable and burdensome for both public and private developers. An appropriate economic objective would be to target at a 30-per-cent reduction in the per capita

costs for infrastructure. For example, if it were to cost $1,000 per capita to build streets and highways and provide water and sewer connections, distribution facilities, and other items, an appropriate goal would be to deliver them for $700.

THE SOCIAL ENVIRONMENT

A new town is more than bricks and mortar. It is individuals and families who interact, recreate, and live in the community. Thoughtful and imaginative management to provide a better social environment is a key to the essential art of new-town development—and another factor that sets the new-town developer apart from the run-of-the-mill subdivider.

New towns may well offer urban society its best chance to de-homogenize the suburbs and relieve the mutual ghettoization and polarization of central-city blacks and suburban whites. At no other time in its life cycle is there so much flexibility in attitude, in governmental forms, and in social configurations as there is at a new town's point of inception. Thus new towns can serve not only as laboratories, but as vehicles for change—change urgently needed in the structure and population distribution of our urban areas.

WELFARE ISLAND

Welfare Island has been described by New York City Mayor John V. Lindsay as "one of the most extraordinary paradoxes in the city—a large tract of relatively undeveloped land sitting only a short distance away from the most expensive real estate in the world."

Now, all that is changing. Through a joint effort of the city, the Welfare Island Development Corporation (a subsidiary of the New York State Urban Development Corporation), and the federal government, Welfare Island is being transformed into a new town in-town accommodating 17,000 residents. Their community will be a strip of land in the East River that is two miles long, 800 feet across at its widest point, and scarcely more than a stone's throw from Manhattan and Queens.

The private automobile will be banned from the streets of Welfare Island. Residents will park at a 2,500-car "motorgate" garage near the Welfare Island Bridge and either walk to their apartments or take electric minibuses. A new subway station connecting the center of the island with Manhattan and Queens is scheduled for completion in 1980. In the meantime, Manhattan express buses, an aerial tramway, and ferry service are being studied as interim transportation modes.

All of the 5,000 dwelling units will be contained in apartment buildings ranging from four to 22 stories high. More than half of them will be for low- and moderate-income families. Schools, shops, and other community facilities will be designed as integral parts of the residential structures.

A Town Center will contain housing, office space, stores, specialty shops, hotels, and schools. More than half of the land will be given over to parks, promenades, streets, and other open space. Existing hospitals, which occupy 21 of the island's 147 acres, will remain, providing jobs for about 5,000 of the 7,500 persons who will work on the island.

The first phase of development, 2,100 dwelling units in North Town, are under construction and scheduled for occupancy in 1974. It will contain 300 units for the elderly and 100 more designed especially for the handicapped, with an additional 150 units scheduled for the later phase. All 5,000 units are scheduled for completion by 1979.

Above: Welfare Island before construction of the new town in-town began in the spring of 1971. Except for large hospital complexes covering 21 acres, the 147-acre island was virtually undeveloped. Right: An apartment complex for low- and moderate-income families overlooks a landscaped park. Approximately 41 acres of the island will be devoted to open space.

Right: Main Street will be a meandering pedestrianway lined with apartments, offices, and stores. Below: A pedestrian arcade will form the spine of the Town Center, connecting with the major public spaces. Below right: A model of the island as it will look when the new town is completed in 1979. The structure in the lower right hand corner is a "motorgate" where residents and workers will leave their cars.

A harbor facing Queens (right) and a
Town Square facing Manhattan (above)
will provide the two major waterfront
open spaces on the island. They will be
linked by a glass-roofed arcade. These
sketches, and those on the preceding
page, are based on a plan for the island
prepared by a team headed by Architects
Philip Johnson and John Burgee.

SOCIAL PLANNING AND PROGRAMMING

Robert Tennenbaum

SOCIAL PLANNING AND PROGRAMMING as an input to the physical design of new towns is rare. Even when it is claimed to have been done, it often is well-meaning lip service on the part of the physical planner. With few exceptions, social scientists have no experience and little interest in applying their expertise to the programming of a new town. The few social scientists who are interested in the field have no material or methodology that they can look to or rely on. In Columbia, where social scientists participated in the work group that contributed to the new town's program and planning, there is no formal feedback process through which they can study the results. Recent studies by outsiders of Columbia, Reston and other communities are only a bare beginning. Much more experience and work are needed if social scientists and the new-town programmer are to be effective.

My office has been involved recently in three new towns where the developer/client has been enlightened enough to include social programming on an equal footing with the economic program and physical design. The social programming is carried out by a team of individuals trained in the social and political sciences, urban planners with a particular leaning toward community programming, and socially and politically oriented members of the client's staff. The process and methodology described below are in their infancy and are being revised daily even as you read this.

SOCIAL/POLITICAL DATA SURVEY

Here the social scientist, through basic field research, describes the existing social service system in the area, identifying programs, policies, and plans as they relate to the community services of health, communications/information, education, culture/entertainment, recreation, religion, and law enforce-

ment/public safety. The physical location and delivery system of existing facilities are mapped in relation to the site of the new town. Normally this covers an area as large as a county or subregion, with highly specialized service systems delivered in the urban core.

Short memos are produced describing the state of existing and proposed facilities and how they might relate to the new town. Valuable initial contacts are made with the personnel of the institutions that deliver social services to the area in which the new town will be developed.

DATA EVALUATION

During this phase, existing facilities and proposed plans for their expansion are carefully related to the phasing of the new town and the full range of services it will need. Large new towns are located in predominantly rural areas where social service systems are nonexistent or at a bare minimum, but highly specialized services, such as medical centers, are available through the urban core.

Here the planning team realizes the degree to which the developer and local government must begin to plan for the delivery of social service systems to the residents of the new town—by attracting regional institutions, expanding existing ones, or creating new ones. Here too certain hints about possibilities for innovative service systems emerge.

As a working tool, a matrix of social service systems is created and the existing conditions and proposals for expansion are noted as a base upon which the new town's social service requirements are added.

CONCEPT DESIGN OF SOCIAL SYSTEMS

Based on the existing situation and the new town's projected needs, a set of planning gols and objectives is projected as a general guide for structuring the community. These goals are based on such considerations as the socioeconomic breakdown of the anticipated residents identified by the economist, the life-style of the metropolitan area, and the physical nature of the site.

A social service system concept is sketched out, identifying basic services required in terms of administration, operations, facilities, and, most important, linkages to other service systems. These variables are set in a group of matrix studies to be used as a tool for refining the basic concept.

During this phase the social scientist will work closely with the designer, both to understand the possibilities of the site and to develop flow diagrams and charts illustrating many complex interrelationships. These visual systems are used not only for notational and design purposes, but to communicate to the client and outside consultants the concepts under consideration. We have found that people respond more creatively to a visually projected social concept.

Sketches and diagrams are prepared to illustrate the diagrammatic relationship between, for example, the total educational system and other community facilities such as recreation or health. Diagrams are generated attempting to structure the various elements of the new town in terms of neighborhoods, villages, open space, or whatever the site characteristics and goals might suggest.

The social scientist recommends to the designer certain broad requirements in order to begin to satisfy the needs of the community. If, for example, conversations with school administrators have indicated that an innovative educational system is possible, then the urban designer is less constrained in approaching the relationship between residential areas and school facilities.

In one new town, the social scientist identified the need for a regional recreation system and recommended that land be set aside for a regional park. This began to suggest a whole series of possible interrelationships between a regional park within the community and the other facilities and activities the developer would provide.

Sometimes elements of the designer's site analysis and sketch concept plans can inspire innovation from a sensitive social scientist. In one recent project the existence within the new town of a highly desirable ecological preserve led to building curricula related to this unique area into the educational system. In another case, an existing rail system suggested possibilities for commuter transit to the urban core and in turn inspired the idea that the educational system could use the trains during off-hours as a classroom-on-wheels, taking students on excursions to the urban core. Thus an expensive commuter transit facility would be used to its capacity and serve purposes beyond its original intent.

During the concept design of social systems, the developer and the heads of the various institutions are involved in the drafting of outline programs and proposals. Where a significant number of residents live within the influence of the new town, their guidance is sought so that proposals can be tested and additional needs identified.

PRELIMINARY SOCIAL SERVICE SYSTEM AND COMMUNITY ORGANIZATION

During this phase broad concepts and approaches are structured and quantified in terms of a physical program, defining and describing in detail all of the systems and related criteria required to serve the new town.

The projected educational system, for example, is detailed in terms of the

number of schools needed at each level; the student population, size, and acreage needed for each school, and suggested physical relationships between the schools and other community services and facilities. A program of the community recreation system is proposed, and its effect on the required community centers detailed, providing input for the designer in locating them at the various levels required.

We have found it useful for the social scientist to write a series of vignettes describing, and thereby testing, the projected life-styles of various socioeconomic and special groups expected to live in the new town. These constitute a verbal description of the new town, just as the designer describes the projected new town in terms of plans and sketches.

FINAL SOCIAL SERVICE SYSTEM AND COMMUNITY ORGANIZATION

Here the preliminary work is refined. Most important is the setting up of on-site advisory work groups of professional specialists for the continuing programming and planning of the new town's social service system. Detailed proposals for the creation of programs relating directly to the physical design and the phased development of the facilities are projected.

Programs are prepared for all of the community service centers, and the detailed linkages between them are clearly identified. The square footage and cost of the centers are estimated, providing input for the economist's economic model. This is a most difficult task because a complex collection of interrelated community services, linked together in an innovative way, must be described in terms of capital and administrative costs. An attempt is made to demonstrate that it is less costly to structure overlapping multiuse facilities serving many activity needs.

THE CLIENT IS
THE COMMUNITY

Herbert L. Franklin

In order to keep this complex set of relationships in a workable form, we have prepared a series of matrix charts which relate facilities to facilities, facilities to activities, activities to needs, facilities to dimensions, and activities to dimensions. One product of this process is a scaled relational diagram of facilities which allows sketch schematics to be drawn for community centers and other related facilities. This tool is as important to the new-town developer over a long period as the urban design plan or economic model.

We must leave the community developer with more than a development plan. He also needs a development *process* that is responsive to the community concept. What we are seeking is a workable technique by which we can marry all of the natural and man-made community structures to a system for continuous programming, allowing for constant feedback and the continuous updating of market data in an economic model that recognizes the dynamic nature of the new-town development process.

IN A RECENT ARTICLE on what it chose to call "the new-towns movement," *Fortune* listed a number of large corporations entering this form of real estate development. They enter it at a time when consumerism is in new vogue. If Westinghouse, Gulf Oil, Florida Gas, Chrysler, Ford, Sears Roebuck, Marshall Field, Aetna Life, Illinois Central and other large corporations are going to build the urban environment of tomorrow, will they be building for communities or for consumers?

My message under these circumstances is simply this: The client *is* the community, the community that exists and that which is yet to be.

There are natural and perhaps unavoidable tensions or conflicts between the developer and the community. They reflect the familiar issues that enliven community development generally: How do we reconcile the private profit motive with social objectives? How do we reconcile regional perspectives with local interests? How do we balance the national objectives of long-term planning with those of responsive democracy, or fit mounting growth pressures into legitimate expectations of stability and tradition? How do we mesh the life-styles of the old-timers and the new arrivals?

The importance of secrecy in the assembly of land for a new town, for example, means that a basic locational decision is made unilaterally and often without reference to any publicly approved—much less debated—comprehensive plan. And even where it may be argued that such a plan exists and the proposed new town accords with it, the very nature of the locational decision will raise questions about "windfall profits" for the developer, higher property taxes for adjacent land, and the like.

Under the existing system of land spec-ulation the removal of the cloak of secrecy is widely and correctly regarded by developers as likely to be so counterproductive financially that it is not entertained seriously. The land for Columbia, for example, was assembled piecemeal through "blinds" over several years, and Howard County, Md., was confronted with the prospect of change willy-nilly. It is fortunate for the county that it dealt with a developer who has a highly refined understanding of how the profit motive can be applied imaginatively to avoid doing social injury and perhaps even provide social benefits.

Columbia and its fairly successful relationship with Howard County at one end of the spectrum should be compared with a proposed new town in Loudoun County, Va., at the other end. An article in *The Washington Post* of February 12, 1971, relates the experience of one new-town developer:

"The Board of Supervisors of Loudoun County, in one of the strongest moves against suburban growth by a Maryland or Virginia locality within memory, have turned down a rezoning plan for a $112-million, 1,270-acre planned community in the county's eastern end.

"Shaped to conform with the county's own master plan and designed to absorb much of the county's growth during the coming decade, the rezoning application submitted by Levitt and Sons Inc. was described as 'technically perfect' by county planners. It was praised by the Supervisors themselves even as they voted 4-2 against it last week.

"Supervisor James F. Brownell of Round Hill appeared to sum up the feelings of the board's majority when he told the meeting: 'It just seems to be time for somebody to say "whoa" ' to the pressures of growth that have come to Loudoun in the last 10 years.

"The plan proposed by Levitt, the nation's largest homebuilder, would have provided 4,235 dwellings for 13,000 people in a mix of apartments, single-family homes, shops, parks, and open space similar to the new towns of Reston, Va., and Columbia, Md.

"The community would stretch from Virginia Route 7 to the Potomac River a few miles west of the Fairfax County Line.

"The Loudoun Supervisors' denial stands as the latest and perhaps most dramatic local example of the increasing disenchantment of suburban governments with the postwar article of faith that 'growth is good,' even the kind of attractively packaged and controlled growth the Levitt plan represents.

"The collapse of belief has been fueled by mounting costs of public services, rising long-term indebtedness, heavier local tax burdens, all of which accelerated on the heels of suburban residential expansion.

"'We're not trying to build a wall around the county and shut out all growth,' said Board Chairman William S. Leach of Middleburg in a recent interview. 'We know it's got to come. We are just buying time.' . . .

"Leach thinks the answer may lie in a program of intensified industrial development for the county—which now has only a dozen small industries—coupled with a land-use tax to assess farmland as farmland rather than potential development land.

"Pocketed between the Potomac and the West Virginia border at Virginia's northern tip, Loudoun County long has been remote from the sort of development pressures forced on Washington's immediate suburban counties. . . . According to Supervisor Douglas N. Myers of Waterford, 'Sterling Park soured the whole

county' on the idea of suburban growth. Myers, a white-haired, 74-year-old retired insurance man who voted against the Levitt rezoning, says Sterling Park 'makes me mad every time I drive past it . . . houses crowded right on top of each other like that . . . no trees . . . I like some acreage.' But he says his overriding objection to Sterling Park is the demand it has put on the county for services.

"To meet the demand for police and fire protection, schools, and utilities—most of it in Broad Run district—the county has contracted bonded indebtedness of $20 million in the past eight years and now faces a projected deficit of $3.2 million in the operating budget by mid-1972.

"'You know what caused that?' said Leach as he waved his hand toward the budget figures in frustration during an interview. 'People. Too many people. Every house built in there created an economic deficit.' . . .

"The Supervisors are friendly about their differences and united in their high opinion of Vose and Levitt, who they said 'bent over backwards to do everything we asked' during the two years the plan was in preparation. . . .

"Levitt spokesman Vose says his firm did everything it could to suit its community to Loudoun's master plan for community land use, including reducing the number of dwelling units by 11 per cent, cutting its projected population by 12 per cent, and eliminating the planned shopping center. To soften the adverse economic impact on the community, he said, Levitt offered not only to donate three school sites but to build the schools as well and lease them to the county at cost." (A lower state court later upheld the county's action. Although Levitt appealed this decision, it eventually dropped the appeal to resubmit plans

under which it would finance facilities such as schools, sewers, parks, and libraries.)

HOSTILITY AND SUSPICION

This story illustrates an obviously bad resolution of conflicts between the existing community and the developer of a proposed new town. Venture capital, which is available only to the larger and more sophisticated developer, takes an enormous risk in dealing with the politics of the Loudoun Counties of this world.

The local people will inevitably view any highly visible agent of change with hostility and suspicion. They will want to know what is going to happen to their real estate taxes, their property values and the level of public services. They will want to know what kinds of new people will be arriving to live in their supposedly tranquil and bucolic setting. They may want to know how newcomers will affect local political decisions and cultural patterns; who will be attending school with their children; how increased traffic loads will be handled, and if a rapid increase in population will bring the social pathology commonly associated with urbanization.

The Loudoun situation illustrates another important point. I have heard it said that one of the problems with our subsidized housing programs is that because they underwrite piecemeal, undramatic, and poverty-oriented developments they will always be regarded as detriments rather than benefits to a locality. This argument goes on to suggest that couching such housing in a broader community-development program will sugarcoat the pill. The Loudoun situation shows that even a presumably well-planned new town will inevitably confront the "power to the people who got there first" psychology.

The poor and the minorities are but the

most visible targets of an antigrowth politics that is sweeping suburbia and will exact a high price from venture capital unless we reform our system of land-use controls. Judging by the landscape we have produced through development business-as-usual, there is room for honest local dismay that is not motivated simply by racial and economic prejudice. The middle-class professional may proclaim that the profit motive must be allowed to flourish through new towns, but the ordinary citizen has not seen much improvement to his environment from current zoning processes which profess to harness that motive to social or public purposes. So there is a great deal of unfinished business, in terms of national growth policy, if at least satellite new towns are to play a role in shaping the metropolitan environment. The agenda for reform must include new processes which both assure citizen protection from rapacious development and give private capital an outlet for responsible, imaginative building of the environment.

Moreover, the natural inclination of most existing residents is to resolve their doubts in opposition to significant and visible change, notwithstanding the inducements a public or private developer might devise. These attitudes are not limited to rural people. The experience with proposed large-scale developments within highly urbanized areas suggests that it is a common phenomenon there as well.

There is, after all, a sense in which confidence by local people in the good faith of a developer is not inspired simply by his largesse in the form of school buildings, open spaces, sophisticated designs, and other professed bonuses for the community. Indeed, the more an apparently highly financed developer promises to dole out such sweeteners, the more

he may engender the feeling that he hasn't dug into his pockets deeply enough.

Citizens who are too busy to oppose the ravishing of their environment in the usual piecemeal ways will thus be inspired to take concerted civic action against a proposal for significant change no matter how well planned, beneficial, and sensitive it might be.

How does a developer, public or private, deal with this situation? Indeed, how do we all deal with it in order to promote a more rational and humane urban environment? In Britain, local residents are actually put on the board of the development group—something that to my knowledge has no parallel in the United States. It is also common for staff members of the development group to live in the town they are developing—an informal but probably effective method of bridging the conflicting perspectives. This practice might help avoid the community referendum that so frequently becomes the vehicle for "citizen participation" in planning and community development.

An August 1971 report of the Twentieth Century Fund entitled "New Towns: Laboratories for Democracy" observed: "The nature and the mechanisms for citizen participation in new-town planning can take many forms. In some cases a system of public and official hearings and review of proposed plans might be adequate; as a minimum, private developers should seek the views of citizens' groups in the areas where they plan to locate new towns. In others, a body of citizens aided by professional planners might be empaneled to participate in the planning process. In an in-town or add-on new town it may be more appropriate to establish a new-town district whose residents or governing board could elect official partici-

pants to the board of the development group. Alternatively, the board of the new-town district could advise the developer on behalf of its constituency."

The above recommendation is based on the premise that "the planning of new towns without some form of (citizen) participation is unlikely to remain politically feasible as increasing numbers of people recognize that the employment of public resources for new-town development is of direct concern to them." Very clearly, a developer will be calling on a federal guarantee or on major local public investments to carry out the project. The fiscal benefits and detriments of the development will be spread unevenly. So there is always a public interest to be legitimately expressed from the earliest possible stage.

The question is, How should the public interest be expressed? Leaving this issue to hit-or-miss arrangements may be in order for the time being, but it behooves some group or the federal government itself to monitor experience in this field to determine just what patterns work and which need improvement.

The Loudoun County experience demonstrates how our existing system of land-use controls is poorly equipped to deal with the pressures of urban growth in metropolitan areas. Had Virginia adopted a model land development code similar to that now under consideration by the American Law Institute, the developer would have been able to appeal the adverse decision of the county to a state body. ALI's proposed legislation would replace existing state laws on zoning, planning, and subdivision control. It would return to the state level powers the states do not now exercise to plan and control the use of land. The code would provide an administrative appeal from local decisions involving proposed developments having state or regional impact. The refusal of a locality to permit the development would enable the developer or other interested parties to appeal the local decision to a state body that would have the power to invalidate the local decision. The ALI proposal has shortcomings, but it is a step in the right direction.

Unless the federal government prods the states to examine and reform their existing land-use policies in the face of the pressures of urban growth, the developer of a new town will find his risks increasing rather than decreasing and his front-end investment growing as he deals with localities that wish to stop the world and get off.

BENEVOLENT DESPOTISM

Royce Hanson has described the relationship of the developer to the governance of a new town as "benevolent despotism." Unlike most small homebuilders, the developer of a new town will have a continuing relationship with his "customers" for some time. The devices he uses to gradually remove the development corporation from the scene as the new town is completed must be delicate enough to handle the peaceful transfer of political power in an absolute dictatorship.

The homeowners' association is the usual device by which a developer relaxes his control over the new town as development proceeds. The developer of Reston, for example, created the Reston Homeowners Association, with each housing unit having one vote, the developer retaining a vote for each unsold unit, and a third of the total votes in any event until 1985. The association operates recreational areas and facilities conveyed to it by the developer.

In Columbia, the Columbia Association has taken on the character of a private government. It has a charter permit-

ting it to do just about anything. The developer appointed the original board, to which one Columbia resident is added for each 4,000 units of housing occupied. Beginning in 1976, one developer representative will be dropped each year until 1980 when the terms of the last three will expire together. The resident directors of the Columbia Association are chosen by the board itself from among nominees of the Columbia Council, whose membership is elected directly.

Thus the Columbia Association is somewhat insulated from the electoral politics of Columbia, is totally divorced from the politics of Howard County, and by 1980 will be divorced from direct developer influence as well. The association builds and maintains community facilities, including recreation and community centers, swimming pools, transportation services, and other quasi-governmental activities. It is financed by an annual mandatory charge on all taxable property in Columbia at a rate of 75 cents per $100 of assessed valuation.

In 1970 the Howard County Council appointed a Columbia Commission to assess the impact of the new town on the county. In its report, issued in 1971, the commission pointed out that by 1980 the Columbia Association's annual budget will exceed $17 million, only $1 million less than Howard County's total revenue in 1969-70. It is not surprising, therefore, that the commission's report observes:

"The commission is concerned, not so much by the size of these figures, but by the fact that there is no formal relationship between the Columbia Association and any branch of the county government, i.e., that Howard County has no way of either controlling or legally influencing the actions of the Columbia Association, and that there is no procedure

to officially oversee the administration of its funds. A similar concern has been expressed by the citizens of (Columbia), who are frustrated in their own efforts to have an effective voice in operations of the Columbia Association. In fact, this concern has been frequently characterized to the commission as being the Big Problem as perceived by citizens of (Columbia). These problems are directly attributable to the unusual organization of the Columbia Association."

The report recommends that the county council take action to assure that at least one representative of county government become a member of the Columbia Association board. The report also voices concern that the divisions between residents of Columbia and residents of Howard County result from the invisibility of the county to Columbia residents, many of whom do not realize that the county, and not the Columbia Association or any other Columbia entity, is the only level of local government and contains not a single incorporated municipality.

At the same time, many of the old-timers are convinced (wrongly) that they have paid for the higher level of services enjoyed by Columbia residents and (correctly) that the presence of Columbia has drawn people of ethnic, racial, and cultural characteristics quite different from their own.

More than 15 per cent of Columbia is black. The developer has gone out of his way to portray the new town as racially integrated. The inclusion of renters on the board of the Columbia Association reflects this commitment. But in different situations homeowners' associations could become devices to insulate new towns from the reach of the Constitution.

We would be learning very slowly indeed if we permitted private associations to assume responsibilities that local pub-

THE RISK OF MEDIOCRITY

Ralph Rapson

lic agencies formerly discharged, especially when the role of local government in blocking the economic and racial integration of metropolitan areas is becoming a major focus of national urban growth policy.

From the standpoint of public policy, the time is approaching when these arrangements can no longer be left to the untrammeled discretion of the developer. At present he is free to view community relations with the same motives of any producer to his consumers. Even the matter of socioeconomic integration can be sidestepped, although the criteria for federal guarantees may force his formal recognition of this goal (yet quietly enough so as not to upset the local authorities).

For in the last analysis, the community of concern for new-town development is a broader one than I have described. Professor Stanley Scott, of the University of California, has identified these interests as legitimately concerned with large new communities and their future: the developer, future residents, residents in the vicinity, the county, the whole metropolitan region, and the larger public interest in the character of future urban growth throughout the state.

American new towns to date have attempted to reconcile the interests of the first four groups. The last two—those concerned with the future of the region and the state—are just beginning to be heard. For the new-town developer of the future, these may be the "clients" to woo as the pressures to stop urban growth, any growth, mount.

IT IS BOTH INSTRUCTIVE AND FRIGHTENING to cite the different disciplines and skills that are being called on to plan and develop new towns. Beyond the traditional architectural, mechanical, electrical, structural, construction, and financial professions and skills, there are management and marketing experts, social scientists, computer programmers and analysts, industrial systems experts, environmentalists, climatologists, data coordinators, industrial designers, and a growing band of such specialists as educational and occupational psychologists who deal with human factors and the interrelations between people and their occupations, equipment, and work.

Moreover, one cannot ignore the authorities on government programs with their seemingly endless hurdles apparently devised to confound and confuse, and the owner-developers who so often impose their limited objectives on the design process.

The theory is that great things can happen if you call in as many experts as possible and let each get into the act. But usually the result is to avoid bold and major decisions, never taking a chance. The result is compromise, dilution, and homogenization.

Expertise is necessary and desirable at all levels and stages as long as the input is meaningful and contributes to creative design solutions. If it is assumed, however, that a good solution will be automatic because data and information are plugged into a systems formula, then the premise is wrong.

At the risk of seeming antianalytical and subjective, let me suggest that, however logical the process, it is fraught with pitfalls and in constant danger of producing mediocrity.

If our new towns are to provide a framework for a better life, then our objectives and our planning must be truly inspired. We have the knowledge and the resources to break with our restrictive and limited past policies. We have the ability to build significant environments. But new towns will fall far short of our aspirations and potentials unless the wealth of wisdom and resource is guided by a firm belief in quality, three-dimensional design solutions. This is the unique expertise of the gifted architect.

THE DESIGN TEAM IN FEDERAL POLICY

Ralph Warburton

A WELL-QUALIFIED DESIGN TEAM with continuing authority to do the job effectively is the first requirement in achieving new towns of high quality. The Urban Growth and New Communities Development Act of 1970 acknowledges this requirement when it states:

"It is the purpose of this Act to provide private developers and state and local public bodies and agencies with financial and other assistance necessary for encouraging the orderly development of well-planned new communities, and to do so in a manner which will rely to the maximum extent on private enterprise, enhance both the natural and urban environment, assist in the efficient production of a steady supply of residential, commercial, and industrial building sites at reasonable cost, increase the capability of the homebuilding industry to utilize improved technology, help create neighborhoods designed for easier access between the places where people live and the places where they work and find recreation, and encourage desirable innovation in meeting domestic problems, whether physical, economic, or social."

Of the seven points included in this quote, five relate directly to architectural concerns. Thus more than 70 per cent of the Act's objectives involve the architectural profession. Moreover, HUD's regulations for implementation require that a new community be "a well-planned and diversified whole so as to create an environment that is an attractive place to live, work, and play. Among the factors which the Secretary will consider in evaluating the plan are the adequacy of controls and incentives for promoting and enforcing attractive land utilization, urban design, and architecture."

In fact, of the total of ten factors to be considered in evaluating the new-town plan, nine require design services. And Secretary Romney has said, "The design and planning activities must result in environments which have an uplifting effect on people's lives."

The high level of design quality in all HUD-assisted work has been recognized for some years through the Design Awards Program. This biennial program stimulates good project design and urban design by giving public recognition to those HUD-assisted activities in which superior three-dimensional form appropriately combines and expresses visual, social, and economic values.

The first new town to receive the HUD Urban Design Concept Award is Jonathan, Minn. The following excerpt from the Project Agreement between Jonathan and the federal government may help to explain why:

"The developer has planned to provide for the preservation and enhancement of the natural features of the area so as to permit the establishment and maintenance of an accessible open-space network. Land-use planning in all cases shall consider the potential of the land to support the various categories of land use to be programmed. These include slope of land, present vegetation, soil considerations, soil conditions, and aesthetic considerations. The developer shall include in covenant with all builders appropriate standards to restrict the indiscriminate destruction of tree cover in residential and industrial areas and to require specific approval of site plans as well as architectural drawings.

Like Jonathan, every new town offers the opportunity and responsibility to develop new design potentials, for the development of new towns of high quality is one of the prime vehicles for stimulating overall environmental excellence

HERITAGE VILLAGE

Considering its small size and the fact that almost all of its residents have reached retirement years, Heritage Village, in Southbury, Conn., is a remarkably diverse new community. It contains, among other amenities, a full-fledged commercial area, an 18-hole championship golf course, a library, and a multiuse activities center that offers everything from badminton to yoga.

Many of the community's activities are contained in buildings that already existed on the 400-acre pastoral site, most of which was once owned by pianist/comedian Victor Borge. The activities building itself was once used by Borge to process frozen game hens. The library, which was organized and sponsored by residents, is housed in a cottage said to be the birthplace of Ethan Allen. And a meeting house and restaurant occupy former residences on the site.

The new structures of Heritage Village, including groups of cul-de-sac town-house clusters that eventually will house 4,200 to 4,700 persons, are sensitively dispersed to protect the natural beauty of the site. One group of new structures forms the Village Green, a 30-acre commercial complex situated a short walk from the residential areas.

A project of Heritage Development Group Inc., Heritage Village enjoys a high degree of community participation in the management of its affairs. A Master Association composed of one representative elected by the board of directors of each condominium association, manages the overall operation and maintenance of all the housing units. Residents also operate a volunteer ambulance association, a minibus service, and a host of civic, social and charitable clubs and organizations.

A cluster of condominium town houses overlooks one of the ponds that enhance the beauty of Heritage Village's site.

All housing in Heritage Village is in small clusters of condominium town houses (right) dispersed throughout the site. A professional building (bottom photo) serves the medical needs of the retirement community. An amphitheater (below) seats 500 persons for a variety of outdoor activities, including concerts and lectures. To the left of the amphitheater is the activities building, and to the right is the women's club.

The activities building (above) offers swimming outdoors and a wide variety of recreational and cultural pursuits inside. Left: One of the 22 shops in the Bazaar, a shopping center that, together with a financial building, a market building, and a professional building, forms the Village Green commercial center.

III. NEW TOWNS AND URBAN GROWTH

THE FOLLOWING ESSAYS deal not only with the future of new towns in America but, more important, with the future of urban growth as a whole—a whole of which new towns are only a part. If our present pattern of sprawling urban agglomeration, with an occasional new town here and there, is allowed to continue, there is little hope that the quality of our total environment can be improved.

The main theme of all the essays is the need for a national urban growth policy that would encourage orderly and efficient development throughout the United States. Though the emphasis is on the physical form that urban growth can and should take, the overriding consideration is the human factors that the physical form can serve. For, as Samuel C. Jackson points out, "The greatest tragedy of current growth patterns is not the physical form of that growth but the fact that it has polarized Americans by race and class. Bankers, real estate brokers, homeowners, and unfortunately even governments seem to have conspired to zone out the poor and exclude racial minorities."

IN SEARCH OF 'NEW' NEW TOWNS

David A. Crane

IF WE ARE TO FULFILL THE PROMISE of truly "new" new towns, we should search for them at least at three levels, each with its own important implications for organizational innovation.

FIRST, we should take a look at *urbanization roles and corporate structure*, matching a more varied vocabulary of environmental concepts with realistic institutional changes in public and private methods of financing, developing, and continuing services. We need to examine critically the persistent but elusive ideals of the garden city and independent satellite town. A wider variety of persuasive, practical concepts and roles for new communities in solving urban problems and realizing urban cultural, social, and economic opportunities must be identified. Without such innovations political and economic incentives for effective forms of new-town organization will not be forthcoming.

SECOND, in developing organizational concepts we should emphasize ways of *seizing the opportunities of scale and environmental innovation* that potentially are available when development occurs at a comprehensive level. When visiting the experimental new towns of the past 20 years one is too often impressed with the fact that, while some useful two-dimensional coordination of land uses has occurred, great opportunities have been missed for new departures in design, community services, or life-styles. Housing types, circulation and parking, utilities and maintenance, schools, recreation, health, and other service systems too often follow the fragmented and stereotyped environmental and service standards of single-purpose bureaucracies and competing developer/designers. Completion rates have been painfully slow, and economies of scale from quantity production of houses

have seldom been realized. Performance in meeting the special needs of either lower- or upper-income groups has usually been disappointing. In fact our prototypes sometimes bear a strange resemblance to urban areas that grew up incrementally without unified planning.

If we are to produce "new" new towns and exploit the intrinsic advantages of large-scale development, we need management, financial, and technological organization capable of moving total environmental packages—housing, infrastructure, community facilities, open space, and commercial/industrial—on a closely integrated volume production basis. We need new thinking about private and public relationships, basic service concepts, and methods of delivery in many community programs, including housing assistance, schools, recreation, health, circulation and parking, and community maintenance.

Administrative reforms in the allocation of development and operating responsibilities for these community systems will be required to permit new conceptual models and more integrated environmental design. Without this level of attack, new towns will continue to fail in offering really new environments for an exciting choice of life-styles, and there will be no savings of cost or time that can be passed on to sponsors or consumers.

THIRD, organization should be looked at in terms of *rational process design*, and this should become a routine emphasis in front-end activity of every new-town project. Designing the total process by which a new town is to be planned, built, and operated is at least as important a task as creating the physical master plan and design image.

In preliminary phase, a rational "plan for planning" should select a basic community development strategy, establish

116

criteria for determining development feasibility, and describe schedules, participants, resources, and procedures to achieve an approved overall plan and make ready for first-stage construction. Indeed in the design of the front-end processes we have the best chance to build in realistic conditions for achievable and profitable environmental innovations, and a great deal of time and public support can be gained if the early phases are organized properly.

Later, with general program and plan concepts in hand, detailed process design for future development and post-development phases should follow. This detailed logistics should build into the future execution process all of the resources, participants, assignments, and controls that are necessary to realize opportunities of scale and achieve significant environmental quality.

DEVELOPMENT OF ROLES, STRATEGY, AND VEHICLES

In the United States there has been no practical example of broad regional or national urbanization strategy involving the use of new communities. Still, we have had many specific community projects inspired by borrowed conceptual formulas that closely reflect peculiarly British national strategy. Sometimes the community roles that have been borrowed from British garden-city and independent-satellite-town theory are extremely difficult to implement under American conditions. Expectations have been raised that often could not be fulfilled, while crucial urban needs were not addressed in our national prototypes. Perhaps the entrepreneurs of Reston have unnecessarily let themselves in for criticism and financial losses by following inapplicable community models.

Responsive strategies and role concepts for new communities in America should pay special heed to some of the following concerns:

● Provision for greater and more profitable involvement of private enterprise to a degree that would not be expected in Europe.
● Confrontation of environmental manifestations of current pressures for racial and social justice, including elimination of the center city/suburban imbalance and a variety of other responses to the complex issues of local community integration/segregation.
● New solutions to the problems of central urban areas, obsolete older towns, or existing areas of scattered development (answering shortcomings in current urban renewal programs).
● Development of greater environmental choices for all sectors of a society that is increasingly pluralistic, less tied by work routines, and more concerned with education, recreation, and travel.
● Creation of new magnets for urban growth in less developed parts of the United States, thus helping to relieve pressure on existing concentrations and making more accessible the great environmental resources of this country.
● Preservation of open space and confrontation of ecological problems, particularly in pollution-ridden metropolitan areas.
● Allocation of vastly increased public financial support for new towns, together with the creation of new types of corporate vehicles which will join private and public initiatives in a wide variety of new-town types.

REPERTOIRE OF SOLUTIONS

This list of goals cannot be satisfied by any one formula for new towns. Indeed, there are potentially conflicting concerns that can be resolved only in the evolution of a highly diversified range of new towns. Some steps toward a broadened repertoire of concepts were taken in Title IV of the Housing Act of 1968 in which four types of new towns eligible for public assistance were recognized: freestanding, independent satellite, add-on, and new town in-town. To these we must add a series of other types in order to complete a repertoire of solutions properly responsive to our urban problems and unique opportunities. Some additional possibilities can be suggested:

1. The *packaged neighborhood*, a development of, say, between 400 and 2,000 houses of varied styles, lower-level educational services, recreation, convenience retail, and other services and amenities. We need antidotes for the "projectitis" and lack of total neighborhood improvement that we have witnessed in both center-city and suburban housing developments. The presence of new-town qualities must be measured less in terms of size than in terms of how much environmental design and social amenity are offered. With an eye to financial feasibility, we may even have to violate sacred cows of planning and admit into the development commercial or institutional uses that can help pay for these amenities.

An example of a packaged neighborhood is the forthcoming 490-unit development of a 6.35-acre site for the Operation Breakthrough program at Jersey City, N.J., where amenities include a Turnkey K-3 school, preschool, swim club, local retail and commercial office space, structured residential parking, and significant open space and recreation facilities. While this example has a rather high density, our firm has designed other packaged neighborhoods for private sponsors at scales of 1,000 to 2,000 units on 70 to 200 acres.

2. The *community backfill*, a develop-

117

ment of any required content and scale to speak to problems of scattered development areas in the urban fringe. In these areas of uncoordinated subdivisions we find lack of housing choices for a balanced population; shortages of schools, recreation, health, and other essential services; increasing service costs; diminishing revenue base or underemployment, or both; problems of traffic and transportation; and inadequate water supply, sewerage, or community maintenance.

While leapfrog development practices have left further areas for development, economic and political obstacles have prevented natural market development of these sites for the missing housing types, amenities, or revenue uses. Public assistance programs for the conversion of these areas into sound social and physical environments are needed.

Examples of such programs do not exist. Santa Clara County, Calif., or Albuquerque, N.M., are two among many places where this treatment could apply usefully.

3. The *regional growth module,* involving opportunistic multiuse development for any workable scale and combination of urban activities that may be required in response to different site circumstances, problems, and opportunities found in a given region.

Near Syracuse, Lysander, N.Y., a 2,-600-acre new town of 5,000 houses and 800 acres of industrial uses, is an example of the regional growth module. As exemplified in this project of the New York State Urban Development Corporation, the regional growth module derives its ingredients and its design structure from the dictates of an unusual natural site, a practical concession to economic and political objectives of the surrounding Syracuse suburbs, and a strong UDC

commitment toward unmet regional housing needs in the low- and moderate-income ranges.

In Lysander, an unusually large industrial program is included, not so much for the home-to-work convenience of residents as for the purpose of contributing jobs to the region and a revenue base to the surrounding locality. This revenue base also helps the sponsor to provide a high standard of onsite open space and recreational amenities. The new town will provide services needed for nonresidents and at the same time existing local governmental systems will be asked to develop and operate many services.

In fact it is UDC's conscious policy to avoid a "walled city" approach to new-town governance. This policy has encouraged a high degree of local acceptance of the development.

Lysander will offer a wide range of physical styles for all income groups, but it will not be "balanced" according to traditional new-town formulas because of UDC's commitment to meeting selected needs. Unlike the satellite town, the regional growth module does not follow a formula of internal balance or self-sufficiency and does not presuppose a cultural or home-to-work dependence on a core city. Rather, it is a pragmatic and circumstantial piece of comprehensive environmental improvement geared to the kind of complex local, regional, and even state-wide relationships that now have superseded the influence of the core city.

4. The *spinoff town,* involving the seizing of opportunities for coordinated environments in areas impacted by major new institutions, economic developments, transportation, or recreational features. There is increasing recognition of the negative impact of urban sprawl surrounding such major new generators as regional shopping centers, resort devel-

opments, airports, or suburban university and hospital complexes. In at least one case, a major regional shopping center developer, Urban Investment Corporation of Chicago, has seen the financial advantage to be gained by comprehensive treatment of areas that have grown in value because of its prime investment.

Employing what it calls the "mini-town" concept, it acquired land adjacent to the prime shopping center site in advance and developed the land for selected residential and community uses.

The approach taken at Walt Disney World, near Orlando, Fla., is a similarly comprehensive example dictated by sound private business strategy.

If the problems and opportunities created by prime generators are to be met in ways that respond to broader public purposes, new programs or incentives (and perhaps public benefit corporations) will be needed. These should encourage entrepreneurs and institutions to look beyond their own narrow corporate objectives and recognize the needs of the impacted communities.

One of the few places where this is occurring is in the Amherst new community near Buffalo, N.Y. This UDC project responds to the situation created by the entry into an upper-income suburb of the new campus for 40,000 students of the State University of New York at Buffalo. Amherst will address the needs for university-related housing and services, and at the same time economic development, transportation improvement, and control of speculative development will be undertaken for the mutual benefit of the university and the existing town of Amherst. Our firm is engaged in a similar project relating to suburban expansion of the Greater Wilmington Medical Center south of Wilmington, Del.

The spinoff-town concept provides a

model that ought to have extensive application in the future, for residential life-styles will be oriented increasingly to unusual educational, health, recreational, or transportation centers.

5. The *new regional city*, involving development of large cities of, say, 200,000 to 1 million population in less developed parts of the United States. Our national urbanization policy will not be responsive fully until we have answered demographic concentration trends on a scale commensurate with our national resources. Obviously, private enterprise will not build such communities without major federal leadership and assistance.

The only U.S. example of a large new regional city of which I am aware is the theoretical project for New City 4-Corners proposed by a group of University of Pennsylvania students and me 10 years ago. This was to be a city of 500,-000 to 1 million situated at the common boundary of Utah, Colorado, New Mexico, and Arizona. A great year-round climate, gorgeous scenery, and undeveloped mineral resources suggested a potential that is still unrealized.

We need not build large new cities merely as a matter of national pride, which was the prime factor in the creation of the new capital cities of Brasilia and Chandigarh. Rather, we should build them for the practical purpose of creating alternative growth magnets. The burgeoning of speculative developments for early retirees and other middle-income groups in Florida and the Southwest already attests to the "push" forces of pollution, work routine, and social conflict in the major metropolitan centers and the "pull" forces of climate, leisure opportunities, and an open social structure available in less developed regions.

Through public intervention it should be possible to respond to these forces with a higher quality of environment in communities of sounder social, cultural, and economic structures than the specialized "resort ghettos" now being built. At the same time, urbanization in virgin regions could bring a broader cross section of the population into more frequent contact with natural amenities and recreational resources. Provided that appropriate conservation measures were taken in these new cities, renewed contact without unusual environmental assets could not help but reinvigorate the receiving regions.

METROPOLITAN STRATEGY

The diversification of types of new towns will not of itself provide effective strategies for solving urban problems. The repertoire of types must be deployed in concerted thrusts at persistent problems within particular urban regions. The "paired towns" concept being looked at in Detroit is an example of such a broad-reaching strategy. An equally interesting theoretical proposal by Bernard Weissbourd and Herbert Channick calls for a wholesale public new-towns program tied in with selective curbs on inner-city housing subsidies which, they say, contribute to a hardening in of racial and economic segregation. This strategy would attack interrelated problems of social imbalance, uneven educational quality, lack of inner-city relocation housing vacancies permitting realistic renewal, and lack of consumer choice in a seller's housing market. The proponents present convincing arithmetic to support their estimate that a new-towns and subsidized housing policy of their type could eliminate black ghettos in 10 years and achieve up to a 25-75 black-white ratio in all parts of the metropolitan area.

These imaginative ideas still lack the thrust of major federal policy. Since 1946 the British have started or completed 24 new towns with an estimated resident population in 1970 of over a million. When we see an American commitment of resources at even a two-per-cent level perhaps we will begin to make a dent in our national urban problems.

NEW CORPORATE VEHICLES

In the meantime, along with further experimental development of new-town prototypes we should look for considerable innovation in the corporate vehicles for financing, development, and management of new towns. The most relevant recent trend is the growth of general-purpose and special-purpose public benefit corporations for urban development, along with new types of tax-free bonding capacity outside the limitations of local debt ceilings.

An early imaginative contribution to these devices was Edward J. Logue's 1968 proposal of twin corporations for development and services in Fort Lincoln. The development corporation would mesh private and public investment in a monolithic financial enterprise. It would be charged with total responsibility for planning, development, design, and construction within the site, receiving delegated powers from local agencies that normally carry out public improvements. It would be free to employ and contract with private or public developers, builders, suppliers of technology, or architects, but it could also retain whatever portion of these functions it deemed desirable. The opportunity for integrated and innovative urban design treatment under these conditions is quite obvious.

The Fort Lincoln services corporation would have a similar mandate for ongoing community services management, including housing management, school administration, recreation, health, and community maintenance. It would contract with District of Columbia agencies to supply these services on their behalf, and it would channel to the public the fees collected from residents. Both corporations were proposed to have as directors a mix of public officials, local citizens, and citywide business and civic representatives. It is unfortunate but in retrospect not surprising that the District's political forces did not go along with these innovative vehicles.

Since then, a number of new public benefit corporations have been set up. The most well-heeled and dynamic is the New York State Urban Development Corporation, a general-purpose organization with an authorized tax-free bonding capacity of $1 billion. UDC's three new-town projects (Amherst, Lysander, and Welfare Island) are only part of a much larger statewide program. Much of UDC's development workload is delegated to subsidiary public and private corporations, and a variety of financial and management relationships are beginning to evolve with private developers.

UDC sees its primary public responsibilities in terms of front-end financing, planning, and design activities. Through these, social policy and environmental quality can be supported, but at the same time assignment of roles in development execution to the private sector can release UDC funds and talents to work in new front-end tasks. This sort of partnership between the public and private sectors, multiplied nationally, should go a long way toward greater profits for private ventures in the new-town field.

OPPORTUNITIES OF SCALE AND ENVIRON-
MENTAL INNOVATION
The nine types of new towns discussed above will obviously present widely varying organizational circumstances, including differences in requirements for public investment, public-private corporate vehicles, political and community pro-

cesses, rates of completion, and scale of front-end land assembly, planning, and development overhead.

Each of these prototypes will involve a unique context for problem-solving, and each will present its own opportunities of scale and environmental innovation. What are these opportunities, how do they vary, and how can they be seized?

INDUSTRIALIZATION OF HOUSING PRO-
DUCTION
A major "opportunity of scale" is to link new-town programs to the industrialization of housing, using large-scale land assembly and development techniques in open areas as a major contribution toward the still unrealized national target of 2.6 million housing starts per year. There is tremendous interest now in the technological potentials for producing housing through offsite prefabrication and factory-type production. But technology per se only saves construction cost and time, and these are not nearly as promising as potential savings on land costs, site infrastructure, interest, and other time costs of delay due to cumbersome red tape.

The new town can pay off handsomely in all of these categories, permitting as it does improved land use, a more efficient infrastructure, and collateral sources of project revenue in multiuse development that can help reduce housing costs. However, new-town development procedures must not be saddled with the time-consuming bureaucracy that prevails in traditional urban development if the costs of delay are to be avoided.

Thus, even if we continued to use conventional building techniques, the new town could contribute remarkable savings in cost and speed of housing delivery. Relatively small builders could be woven into an effective production system offering wide variety in design—given

well-coordinated central management, comprehensive financing, sitewide design and construction of the community infrastructure, and well-orchestrated parcelization and staging of assignments among the builders.

Industrialization of housing could go even further by linking specific new towns to market aggregations for selected housing fabricators, assuring enough demand to justify the heavy cost of housing factories. While market aggregation is one of the key ideas in HUD's Operation Breakthrough, an important link between policy in this area and public policies for new-town development has yet to be made. The opportunities of manufactured housing technology are, of course, quite different in the large new regional city, spinoff town, community backfill, or packaged neighborhood. There are hard tradeoffs to be made among production quantity, numbers of building participants, variety in housing design, social diversity, and balanced staging of community ingredients. These tradeoffs are less difficult in large new towns with a wide range of housing that can be marketed quickly.

On the other hand, certain types of more flexible housing systems permit wide variations of building types, cost levels, and environmental quality, and some of these technological concepts allow for customized site design applications. Careful matching of different types of housing producers and systems to the new-town variables of size, site, social and physical profile, and timing should permit an effective basis for supporting development of the manufactured housing industry through new-town programs.

Indeed, private producers of manufactured housing increasingly will have to look to devices like the new town in order to compete with conventional building.

Through comprehensive community planning and environmental design they will be able to produce a better product, overcoming current consumer resistance to the prefab image. They also will be better able to control the time element in housing production, and they can pass on to the consumer some of the savings not attributable solely to housing fabrication. These factors already are encouraging some manufacturers to participate directly in large-scale land development.

One large national industry recently commissioned our firm to identify prototype resident environments in a wide range from 20 to 5,000 houses and suggest an operational model of a corporate market aggregation program based on its direct participation in land assembly, design, and development. The corporation owns a number of subsidiary real estate and housing fabrication companies which it intends to weave into a unified national housing system. We were able to suggest that factory production of the subsidiaries could be provided with outlets in workable regional concentrations of noncontiguous sites. At the same time, the corporation's environmental packaging of technologies, building types, community facilities, and site design could respond to extreme variations in sites, community needs, consumer requirements, and political/fiscal factors.

INNOVATIONS IN COMMUNITY SERVICES AND DESIGN STRUCTURE

Our excursion into a private corporation's possibilities for involvement in residential packaging has confirmed the feeling that savings in time and money need not be in conflict with the search for environmental quality in our communities. The "opportunities of scale" are of several distinct types, and we can seize all of them if we will.

Apart from opportunities for housing

industrialization, new towns offer the opportunity to alter substantially the institutions that provide urban services and give these a wholly exciting new design structure. Perhaps our firm's experience in designing several new towns of widely varying scales can point to the possibilities of worthwhile innovation.

LYSANDER NEW COMMUNITY

This new town of 5,000 homes will be developed on a beautiful virginal site of 2,600 acres next to a large game preserve and the Seneca River in the township of Lysander and next to the village of Baldwinsville. Through public assistance of various forms, fully 50 per cent of the housing will serve needs not now being met in the natural housing market. At the same time, the new town will aim for a larger share of middle- and upper-income families than are now being attracted to this part of the Syracuse region.

Fulfillment of these objectives demanded a plan with dramatic environmental design choices, outstanding services and amenities, and a scheme for making these assets available to everyone without physically setting one group apart from the other. This challenge was met in an urban design concept providing two towns in one.

Almost half of the housing will be developed in moderate densities on exciting topography and within walking distance of a quite urbane town center. Formal architectural qualities and a concentration of vitalizing facilities will be found in this pedestrian environment. Around this core will be a more traditional suburban area of lower-density homes, a golf course, marina, small subcenter, untamed woods, and open spaces. Housing types and assistance programs will fit a balance of family groups in both areas so that esthetic and cultural choices are equally available to all social groups. In

order to produce this kind of integration, public housing will be excluded and different forms of financial assistance will be used.

The desired vibrancy of the town center and a most unusual school system will be achieved through centralization of all except the earliest grades in an education park at the center. Because a small community of this scale cannot support extensive commercial or public buildings, joint community use of the school's cultural and recreational facilities will greatly enhance the vitality of the core. At the same time, this will provide an unusual urban educational milieu accessible to all parts of the community and to nonresidents.

Lysander's rural image will be preserved through a major open-space reserve and a structure of main roads passing through wide, dense bands of woods. Circulation will, however, follow a systematic multivector geometry to assist the sense of orientation.

A "main street" will expose to everyone's view the formal architectural crescent of the town center. This "capital design" system anticipates the need for a coherent overall physical framework to coordinate the future efforts of many developers. Development controls will encourage varied treatment of subareas within the overall structure.

The greatest freedom of design will be granted to those developers who employ outstanding design talent and do comprehensive environmental treatment of the broadest parcels. In selected areas where particular quality or economic objectives can be met only through closer UDC intervention in the design process, the plan foregoes restrictions and anticipates that UDC will select architects and pay for their services before it disposes of the parcels and the designs to developers.

FORT LINCOLN

According to a White House order given in 1967, this new town in-town was to provide a national model for urban racial and social integration, demonstrating advanced concepts of community services, design, and technological innovation. The 335-acre site has a dramatic topography with excellent views in all directions. Given a District location on the Maryland line, with concentrated black and white neighborhoods on both sides of the line, the mission of producing a socially balanced community of 4,500 families was enormously difficult. Low- and moderate-income families (who inevitably would be largely black) had to be provided for despite opposition from residents of adjacent middle-income black neighborhoods, who feared an impact on already overtaxed schools, recreation, and health services. Middle- and upper-income groups of both races had to be attracted to the community, overcoming the effects of both racial and economic prejudice. The response to this dilemma had to take radical departures if the President's mandate was to be fulfilled.

First, a solution was sought in terms of a *surplus* of community services, providing not only a remarkable level of service to residents, but offsetting surrounding neighborhood deficiencies. An outstanding education concept was developed, based on general and special "learning centers," each integrated with other community activities for all ages. The schools were programmed for 11,000 children, of whom only 7,400 would be residents.

The surplus would not only serve adjacent areas, but permit citywide and regional enrollments needed for a 50-50 racial balance in the schools. Other shopping, health, recreation, and social services were programmed at similar levels.

Federal office employment and a branch of Federal City College were proposed, to promote regional interaction through outstanding cultural and economic activities and to attract middle- and upper-income residents of both races from employees in these institutions.

The size and composition of the proposed 4,500 housing units—rather dense for a family-oriented living environment—were derived from a complex process of balancing a fair burden of the elderly and low- and moderate-income families with other groups to get a predominance of middle- and upper-income families and a desired minimum of at least one-third whites.

Twelve different housing types, heavily emphasizing private access to open space, were developed. None of them would be identified exclusively with a particular social group. Each of the five major subareas was assigned a microcosm of the total population. They would be encouraged to live together because of unique and varied neighborhood sites, views, services, and architectural quality.

The Fort Lincoln design concept had to reach for quite audacious new space-saving devices if that many housing units and the surplus of community facilities were all to fit on 335 acres of beautiful but rough terrain. An onsite minirail transit system was proposed to reduce the need for cars and thus space for streets and parking. The minirail was structured to serve eight key multiuse subcenters based on the specialized learning centers, thus encouraging social integration.

Innovations in financing were proposed to permit multilevel parking structures for all nonresident cars and more than 40 per cent of resident cars. The additional capital costs of minirail and parking were more than offset by re-

ductions in roads and gains in developable sites and open space. Thus a financially feasible high-density scheme of relatively few high-rise apartments was nevertheless able to reserve more than a third of the site for open space.

Because of the tight fit between all of the problem-solving strategies, Fort Lincoln front-end planning included a more detailed comprehensive design framework than normally would be expected in planning a new town. It was also necessary to anticipate the demands of new demonstration technology systems during construction, so planning was accompanied by in-depth process design for future development, design, and construction.

Parcelization, development controls, construction staging, and the assignment of roles to different types of developer/technology groups optimized the requirements of industrialized building against the indispensable objectives of architectural diversity and varied user needs. Special attention was given to structuring different kinds of architectural roles and assignments to physical subsystems. In addition to a strong centralized design coordination group, sitewide design responsibilities for the entire development period were to be allocated to a relatively few qualified architects.

These unifying design roles were identified in terms of (1) circulation, utilities, open space, and graphic systems; (2) schools and related multiuse centers, and (3) development of housing system prototypes. In addition, a variety of architectural roles for specific parcels and local sponsors were identified. This architectural participation program was designed to support the equal needs of industrialized building, unified design, and responsiveness to particular design needs and opportunities in every parcel.

OPERATION BREAKTHROUGH, JERSEY CITY

This example, a prototype of the packaged neighborhood, has parallels with the Fort Lincoln problem but on a smaller, more intense level. On a 6.35-acre site near downtown Jersey City, HUD wants to demonstrate as many as four new building systems plus varied building types, and at the same time illustrate new standards of overall environmental design. New solutions for family living conditions in high-density inner-city areas is a key objective, as is demonstrating that social integration can be accomplished in a compact development.

Attractions of the site include a 20-minute connection via the PATH rapid transit system to Lower Manhattan and excellent views of Manhattan and the Jersey Meadows—provided the viewer can be lifted several levels above a tawdry Jersey City street scene. Obstacles to development include heavily overcrowded schools and a total lack of open space in the surrounding area, together with no local financial capacity to provide additional facilities for families housed on the site.

Again, the search for a solution started with finding programmatic ingredients internally sufficient for family living and overcoming deficiencies in surrounding areas. A K-3 school for resident and nonresident children was proposed. This would be capitalized by the development and leased to school authorities on a Turnkey basis. A small playground, extensive playlots and pedestrian areas, a swim club, and an extensive preschool facility will also be included.

Given these extensive and costly amenities as a precondition for developing the site, analysis then turned to finding the most housing and highest densities, multilevel parking (space-saving but cost-producing), and commercial uses that could combine in a feasible mortgage package. With the aid of a computerized space-allocation model and cash-flow testing, a large number of alternative program mixes and physical arrangements was evaluated. A feasible configuration was determined of 490 dwelling units in low- and high-rise variations by three different systems producers with an unusual percentage of large-family units not dependent on elevators.

Most housing will have dramatic views. Two-thirds of the required parking will be under the housing units or on raised open spaces offering good external views for the pedestrians. Pedestrians will be extensively separated from traffic. Also added was a sizable mix of shopping and local offices, which will not only be a convenience to residents, but also will enable a financially feasible development.

Given a small, intense, multiuse environment to be produced by a complex group of participants, the overall design had to be closely tailored and processes of coordination in execution had to establish a clear hierarchy of responsibilities. The initial design concept assigned one of the more flexible systems types to produce a continuous "route building" of medium height linking all parts of the site. A raised pedestrian open-space system was proposed in parallel. Variations have since evolved, but the principle of a continuous architectural "glue" to hold the parts together has been maintained. This is essential in any community design that is truly responsive to collective living.

Clarity of collaborative process was aided by the assignment of our firm to execute architectural designs for all nonresidential buildings, parking, access, open space, landscaping, and community graphics. In addition to design control over these unifying elements, we have provided program assignments, performance specifications, and design review and coordination as a context for the talented efforts of four other groups of designers.

Development leadership by Volt Information Sciences Inc. and centralized construction management by their subcontractors have also played a key role in unifying this complex effort. HUD's own imaginative support for the broader environmental demonstration aspects has enabled the project to reach for a sum greater than the individual parts.

RATIONALIZING PROCESS DESIGN

In the foregoing discussions of the opportunities of scale and innovation there is an inescapable point being made: The performance of the urban environment is the result of processes by which it is manufactured. If we want better performance we must have better processes.

The concern with rational and continuing planning processes goes back to early days of modern city planning. Leading urban activists like Edward J. Logue, the late Justin Herman, and William L. Slayton (all nonarchitects with close ties to the profession) have greatly expanded the range of thinking beyond rational planning to a more complete attack on development and community management processes. Over the past 20 years of urban renewal, and especially during the recent frustrating five years of tight money and violent social change, urban manufacturing processes and mechanisms have become extremely sophisticated. In fact we often have seen too much conceptual sophistication and not enough simple commitment of the indispensable resources: money, time, talent, coherent decision-making structures, and meaningful participation in process. The next steps in development organization will have to emphasize simplification and much greater resource commitments if our processes are to perform adequately.

Apart from overall organizational simplification and commitment, process designs tailor-made to individual new-town prototypes and unique local circumstances will greatly rationalize environmental manufacturing and provide greater assurances of performance. This step of conscious process design should occur at many levels, the first of which is preparation of a "plan for planning."

PLAN FOR PLANNING

It has become routine in our firm to develop detailed process design, scheduling, and task programming for our own planning and design activities and those of other professional collaborators. We hope to see this kind of plan for planning undertaken more often as a joint effort with the client, for realistic process organization depends more on the decision-maker than on the designer.

From our firm's experience with new towns and organizing the front-end steps, a few recurring principles for the plan for planning have emerged. These might be listed briefly as follows:

1. The planning process must lend itself to reiterative, cyclical phases of professional activity, reviews, and decision-making. A plan must evolve through successive approximations and result from the exposure of concepts to rational economic and technical evaluation, as well as the reactions and commitments of sponsors, officials, or interested sectors of the public.

2. New towns should be planned in the alternative until a clear and feasible direction for action has attracted the support of everyone concerned. Conceptual development of alternatives cannot wait until after there is complete information

because it is through this early problem-solving strategy that we can put practical limits on time-consuming research efforts. As cyclical planning proceeds, it should progressively examine program options, site organization concepts, architectural alternatives, and alternative general models for development operations.

3. New-town planning requires a broad-gauged and closely coordinated team with expertise in physical planning, ecology, economics, transportation, engineering, administration, finance, housing, and various community services and social evaluation specialists. While there is a tendency among sponsors to place market studies and financial feasibility studies first in sequence, a lack of close collaboration from the start between the planners of hardware and software will almost always be a waste of time.

4. If there is any group within the team that must move first, it is the one that can make decisions on operations strategy and policy. Early clarity of approach to resource commitments, management organization, corporate vehicles, and the distribution of responsibilities and opportunities in development planning and execution will save time and money during the economic and physical planning studies. The typical development administrator has approached the new-town enterprise with the idea that economic studies and a physical image are needed before he can swing into implementation. *He puts plan-making before process design*, and as a result he offers little contribution to the key instrumentalities that so much affect feasible and innovative community design.

5. To the extent that early phases emphasize the creation of processes rather than the making of definitive master plans, time and money spent on the front

end can be minimized. The early phases should emphasize the selection of a feasible general program and physical concept, followed by detailed design of the logistics of project execution. Definitive overall master planning often can be undertaken at a later stage in parallel with detailed design and site preparation of first-stage construction. Master planning might even be stretched out over the entire execution period. Telescoping the front end can stimulate cash flow, and when definitive planning occurs it might be both more realistic and more easily supported by project revenues.

A plan for planning implies effort to rationally anticipate and sequence all of the steps required from beginning to end. While this kind of forethought is difficult and is subject to change as the process goes along, it can provide a context for effective and creative results in each phase. The phasing of operations must vary with the prototype, the local situation, and the nature of the sponsor so that every plan for planning ought to be special. But if we can generalize we might think of a total process sequenced in major phases as follows:

1. *Plan for Planning.* Irrevocable commitments will be avoided, but preparatory steps might include site identification and evaluation; urbanization strategy and assumptions for future public/private vehicles; preliminary allocation of development and operating responsibilities and prerogatives, including the assignment of front-end tasks to entities; long-term operations scheduling; a specific plan for decision-making and review procedures, including the nature and timing of citizen participation; assembling initial interdisciplinary expertise; and detailed programming and budgeting of front-end activities.

2. *Concept/Feasibility/Commitments.*

Here the steps are the minimal ones to justify and channel further actions and expenditures. Operations to be emphasized are marketability and site analysis studies; conceptualization, testing, and reviews of program, plan, and operations alternatives; selection and schematic design of a preferred conceptual alternative, including preliminary staging concepts; modelling cash flow and public fiscal impacts of the entire development operation over time; negotiation of all types of general financing and development agreements dictated by the conditions for feasibility, including any needed waivers of red tape; and finally formal public proceedings if required for approval of the development.

3. *Process Development/Early Action.* Assuming positive go signals have been received at this point, early actions would include land acquisition; preliminary site preparation; permanent staffing of the development management vehicle; and early organization of a marketing program. It may be possible in some circumstances to begin an immediate land-disposition or construction project, or both, to yield early development revenues. In this event, we can think of the front-end phase as ending here.

Paralleling these action-oriented steps would be detailed process design for the logistics of project completion, including articulation of development parcels, sitewide systems, and their program requirements; definition of central management's development and construction roles; detailed staging of facilities, sitewide systems, and parcel development; assignment of development roles by stages to different types and size of sponsor/developer/builder teams; programs and criteria for building systems and technology; development of an organization and criteria for assigning archi-

tects to the sitewide infrastructure, technology development, and particular site and building design opportunities; environmental and building standards and controls for sitewide systems and specific development parcels; and design review procedures. This further development of the process will establish an effective context for later definitive planning and design activities. If what has preceded is a plan for planning, this will be a design for designing.

4. *First-Stage Development/Comprehensive Design.* The master planning might be combined usefully with specific first-stage development, and it might include selection of major developer/builder/technology consortiums and definition of their requirements and capabilities; development of housing prototypes and technology; sitewide design of open space, roads, utilities, schools, and other community facility systems; detailed subdivision planning and cost estimating; and the refinement of inputs to the ongoing models of cash flow and fiscal impacts.

Many of these systems will require major collaboration between the sponsors and other agencies or developers to arrive at mutually agreed upon programs for services and facilities and comprehensive design solutions. These collaborative individual systems will make a more meaningful and realistic master plan than would result from superficial front-end physical planning. In parallel with this activity, emphasis would be placed on revenue-producing first-stage development, especially marketing, land disposition, design review, and contruction by developers not bearing the main financial burden. In order to stimulate sales, central management would develop supporting improvements and facilities.

5. *Staged Construction/Interim Man-*

agement. The remaining development and construction would be sequenced in a few or many subphases, depending on the size of the new town and the pace feasible for its completion. Ongoing activities would include not only the development of individual projects and systems but also continuous revision of the comprehensive design, its staging, assignment to developer/builder/technology groups, and cash-flow modelling. From the beginning of occupancy, new residents and business interests will demand many community services and a share in community planning and operating decisions. Interim management and self-government vehicles established at this time should respond to these desires, but one should be careful to protect the interests and objectives of citizens and businesses that have not yet arrived. It is a truism that the strongest opponents of a "balanced community" are the first to arrive. Predominant control should reside in external, objective hands until the total job of building is done.

6. *Permanent Inhabitation and Management.* The variables among new-town prototypes, sponsors, and local governmental situations are too wide to permit many useful generalizations about this final phase of the community manufacturing process. We can stress the importance of anticipating far in advance, even in the plan for planning phase, the kind of community management and government that will be needed. Planning by the software experts will be needed from the earliest phases. And if the unusual sense of social adventure and experimental services of Tapiola or Columbia are any guide, we can emphasize that management structure will usually have to supply services over and above those provided through normal local government agencies. Even if there is no complete self-

THE NEXT GENERATION OF NEW TOWNS

Lloyd Rodwin

Lawrence Susskind

government within the new town, resident associations or an internal structure of some kind will be needed to supply the extras that are expected from a "new" new town.

Perhaps what we all look for in the new town is what we have failed to produce in our existing communities. Certainly we must not encumber the making of a new town with the outworn values, forms, and urban processes that have produced the urban America we already know. If we will seize these fresh opportunities with audacity of concept and organization, we may produce truly "new" new towns. When we can see a wide range of new models for this ancient urban dream, with a thrust of policy and resources of meaningful scale, then we shall have brought some answers back home where we live.

SUPPOSE THAT 25 YEARS FROM NOW 60 federally assisted new towns will have been built in the U.S. That would not be an unreasonable estimate. After all, it took the British just about 25 years from the inception of the New Towns Act of 1946 to build 25 new towns. With a population that is four times greater and a per-capita national income more than twice that of Britain's, we ought to be able to build more.

Of course we won't do half as many, but why quibble about numbers, especially since it is the scale and quality of these towns that will be so important. Let us consider instead what the more articulate and perceptive critics may and perhaps will be saying about these communities, assuming they are built. This perspective might furnish helpful insights into the different ways of evaluating alternative new town plans. It might even give us a lead on what we can do now to forestall the criticisms that are otherwise likely to be leveled.

We guesstimate that more than half of the new towns completed 25 years from now will be the suburban type closely dependent on older urban centers. All of these communities, built in the style of Columbia, Jonathan, and Lysander, probably will end up with populations of 100,000 to 200,000. Although most of these new towns currently are being planned for somewhat smaller numbers of people, they all are in rapidly urbanizing areas and our expectation is they all will exceed their population targets.

Less than a third will be self-contained cities with population levels of 50,000 to 100,000. More often than not, independent new towns in lagging areas are thought of as large, self-contained developments. This is dead wrong. Unless very special steps are taken, new towns designed as growth centers in lagging areas

are likely to be smaller rather than larger. Lacking an existing economic base and being too distant from the central city to permit a substantial portion of the labor force to commute, such cities will face the difficult problem of attracting employers, and residents will be hard to attract unless jobs are available. Moreover, even with substantial federal support, such new towns will grow very slowly as they try to develop new markets.

Perhaps as many as 10 new towns will be of the new-town-in-town variety. Cedar-Riverside, Fort Lincoln, and Welfare Island are examples. Basically such developments will seek to revitalize sagging inner-city economies. They also will try to provide desirable living spaces for high-income residents and to promote racial integration in the central city.

THE FINANCIAL WRINGER

How will these communities fare? Some of them, financed largely by private investors, will be abandoned halfway through the development process because they will fail to yield a handsome profit. Like Reston, they will go through the financial wringer and simply fade into the usual pattern of speculative developments.

A few will be straight-out economic failures. In some, development costs will exceed the returns on the sale of housing units and the leasing of industrial and commercial properties. In others, the pace of development will be too slow or the turnaround time on investment will drag out long beyond the point at which repayment of borrowed money is to begin.

What might be surprising—and sad—is that most of the new towns completed 25 years hence will not fail; they will succeed—in a moderate and dull way. They will yield a small profit, provide a modicum of low- and middle-income housing, manage to stick fairly close to the original development plans (having overcome the objections of various pressure groups), and present no particular threat to the natural environment.

The way of life for residents of these new towns will not be too different from that of other suburban dwellers. More persons may live comfortably, walk to work, have easier access to assorted recreational facilities, and perhaps even feel a greater sense of belonging because of their participation in a "social experiment."

What is far less certain is whether these new towns will serve the poor and disadvantaged, achieve a greater socioeconomic mix, spur significant innovations, or even more important, serve broader ends. In other words, will these new towns have a significant impact on the larger population in the areas outside the communities themselves?

The future of most new communities completed during the next twenty-five years will no doubt depend on their financial, political and social feasibility. In terms of financial feasibility, new communities will have been successful only if they have paid careful attention to a number of factors such as *location* (selecting a site easily accessible to growing markets), *front-end financing* (making sure that considerable financial support is available at the outset), *federal loans and grants* (working closely with federal, state, and local governments to secure whatever supplementary funds are available), *reasonable tax agreements* (securing favorable assessments, easements, tax credits, or other abatements if they can be arranged), and the *pace of development* (working to achieve as rapid a "turnaround" time and positive cash flow as possible).

FRAGMENTED AUTHORITY AND CONTROL

The plans for most new cities completed 25 years from now will have run the gauntlet of various community groups and politicians. "Abutters" trapped between various parcels pieced together to form a new town will have expressed vociferous views about what the proposed development should look like. So too will local, county, state, regional, and federal officials. Each will have exerted whatever influence he has over zoning, tax rates, assessments, utility extensions, transportation plans, and industrial location decisions. The first residents will also have demanded a significant role in decision-making, and at some point the developer will have been forced to turn over decision-making authority to an elected body. With authority and control so fragmented, we can take for granted that the majority of new-town projects will not have developed according to plan.

Successful communities, to be sure, will have benefited from a managerial team able to gain zoning and building code clearance (by arguing for new approaches such as density zoning and PUD) and able to deal with political opposition (by building a coalition of local, state, and perhaps national supporters). The team also will have devised an effective bargaining strategy (by offering to be responsive to local needs and by offering something in return for local support). But there will be few such teams, and in retrospect we will wonder why we ever thought the homebuilders and large-scale developers of the 1970s (even those with successful track records) were equipped to manage the complex process of new-town development.

GLORIFIED SUBURBS

To meet the financial strains of early-stage development even the best-inten-

tioned developers will decide to build high-revenue-producing housing first. Once the first wave of high-middle- and middle-middle-income families has been served, however, resistance to low- and middle-income housing will heighten. And so most new towns 25 years hence will have ended up catering to a clientele not much different from that of the customary suburban developments. Glorified suburbs, they will have had a negligible impact on the problems of providing decent low-priced housing and easier access to new jobs for low- and middle-income families. This is likely to be true despite some low-cost, even public, housing tucked away behind or alongside industrial parks or a few scattered subsidized units physically indistinguishable from the moderate-cost unsubsidized units.

To cope with the problem of providing a better-economic mix, a few communities will have sought help from public entities (such as the New York State Urban Development Corporation) which will have built housing for all economic classes by using a quota system—not because quotas are desirable but because they may be the only means of eliminating "de facto apartheid" housing patterns.

DIVERTED RESOURCES

One could continue this accounting, but what it all adds up to is that some 25 years from now we are likely to find critics of the new-towns program arguing that public investment in these projects had merely diverted resources from inner-city redevelopment efforts and that our largest central cities are worse off than ever. They will be pointing out that our new towns had accommodated a tiny fraction of our population growth over the last quarter of the 20th century—perhaps only five per cent, possibly even only two or three per cent.

Other critics will be reminding us that back in the early 1970s it was pointed out that new towns never would provide us with significant alternatives to conventional urban development. And the more radical commentators will be asserting that new towns are not (and couldn't be) a solution to urban problems because fundamental shifts in the distribution of resources and power are prerequisites of effective social change. And the new-towns program certainly does not imply a significant redistribution of money or power.

SEVEN CRITERIA

This scenario is not altogether fetching, but perhaps it may provoke a hardboiled reconsideration of what government intervention in the design and development of new towns can be expected to achieve. Suppose we were in the unenviable position of those federal decision-makers responsible for the administration of the new-towns program. How would we run the program to ensure that we got the kind of cities we needed and wanted? There are at least seven criteria that would govern our decisions:

1. New towns ought not be built when the expansion of an existing community will serve the same purposes. But they will be built when they shouldn't if our principal focus is on new towns and not on the urban growth objectives we are trying to achieve.

2. New towns ought not lose money. But they might unless a reasonable proportion of the appreciation in land values or earned income (realized through the sale or lease of commercial properties and the rise in land prices) can be captured by the developer. This holds true especially for new towns built by public development corporations.

3. New towns must provide a choice of jobs for all primary and secondary wage earners. But they won't unless the number of new-town developments is restricted and each is large enough to support a diversified set of economic activities, businesses, and social services.

4. New towns have to be socially acceptable in the second half of the 20th century. But they won't be unless they serve a reasonable proportion of disadvantaged minorities and middle-income families directly and also create reasonable economic and social opportunities for other disadvantaged groups in the surrounding metropolitan area.

5. New towns should help reduce congestion, and slow down growth in our biggest cities, and reorganize development patterns in metropolitan areas. But they won't unless they are conceived as a means of achieving these ends. Until a special effort is made to relate new-town development to such things as national, state, and regional planning for transportation, capital improvements programming, welfare policy, and industrial development strategies, metropolitan growth patterns and current development trends are unlikely to be reversed.

6. New towns should help encourage the development of growth ceners in lagging regions, especially in regions with large unemployed or underemployed populations. But they won't if undue emphasis continues to be placed on maximum returns to the developer or if new towns are planned without full recognition of the forces that impel migration and the location of economic activities.

7. Aside from these minimum conditions it would be wonderful (and astonishing) if we could somehow produce two or three brilliant showpieces—breathtaking examples of more responsive and elegant ways of organizing our physical environment. New towns might, for example, re-flect the "educative city" of the future. They could demonstrate a number of ways in which client groups of all incomes and educational backgrounds might participate in the design of services and facilities, such as schools, health programs, day-care centers, and possibly even shape the decisions affecting the financing and day-to-day management of programs at the neighborhood level. They might provide unique educational workshops outside the traditional classroom (nature and wildlife observatories, opportunities to observe building and planning processes, etc.). They might even offer a number of opportunities to experiment with unusual building, highway, street, or area designs, as well as alternative models of entire communities.

The hitch is that it's incredibly difficult to ensure a brilliant performance. An unusual blend of initiative, rare ability, and hard work (as well as a good measure of luck) will be required to produce two or three outstanding new towns. Penny-pinched programs and a fear of anything too different or out-of-the-ordinary will tend to wipe out even these slim chances.

KEY IDEAS

This all leads us once again to wonder about the likelihood of realizing these aims. We find ourselves in a dilemma. From the conditions we have set, it looks as if we are guilty of advocating the best and making it the enemy of the good, and in the process vitiating the entire new-towns program. It's just not so. We want a program that will work and that we can be proud of. The conditions we have posed cannot be met overnight—we acknowledge that. Nonetheless, the prospects for the future are uninspiring unless we can muster considerable political support for the following key ideas:

1. The desirability of focusing on the

expansion of existing communities as well as the building of new ones. Planners, designers, and politicians cannot be allowed to use new towns as a shield to fend off the problems of the central city. They must collaborate with local, regional, and state officials.

2. The need for a limited but strategic increase in the public ownership of land to harvest the full economic and social value created by new-town projects. Public landownership is hardly a cherished institution in this country, but we have to learn how to use the tricks of the private developer to serve the public interest.

3. The importance of limiting the number and augmenting the size of new towns. Given our egalitarian system and the normal pattern of political pressures, it will be quite a feat to develop a significant program in which costs are shared nationally but the visible benefits to particular regions are limited sharply.

4. The obligation of new towns to serve the needs of the disadvantaged—both as consumers and producers. This means reversing or overriding prevailing suburban attitudes.

5. The immediate as well as long-term significance of relating new towns to the needs of the existing metropolis. Most new-town planners and developers think their problems are harrowing enough without having to take on the burdens of existing central cities, but unless new-town development on the metropolitan fringes and in lagging regions is linked to the depopulation or redevelopment of inner-city neighborhoods, these efforts will be trivial.

6. The reminder that new (or existing) towns must serve as chosen instruments to help spark the growth of selected urban centers in Appalachia or the depressed areas of the Deep South. Most planners rarely see the need, let alone the desira-

bility, of getting entangled in the problems of lagging regions, for it is much easier to build new towns in high-growth areas where there is a guaranteed market.

7. The need to spend generously and imaginatively, recognizing all the while the existence of a tradition and a culture that would tend to deplore a consistent and long-term public policy in pursuit of the objectives described above.

NEW TOWNS AND MINORITIES

Finally, we are loath to conclude without voicing some additional hopes and forebodings that we suggest ought to be inscribed in the minds of new-town enthusiasts.

New towns will become odious symbols if they are identified as devices for diluting the power of emerging inner-city majorities. There must be provision for neighborhood government and local control over key public services in each new town if we expect to convince large groups of people to move to them from the inner city.

On the other hand, many new towns can become attractive territories for investment in minority enterprise. They can provide capital investment opportunities as well as guaranteed markets for goods and services. The vehicles by which this can be achieved are federal contracts and purchasing agreements that can encourage minority-run businesses. The lure should be the new markets for inner-city entrepreneurs—not to entice them out of the inner city but to allow them to generate additional resources for reinvestment.

TURNING THE PROGRAM AROUND

What are the chances of turning the program around at this stage of the game? When we say that it ought to be turned around we mean that instead of building 60 new towns—mostly in suburban loca-

tions at somewhat lower densities—we ought to be building only about 20 or 30, but much larger, with higher densities designed to deal with interregional development problems. Instead of overemphasizing the financial feasibility of proposed new towns, we ought to be concentrating on the extent to which each new town will reinforce national urban growth objectives. Instead of funding new towns mainly under the control of private development groups we ought to be favoring public-development entities. Instead of supporting new towns that promise to test a great number of technological innovations, we wought to be encouraging efforts to monitor only a few well-designed experimental approaches to the delivery of services, and we ought to put a premium on experiments in citizen participation. Moreover, we ought to provide special assistance to those efforts that focus on the needs of the poor and the disadvantaged and that emphasize not only the end result but the processes and strategies by which the development of new communities can be controlled more carefully.

When goals are set too high, they must be trimmed down. In our case this means recognizing that new towns will serve simply as another string in the planner's bow, another way of organizing growth and developing resources in the suburbs and central cities, as well as in poorer regions, and that we will be very lucky indeed if the tools are used well or at least not misused. We know that in a new program the language of hope is more appealing than the language of regret, but we would remind those whom we disappoint that the disillusioned generally suffer from illusions to begin with.

PROSPECTS FOR INNOVATION

HUD officials have expressed a keen desire to ensure the financial success of federally supported new-town development efforts, hoping that a few early successes will attract the long-term support and the involvement of the private money markets. At the same time, various administrative spokesmen have encouraged new-town developers to undertake socially and technologically innovative experiments designed to test new ways of designing, building, and/or organizing urban service systems. It may well be, though, that these two objectives are incompatible; and, in the long run, a policy that pursues both objectives may be self-defeating. The factors that determine financial success may inhibit or even prohibit innovation, and the new towns most likely to be financially successful may also be those least suited to producing socially significant results.

It has taken almost 10 years for the new-towns program in the United States to evolve. Along the way many of its strongest advocates have felt obliged to embellish the potential advantages of new towns and to exaggerate the contribution they might make to the resolution of various urban problems. There will be a substantial mismatch between the claims of the most avid new-town proponents and the actual results of our first round of development efforts under Title VII. It might be a good idea to tone down some of the wilder claims.

For this reason particularly we caution against exaggerating or deluding ourselves about the prospects for innovation. Not that we do not welcome or appreciate the need or apparent opportunity for such innovations but, contrary to the conventional wisdom, we do not think the circumstances under which new towns are built are altogether conducive to innovation. The pressure to make a killing or avoid a disaster drives out most high-risk activities and provides power reinforcements for hard-boiled, conservative, not to mention backward and prejudiced judgments about what will work.

Despite this forbidding reality we believe—or hope—that some public development corporations and even a few private ones will support limited risk-taking in a few areas. In one case the focus may be on the design and delivery of novel health and educational services. In another it may be a disposition to experiment with new approaches to urban design and transportation. In still another it may involve innovative factory or site fabrication methods for building houses. In all of these cases the risks are real, but the prospects for some success or for minimizing failure are real too—provided the experiments are few and that in each a careful effort is made to monitor and evaluate the results.

GOVERNMENT POLICY AND ADMINISTRATION

Another easy mistake we warn against is to assume that the government, because it is providing some backing for new towns, will guarantee the kind of benevolent and enlightened leadership that can sustain the program through periods of difficulty. There is much disconcerting evidence to show that even in the short run, changes in government policy and administration can cause perilous lurches and lags in patterns of development. Changes in leadership, values, and purposes can, as Charles Abrams often reminded us, convert measures of reform into instruments of reaction. Without unremitting vigilance the new towns program is hardly likely to be the exception, and the danger is real that if new towns become the symbol for government's turning its back on the problems of existing cities or diverting resources from lagging regions, then new towns will become as unpopular as public housing projects are today.

URBAN GROWTH POLICY

Finally, because the idea of new towns is becoming fashionable and national officials now intone many of the more euphonious phrases describing what such communities are all about, we ought to point out that the government still has no national urban growth policy. We applaud—mildly to be sure—the current draft regulations accompanying the 1970 Urban Growth and New Community Development Act recently released by the Department of Housing and Urban Development, for the regulations outline a host of sensible criteria that will be taken into account in selecting projects for governmental assistance. We cannot quarrel with indexes such as economic soundness, contribution to the social and economic welfare of the entire area affected, increasing the available choices for living and working, making provision for housing of different types and income ranges, serving a wide range of families, and taking account of the location and the functions of new towns in combating sprawl, reorganizing inner-city development or helping lagging regions. The size of the town, the adequacy of transportation connections and services, the quality of planning and the capabilities of the developer are additional considerations (among others) which are appropriately underscored, as indeed they should be, when administrative regulations have to be applied across the board. But this facade of knowledgeable and comprehensive regulations is hardly adequate if the government has no sense of direction. Regulations in these circumstances are like the sky: They may cover everything and touch nothing; and meanwhile in an effort to get the program off the ground, the range and multiplicity of criteria can easily offer more rhetoric than results. What is needed is an unrelenting

THE PUBLIC INTEREST IN LAND-USE CONTROLS

William J. Nicoson

focus on the relationships between the reorganization of our inner cities and the organization of growth in our outer areas, between the slowing down of growth in our largest megalopolitan areas and spurring growth in a few key portions of our lagging regions.

Great leadership can electrify these themes, forge the necessary alliances, focus the agenda, and spur the necessary research. In our judgment the greatest service we can give our political leaders is to sensitize them to the dangers yet point out clearly the nature of the problem and the job that has to be done.

WE HAVE COME AT LAST to the collective realization that, in Russell Train's words, "Land is our most valuable resource." Like all valuable and finite resources, land should properly be the subject of intense public concern and its uses the subject of close public scrutiny.

In view of the fundamental state and national interests in land use, it is anomalous that land-use policy and controls in the United States have generally been the exclusive province of local government. While a number of the shortcomings of traditional zoning ordinances have been so egregious that reform was sometimes possible at local levels of government, others will undoubtedly require state or even federal remedial action.

A summary of selected shortcomings may be useful by way of background:

TRADITIONAL CONTROLS BY TRACT

Zoning, as the name implies, was conceived as a means of isolating varied uses of land in discrete tracts. It serves the important public interest of separating conflicting or antagonistic uses. What we have not always recognized, however, is that uses are not incompatible merely because they are different.

A residential neighborhood gains character as well as convenience from the presence of commercial uses. Centers of activity characterized by mixed uses of land (residential, commercial, religious, recreational, municipal) bring cohesion and identity to a neighborhood. Some planners now advocate the sprinkling at neighborhood scale of primary job-producing uses as well, elevating each neighborhood to the status of a miniature community.

Within the residential zoning categories of a traditional ordinance, restrictions on lot size have frequently operated to separate dwellings as well as land uses. Under such an ordinance developers had

little choice but to proliferate construction of detached units, feeding what Kenneth Schneider calls the "tyranny of minispaces." There was no opportunity to combine structural mass and liberate related open space from fragmentation. Nor was there an opportunity to combine varying types of residential construction at the neighborhood scale to achieve greater architectural interest.

The worst feature of traditional controls, however, has been their application to segregate, not activities or dwellings, but people. Zoning became a device to screen out undesirable residents, assuring the homogeneity of the neighborhood or community. Controls of land use were thus transformed into controls of land users, feeding still another tyranny of our times: exclusionary values.

A city council that suddenly rezones the proposed site of a low-income housing project to open-space or park use may be acting in what it takes to be the public interest of its constituency (*Kennedy Park Homes Association Inc.* v. *City of Lackawanna*), but state as well as federal courts have discerned a high public interest in preventing the discriminatory application of land-use controls. The Supreme Court of Pennsylvania has gone so far as to strike down as unconstitutional lot size requirements of two and three acres as an unreasonable restriction on growth. The court held that compelling people to live elsewhere was not a decision that the "township should alone be able to make" (*Appeal of Kit-Mar Builders Inc.*).

Some states, however, have explicitly abdicated review of exclusionary practices. The state constitution of California requires the approval of low-income public housing projects by local referendum. The United States Supreme Court has upheld (5-3) the referendum requirement, at least when directed against the income rather than the racial status of potential residents *(James* v. *Valtierra)*. In this one respect, the national interest has not been found to require that local exclusionary practices invited by state constitutional provisions be overturned.

It is evident, however, that state and federal interests in the review of local exclusionary practices could be served with greater certainty and uniformity by administrative rather than judicial action.

A final shortcoming of traditional zoning ordinances has been the imposition of procedural obstacles to large-scale development. The uncertainty of zoning approvals for future stages of development and the recurrent obstacle course of filings and public hearings for each successive tract have added significant risks and burdens to the already risky and burdensome undertaking of community-scale land development.

CONTROLS AT THE COMMUNITY SCALE

The early 1960s saw the addition to many zoning ordinances of a special category for planned unit development, under which general restrictions on lot size were replaced by restrictions on gross densities within areas identified in a specific approved plan.

In 1965 Howard County, Md., added to its zoning ordinance a provision for a "new-town district." Under this ordinance a new-town district is created upon approval by the county commissioners of a conceptual plan for a community of at least 20,000 persons with a full range of specified land uses in specified proportions. Gross densities within the total community and within specified residential categories are restricted. The entire district may be rezoned at the outset or in phases of 2,500 acres each. Zoning is perfected by approval of subsequent site

plans consistent with the conceptual plan. A public hearing is required on the conceptual plan but not on site plans unless a specified degree of variation from the conceptual plan is requested.

Planned community zoning permits compatible land uses to be mixed, net densities to be concentrated, open space to be unified, and residency to be open. It provides the developer with reasonable assurance that the community may be developed under his plan in future years without delay in zoning approvals.

With a stroke Howard County swept away many of the shortcomings of traditional zoning—at least for land development at community scale. A framework was provided for the orderly accommodation of regional growth. The influence of Columbia has been felt throughout the Baltimore-Washington corridor.

The Howard County experience is a rare instance of zoning reform with regional significance initiated and effected by enlightened local government. Since land-use controls facilitating large-scale balanced development are of obvious importance in the formulation and implementation of growth policies at the state and federal levels, it is easy to conclude that state and federal governments should not rely for reform entirely on local government, enlightened or otherwise. While today most states and the federal government play no role in controlling land use, a basic reassessment of responsibilities is under way in Congress and across the country. Significant changes are anticipated in the near future.

CONTROLS AT THE REGIONAL SCALE

One alternative for state involvement in land-use controls has been detailed in the American Law Institute's Model Land Development Code, which would establish a state land planning agency with the responsibility of formulating standards

for developments having regional significance. The ALI proposal has little precedent in the United States. Massachusetts and New York have requirements that local land development regulations take account of regional needs; Maine and Vermont have imposed state controls on large-scale development; and Colorado and New Jersey have enacted legislation establishing areas of "critical state or regional concern." The Massachusetts law establishes a review procedure somewhat similar to that proposed in the ALI Model Code, but none of these laws provides the comprehensive regulatory framework offered by the Model Code.

A second obvious alternative for state action is the exercise of full state controls over land use. The equally obvious objection is that many matters of exclusively local concern might better be resolved at the local level. Only in Puerto Rico am I aware of a fully centralized state system of land-use controls. It is doubtful that state legislatures would find such a system acceptable, whatever the showing of need.

A third alternative is my own personal choice: combining the first two alternatives in a two-tier system. Zoning responsibilities would be divided into coarse controls and fine controls. A state planning agency would have responsibility for decisions involving coarse zoning; local planning agencies would have responsibility for fine zoning.

Using criteria approved by the federal government and developed with federal financial assistance, the state agency would divide all land within its jurisdiction into three categories: urban, rural, and reserve. The reserve category would comprise ecologically sensitive land to be withheld permanently from development. Only agricultural and related uses would be permitted for land in the rural category. All other uses would be permitted for land in the urban category, determined by local agencies under state standards and subject to state review. State classifications would be revised annually—or more frequently on a showing of special need by a local agency—and would be subject to federal review. A system for compensatory payments in respect of uses below the highest and best use in an economic sense undoubtedly would be required.

The only precedent for coarse zoning at the state level is that of Hawaii. More research and analysis are needed concerning the system's advantages and drawbacks.

LAND ASSEMBLY IN LIEU OF CONTROLS

State and local governments have still another option in rationalizing land-use patterns: public land assembly as an alternative to statutory or regulatory controls. Because land is such a vital resource, some experts have recommended that public management be substituted for public controls.

The theory of land assembly in advance of development is attractive. The exorbitant profits of private land speculation would be turned to public benefit, financing additional public acquisition of land in advance of need. Government, through landownership, would exercise much more effective control over the quality, location, and pace of future urbanization in the furtherance of growth policies than could be possible through zoning, subdivision regulations, and building codes.

It is essential, of course, to analyze the promise of public land assembly on its merits, free of ideological labels. In fact we are already engaged in much more than analysis: We have begun direct experimentation in public land assembly for community development. The New

York State Urban Development Corporation has acquired land for three new towns and countless smaller projects. It is significant that the UDC has power to disregard local zoning and other regulations. It also has eminent domain powers, though all land to date has been acquired by negotiation. In UDC's Welfare Island project, the land is held under long-term lease from the City of New York, and leasehold interests will be conveyed to the ultimate users.

The New York experience indicates that public land assembly is entirely consistent with our system of free enterprise. Private developers and builders involved in UDC projects have found risks reduced and construction spurred through land acquisition and planning of the state agency. No complaints from landowners have been heard regarding the fairness of land prices.

In 1970 Congress enacted landmark legislation making federal guarantee assistance available to state and local government agencies to finance land acquisition and improvements for approved new towns. Legislation creating a state capability for new-town land acquisition and development has been introduced or is being drafted in most of the urbanizing states primarily as a result of the new federal incentives and the UDC experience.

Of course, public land assembly for new towns is a severely limited form of the landbank concept because new towns are expected to accommodate only 10 to 20 per cent of the nation's population growth over the next 30 years and the incidence of public sponsorship of new-town development during this period is still unclear. In the field of public influence over land use, however, new towns offer the same prospect for experimentation as in the many other fields where urban problems demand innovative solutions.

THE FEDERAL ROLE

Almost everyone agrees that the federal government should neither control nor manage, but should instead prod, inspire, and finance the states and municipalities. Discussion of appropriate federal action has been generously informed, if not preempted, by the superb legislation on national land-use policy proposed by the Nixon Administration.

Lest my praise be regarded as isolated chauvinism on the part of an Administration servant, let me by way of parenthesis quote Richard Babcock, the preeminent legal authority on land-use controls: "As a card-carrying Democrat, I state categorically that no administration since World War II has made such a far-reaching and sensitive legislative proposal to encourage the restructure of the institutional system for public regulation of our wasting and wasted resource of land as is reflected" in the Administration bill.

The bill would fund with 50-per cent grants two years of state development of land-use control programs and state management of the programs thereafter. In order to qualify for management grants, the state programs would be required to provide for:

1. The identification of areas of "critical environmental concern," including coastal zones and estuaries, shorelands and floodplains, rare or valuable ecosystems, and scenic or historic areas.

2. The identification of areas impacted by public facilities inducing regional urbanization, including major airports, highway interchanges, and major recreational lands and facilities.

3. State regulation of land use in areas qualifying for both categories.

4. State assurance that development and land use "for which there is a demonstrable need affecting the interests of con-

stituents of more than one local government which outweighs the benefits of any applicable restrictive or exclusionary local regulations" will not be restricted or excluded by such regulations.

5. A policy for influencing the location of new towns and controlling surrounding land use.

6. Regulation of large-scale development with regional impact on the environment.

7. Regulation pertaining to all the above areas and activities assuring compliance with applicable air, water, noise, or other pollution standards.

Techniques of state regulation may include:

1. State establishment of standards subject to review and enforcement of local compliance in the courts.

2. State administrative review of local regulations and compliance "with full powers to approve or disapprove."

3. "Direct state land-use planning and regulation."

These techniques may be used singly or in combination, and are not apparently intended to exhaust the acceptable forms of state action. Commenting on the absence of any reference to public land assembly, Russell Train, chairman of the Council on Environmental Quality, indicated that a state regulatory agency would not normally exercise eminent domain powers but that other state agencies "supported by other federal programs" could continue "to acquire land in the public interest."

This legislation would establish the principle that ecologically sensitive areas, areas of publicly induced urbanization, new towns and other large-scale development must be made subject to a state-devised system of land-use regulation. It also would establish the principle

that local exclusionary practices in the administration of land-use controls, however consonant with local public interest, must not be permitted to frustrate development or land use in the public interest of the larger state or national constituency. These are fundamental principles which should long ago have commanded the attention of state governments, and in my opinion the legislation should not only provide incentives for appropriate state action but also penalties for failure to act.

The Administration bill recognizes that land-use controls serve a complex mix of ecological, economic, and social purposes and that the uses we make of land are central to policies of state and national scope concerning environmental quality, urban growth, and equal opportunity.

Following the years of traditional land-use controls by tract and in the light of the recent promising introduction of flexible controls at the community scale, it will be exciting to witness the operation of a federal initiative inviting controls at the regional scale for land use of significance to state or national purposes.

PUBLIC CONTROL VS. PUBLIC ACTION

James McKeller

NEITHER GOVERNMENT NOR PRIVATE IN-DUSTRY nor some combination of the two can "create" communities. They can only prescribe the grounds through which people will come to sense that they have enough in common to live together in new types of environments. It is time to think of the institutions that will connect society to the new communities we are so anxious to build.

Private enterprise alone is not going to counteract the traditional desire of Americans to control their own small parcel of land and their own small local government, and to gain from speculating in land values. Nor is government going to legislate broad public purpose into large-scale real estate ventures. Government must create new institutions to work with the initiatives of private industry, but more important it must match controls with more discretionary intervention to tailor the product to society's needs.

These new institutions should emanate from a partnership among the three levels of government—federal, state, and local—and between government and the private sector.

Operating development organizations created to plan, build, or intervene in some direct way in large-scale developments are a prerequisite to any new framework for regulation. These could be fully public corporations like the New York State Urban Development Corporation, or quasi-public or fully private organizations benefiting from some special powers exercised by the state.

The strength of such an institution would be its ability to undertake varied developments in strategic locations and in a timely manner, including initial planning, land assembly, public infrastructure construction, low- and moderate-income housing, recreation and open-space development, and other selective pieces of large-scale new developments. It should be able to form partnerships with private enterprise and create subsidiary corporations for special purposes, thus strengthening collaboration among government, private enterprise, and community groups.

The second type of new institution should be state or regional enabling organizations. They would make it easier for private or public developers to overcome existing institutional obstacles to large-scale development and to take full advantage of the enabling powers of the state. It is at this level and through this kind of institution that basic changes in zoning, subdivision and building codes, and other regulations must be sought.

Other functions could include controlling the distribution of universities, highways, and other major public investments within a larger-scale public infrastructure; establishing multipurpose tax districts to help finance and maintain elements of the "public environment" in a cohesive and unified manner, and encouraging building and technological innovation, economies of scale, or other mass production techniques through uniform codes or other mechanisms based on performance requirements.

The most important form of partnership that the federal government could offer to the states would be national legislation designed to encourage many different kinds of enabling and operating development organizations to secure a full range of direct public-action programs at the state level. This would provide a more creative context for returning local powers of control over zoning and development to the states.

There is a third institution whose absence would nullify the whole concept of new towns. In Thomas Jefferson's words: "I know of no safe depository of the ultimate powers of a society but the people themselves, and if we think them not enlightened enough to exercise their control with a wholesome discretion, the remedy is not to take it from them, but to inform their discretion by education."

There remains the task of animating the citizen to his duty to participate in the democratic process of which he is the heart. The most crucial institution is that of self-government in town life. Without equal concern for the democratic processes and procedures that allow citizens to seek their own objectives, government actions and controls will end up imposing "solutions" on the people.

NEW PATTERNS
OF URBAN GROWTH

George Romney

THE RECENT REPORT of the President's Commission on Population Growth and the American Future has focused attention on forces creating America's tomorrow and where these forces are taking us.

The most important piece of information is the fact that the changes we are experiencing have been under way for 30 to 40 years. The rate—the speed of change—was altered in the 1960s, but the basic direction has been the same since mass ownership of the auto in the 1920s became a reality.

The reality and stability of these long-range trends tell us three important things:

1. They are due to deeply rooted basic forces in our society.

2. They are not primarily the result of federal or other government policies, but of decisions by millions of individual citizens and business and industrial leaders who were creating fundamental trends in our society.

3. It is therefore likely that these long-term trends will continue and we must adapt our goals and policies to the realities they indicate.

The commission's report emphasized that America's population is concentrating in metropolitan areas (in 1970 four out of every 10 persons lived in 29 Standard Metropolitan Statistical Areas [SMSAs] of a million or more persons), that by the year 2000, six out of 10 Americans will be living in 44 to 50 SMSAs of over a million population, and that these metropolitan areas are themselves part of 16 urban regions where 75 per cent of the population lived in 1970.

The report stated: "An urban region is not a single 'super city'; it is a regional constellation of urban centers and their hinterland. . . . Even in the largest urban region, running along the Atlantic Coast from Maine to Virginia and westward past

Chicago, it is estimated that only one-fifth of the area is currently in urban use." The commission expects the urban regions to grow in number from 16 today to at least 23 by the year 2000, and to increase their geographical coverage from approximately 300,000 square miles to 500,000 at the turn of the century—or a sixth of the continent (excluding Alaska and Hawaii). It is estimated that, by the year 2000, five-sixths of the nation's population will live in these 23 urban regions.

The final point from the commission's report is its projection that 85 per cent of the population in the year 2000 will live in metropolitan areas.

On the surface these projections seem to provide pretty grim reading for those interested in nonmetropolitan growth. But I believe additional facts will indicate this is a superficial misreading of the future. Let us look at some of the facts:

The first fact is the statistical misconception we have adopted by developing the concept of an SMSA. There is no sharp break between counties on the edge of a metropolitan area and those within it. What we see actually today is a crazy-quilt pattern of population expansion away from our central cities and core counties of the old metropolitan area. Periodically, as these adjacent counties pass a statistical threshold, we add them to the metropolitan unit.

But a new factor is emerging: the leapfrog factor. People are now able and willing to commute 30 to 50 miles or more to work in the metropolitan areas. And this becomes increasingly important as jobs decentralize out into the suburban counties—and the commuter no longer needs to drive all the way to the heart of the city.

This leapfrog factor is revitalizing small towns and cities that our statistical methods have assigned to nonmetropoli-

tan, but that are in fact vital elements in the orbit of our metropolitan areas. Between 1940 and 1970 the number of nonmetropolitan places increased from 12,800 to 13,800, and their total population grew from 23 to 33 million. Most of this growth occurred in small cities and towns experiencing the outflow of metropolitan populations and economic growth.

This then is the first element in the nonmetropolitan growth strategy: We must facilitate and encourage the spillover of metropolitan growth dynamics into the surrounding nonmetropolitan areas.

That this is a realistic possibility is shown by the commission's study of public preferences of living environments. Of those surveyed, 34 per cent wanted to live in open country. Another 30 per cent wanted to live in a small town or city. In short, 64 per cent wanted to live in areas characteristic of the nonmetropolitan parts of the nation.

Another 22 per cent wanted to live in a medium-sized city or suburb. There is clear evidence that our new-towns policies and programs have a growing market—perhaps 45 million Americans. For that is what these new towns will provide: a medium size combined with suburban low density and life-style. But these new towns must be located strategically within commuting distance of one or more of the metropolitan areas, yet far enough away not to be absorbed in the expanding metropolitan field and thus lose the attractiveness of the nonmetropolitan living environment.

Our third focus is the growing importance of leisure and recreation. Two factors will cause this new industry to grow more rapidly than perhaps any other element in our economy.

The first is the rising discretionary income of the American family. Family income should increase from a mean level of nearly $12,000 in 1969 to $16,000 in 1980, $20,000 in 1990, and above $26,000 in 2000. We are witnessing but the early stages of a fantastic boom in leisure and recreation.

The second factor is the probable growth of the four-day work week and the three-day weekend. Many industries are discovering that the four-day week increases productivity. And the broad desire for recreation and leisure away from home will accelerate this development.

The direct beneficiary will be the non-metropolitan area, which will become the recreation and leisure hinterland of the nation. We will see vast population flows each three-day weekend between the metropolitan and nonmetropolitan areas.

One of the first consequences will be the erection of millions of second homes for metropolitan families in the mountains, forests, and lake areas of the non-metro regions. This will create an expanded construction industry in these areas.

In the north, ski and other water sports will be expanded, and in the south, artificial lakes for water sports and the esthetic delight of lakeside views will be added to the existent natural attractions of mountains, forests, rivers, and natural lakes.

Tremendous demand will develop for trailer camping grounds, and motor home facilities. Motels and hotels with a wide range of associated recreational and leisure facilities will be built.

And a large business and industrial structure to support the building and operation of this vast recreation and leisure industry will emerge to provide some of the essential economic vitality for the small towns and cities in the nonmetropolitan zone.

In addition the weekly influx of tens of millions from the metropolitan areas will call into being a retail-wholesale and service industry to provide more economic dynamics for the nonmetropolitan areas.

Many small towns and regions will adopt the Vermont model, where the human tendency to nostalgia and fascination for an older, simpler way of life is made the basis for the preservation of the old architecture and the atmosphere of small-town simplicity. The antique industry probably will flourish in new and unexpected places.

In addition to the stimulation of the recreation and leisure boom, we must recognize the growing impact of a retirement population that will be better financed in years to come. The gradual built-in increase in Social Security, the efforts to improve and expand the pension systems, and improvement of the welfare system benefits for the aged will be a major factor in determining where retirees decide to live the remaining years of their lives.

We already see the potential in the vast migration of retirees to Florida and Arizona. People are retiring to more quiet, tranquil areas all over the nation. And this too can become a nonmetropolitan growth strategy.

What are some basic keys to this strategy? Number one is a fast, efficient transportation system out of our metropolitan areas and into the nonmetropolitan regions. This is the key to realizing every one of the potentials I have described:

1. It accelerates the spillover from the metro areas to the open country and small towns and cities in the nonmetro areas where people clearly prefer to live—even if they must commute 50 miles or more.

2. It makes possible a new-town strategy by tying potential new-town sites to the metropolitan areas from which they will draw their economic and population life.

3. It expands the weekend reach for recreation and leisure for millions of metro residents by extending for several hundred miles the areas they can reach in three or four hours of driving or riding.

4. It decreases the contact time between the retiree and his children and friends back in the metropolitan areas.

Up to this time we have designed our transportation system to connect major metropolitan areas around the nation. New we must relate it to the nonmetropolitan areas of the nation so that the metropolitan population—where 85 per cent of our people may live in 2000—may have full use of the nation's natural heritage in the nonmetropolitan areas.

Equal in importance to the extension of fast, efficient transportation systems from metropolitan to many nonmetropolitan parts of our country is the build-up of adequate public services, and the preservation of those environmental qualities that are the basic attraction for metropolitan populations, as well as those living there now.

The key strategic next step, in my judgment, to bring all these forces and factors together for the dynamic development of the nonmetropolitan areas is the creation of the new Department of Community Development proposed by President Nixon. In his March 1971 Federal Reorganization message to Congress, President Nixon said: ". . . the process of community development is becoming more complex, particularly as the problems of urban and rural communities begin to merge. . . . A community that seeks development assistance . . . finds that it has to search out aid from a vast variety of federal agencies. . . . Basic community development programs of the federal government are presently divided among at least eight separate authorities—including four executive departments and four independent agencies. . . . The mayor of one small town has ob-

TOWARD AN URBAN GROWTH POLICY

Samuel C. Jackson

served that by the time he finishes dealing with eight planning agencies he has little time to do anything else. . . To help correct such problems I propose that the major community development functions of the federal government be pulled together into a new Department of Community Development. It would be the overriding purpose of this department to help build a wholesome and safe community environment for every American. This process would require a comprehensive series of programs which are equal to the demands of growing populations and which provide for balanced growth in urban and rural areas."

It is clear that we are on the verge of a new evolutionary step in the civilization of the North American continent. We can combine the advantages of population concentration for certain purposes, and population dispersal for others. These are not incompatible but complementary.

AT LONG LAST, forces have been set in motion to permit the establishment of a national urban growth policy—a policy that will not view new towns as isolated developments responding only to local market forces, but as parts of a broader national and state framework for urban growth.

A national urban growth policy is essentially a concern for achieving more efficient and desirable patterns of human settlement than would occur without conscious effort. It recognizes that virtually every major federal and state action that allocates resources on a significant scale has implications for settlement patterns, whether intended or not.

Two decades of false starts have taught us that we cannot solve city problems in an uncoordinated city-by-city approach within each separate political jurisdiction. The roots and the potential solution to the urban crisis lie not only in the city, but in the suburbs and countryside. Unless we mount a coordinated attack on the problems of rural, suburban, and urban development, we will continue to be disappointed by the small return on our public investment for problem-solving in the cities.

URBAN-RURAL BALANCE

One of the key objectives of a national urban growth policy must therefore be to reverse or slow down the migration to larger cities, which damages both the cities and the countryside from which the migration springs. New towns can play a significant role in solving this problem, because:

1. They provide a framework for simultaneous development of all the facilities and services needed to support a primary job base.

2. They are not entrapped in the cycle of decay and inadequate institutions and facilities often associated with existing communities in rural or depressed areas.

3. They can be built on a scale large enough to support specialized services necessary for economic "takeoff."

4. They provide a framework for concentrating a tax base and federal aids.

CONTROLLING METROPOLITAN GROWTH

A national urban growth policy also must address itself to the problem of uneven population distribution within large metropolitan areas. According to a study of 10 metropolitan areas almost 80 per cent of employment growth in manufacturing between 1959 and 1967 took place in the suburbs, yet 80 per cent of all blacks in metropolitan areas lived in central cities. Many of the suburban jobs would represent opportunities for minority residents were they not immobilized by racial and economic discrimination in sprawling suburbia.

The control of massive growth in metropolitan areas cannot be accomplished by new towns alone. We need effective regional government, revenue policies and land-use controls responsive to local needs, transit tied to and planned with community development, and more effective techniques to preserve land in open space and control the pace of development.

But new towns are an essential part of this larger effort. And even if the larger effort is not mounted in this decade, new towns can, by themselves, set a standard of excellence for other land development within the metropolitan market.

Metropolitan new towns attack urban growth problems from two angles: revitalizing center cities and smaller suburban towns, and concentrating growth on undeveloped suburban land where urban sprawl would have been the predominant pattern of development. Under Title VII, new towns in-town can help with the first half of the job by developing center-city areas with a minimum of bureaucratic controls and without dependence upon the vagaries of the annual appropriation process. Suburban new towns can help with the second part by focusing growth into more efficient and desirable patterns with jobs and housing for all races and economic classes.

CONSERVATION

One of the tragedies of unbridled urban growth is the destruction of our irreplaceable natural and historic resources. The new growth of the South, the Southeast, and every suburban area of the country has been welcomed by some, but the welcome may be short-lived. The visitor has bad manners. Growth has filled the floodplains, stripped forested slopes, and polluted the air and water.

Because of their large planning scale and their control by a single developer, new towns can provide a greater opportunity than conventional urban development for reducing the pollution of air and water, preserving generous and accessible open space, promoting attractive architecture, providing recreational facilities, and restoring and preserving the man-made environment.

SOCIAL CONCERNS

The greatest tragedy of current growth patterns is not the phsyical form of that growth but the fact that it has polarized Americans by race and class. Bankers, real estate brokers, homeowners, and unfortunately even governments seem to have conspired to zone out the poor and exclude racial minorities.

An essential feature of new towns assisted under Title VII is that they must be designed to benefit all Americans. Most of these new towns will have at least 25 per cent subsidized housing, some as high as 40 or 50 per cent. And current

policies prevent the concentration of this housing in any one location to avoid the debilitating isolation of different groups in our society.

Not only must developers comply with all the civil rights laws and executive orders, but they must take affirmative steps to make sure minority groups are welcome. Both employment and housing must be marketed affirmatively to insure equal opportunity. Participation by minority builders and other businesses is encouraged.

INNOVATION

We have only begun to apply the full genius of American enterprise to housing production. The movement started in motion by Operation Breakthrough could have a lasting impact on the homebuilding industry. Now we must turn to the even more challenging task of applying this same genius to new-town building, which is many times more complicated.

We must test new concepts of community building on a larger scale than ever before, and we must combine these concepts into an integrated whole. They must not be in the realm of physical design alone, but also in social-service delivery systems and forms of governance. The Title VII new towns are all exploring new avenues for research and demonstrations in community building.

THE NEW-TOWNS PROGRAM

The major objectives of the new-towns program are sweeping and ambitious. The stakes are high and the outcome uncertain. The prospects for both accomplishment and disappointment have rarely been so great for a new government program. The sad fact is that other programs starting with high hopes have too frequently become diverted from their original objectives when the going got tough, or the operation became ossified

by too much red tape.

In administering the program, we at HUD have attempted to set the highest possible standards, and to define these standards in terms of performance so that the hands of the developer are not tied with second-guessing from Washington.

The project agreement and development plan that each developer signs with HUD sets forth the 20-year program of the developer in general terms but makes provision for a specific commitment in one- and three-year segments. Built into this administrative mechanism is a provision for updating the plan, taking into account changing conditions and feedback from each year's experience. Carefully defined changes of minor impact need not be approved by HUD at all.

Among the performance standards that developers must agree to meet in order to qualify for Title VII assistance are these:

1. The project must have a general plan and development program designed to maintain an attractive environment, including a suitable site, an effective land-use and transportation plan, adequate environmental protection measures, adequate public facilities, architectural controls, and provision for relocation.

2. There must be a substantial amount of housing for persons of low and moderate income.

3. A full range of governmental services must be provided.

4. The new-town plan must be consistent with areawide planning and must have complied with the requirements of Office of Management and Budget Circular A-95 in terms of notifying appropriate regional clearinghouses before a full application is submitted.

5. The developer must secure all state and local reviews and approvals required by law or determined by the Secretary to be necessary.

6. The developer must have or show that he will have the financial, technical, and administrative ability and background appropriate to the size and complexity of the project.

7. The project must be feasible in terms of its economic base or potential for growth.

8. The developer must have a financial plan or program demonstrating that the project is and will be financially sound and have a long-term favorable impact on the area in which the new town is located.

9. The developer must comply with all applicable civil rights laws and adopt an affirmative action program for equal opportunity in employment, housing, and business enterprise.

When a developer has convinced us that he has the capacity to achieve these performance standards, the work has only begun. Without reducing his freedom of action, we must insure that he actually meets expected performance.

In addition to the basic requirements of the law and regulations, HUD applies certain priority considerations that exceed available authority. We give special preference to projects that are especially innovative, to those of a type (e.g., free-standing communities) represented by few applications, and to those located in regions from where there are few applications.

CONTINUING SEARCH

One of our most important activities is the continuing search to improve the new-towns program. In this context, I offer the following ideas for debate and consideration.

1. In partnership with HUD, the Department of Commerce should be given the authority to provide a full system of incentives to encourage expanding or newly established industries to locate in approved new towns under conditions that meet the requirements of our act and of state urban growth policies. This must be done to avoid erosion of the existing community's tax and economic base.

2. We should encourage the private sector to create one or more new-town financing institutions which could offer credit resources supplementing Title VII, equity participation, technical assistance on a contractual basis, and access to industrial location decision-making.

3. We should take steps to provide greater assurances that continued federal assistance is available to new towns approved under the act so that developers can meet their obligations to provide low- and moderate-income housing throughout the life of the project, either through the use of conventional or newly developed programs.

4. To encourage the formulation of state strategies of community development, we should assist state agencies in the implementation of an approved strategy rather than the development of each individual project as required under existing legislation.

These steps are critical if we are to make reasonable headway in achieving the broad goals of a national urban growth policy. We must realize that the job of creating new towns and implementing an effective national urban growth policy cannot be accomplished by a single agency. Secretary Romney summed it up when he said, "Because the varying local problems have their origin in powerful interrelated national forces, their solution will require a national effort that draws on the resources of federal, state, and local governments and the private sector."

THE PROMISE OF TITLE VII

Thomas L. Ashley

THE ORIGINAL SPONSORS of the 1970 Urban Growth and New-Communities Act sought to create in Part A of Title VII a national urban growth policy that would encourage more rational, orderly, and efficient development throughout the United States. (And I emphasize that this was Part A as distinct from Part B, which provided for assistance to new towns, it being understood that new towns are no more than one component of a national growth strategy.)

We believe this policy shoud serve as a guide to making specific decisions at the national level that would affect urban growth and should coordinate federal programs to encourage desirable patterns of growth and stabilization, the prudent use of land resources, and the protection of the physical environment. In addition, we feel it should set a framework for the development of interstate, state, and local growth and stabilization policy.

In section 703 of Title VII, the President is given the responsibility of transmitting to Congress a biennial report on urban growth prepared by an identifiable unit of the Domestic Council in the White House and the departments and agencies of the Executive Branch. The report is to contain a summary of problems facing the United States as a result of growth trends and developments, together with a review and assessment of interstate, state, and local planning programs and specific recommendations for programs and administrative actions for carrying out this emerging national urban growth policy.

It is our conviction that if the Executive Branch fails to perform this task the country cannot achieve the national goal of orderly and efficient growth. Without government efforts to assure adequate planning, present trends of haphazard, ad hoc development will continue, and the results are certain to be catastrophic.

The Administration's record on this part of Title VII has been disappointing. In the first place, few substantive additions, if any, have been made to the language of Title VII itself, either by the President in his messages to Congress or in the Administration's specific legislative proposals. To the extent that growth policy guidelines exist, they are to be found largely in Title VII and only occasionally and minimally in pronouncements from the Executive Branch.

Second, even if the Administration's legislative package, including revenue sharing, were adopted, a coherent national growth policy would not result. The large degree of emphasis on state responsibility would make national coordination difficult and the results disparate and uneven among the 50 states. The idea of aggregating whatever the states do and calling it a national policy isn't exactly what we had in mind.

Third, while the creation of a Department of Community Development as proposed by the Executive Branch could strengthen considerably the ability of the federal government to develop and implement a growth policy, the prospects that Congress will approve this proposal in the near future are extremely dim. Therefore it should not and cannot be relied upon as an anchor for an emerging growth strategy.

In short, the nation still lacks a detailed and comprehensive growth policy because to date there has been no commitment to a national urban growth policy. It would be hard to imagine a narrower construction of a legislative mandate calling for the creation of a national urban growth policy.

But there is still some reason for optimism among those interested in new towns. Most important perhaps is that some excellent projects are under way.

There is also a growing body of interest and commitment at HUD and throughout the country. I think that the board of the Community Development Corporation and its managing director are first-rate and, generally speaking, anxious to unshackle the program and give it a chance.

Good projects make effective advocacy easy. If congressional interest and support can be strengthened through individual and organizational efforts, then I think a change in the level of the Administration's involvement and commitment can be brought about.

And if an effective constituency for new towns can be developed from New York to California to support congressional efforts, I am confident that Title VII will then assure the better patterns of urban development and revitalization that are necessary if we are to improve the quality of our national life in the years to come.

ELEMENTS OF AN URBAN GROWTH POLICY

Carl Feiss

OUR SUBJECT MATTER has to do with well-planned, well-designed, well-balanced, attractive, and presumably permanent new places in which people will live, work, learn, play and go about their business until, it is hoped, they will die comfortably in their own beds at a ripe old age and get buried at the still-to-be-built community crematorium.

"Well-planned," "well-designed," "well-balanced"—these are all terms that we use constantly and barely understand. They are word symbols for concepts and criteria that have seldom been identified mathematically, physically, socially, culturally, environmentally. Nor can we actually put our fingers on any specific community that embodies all of these standards or distinctions. If such an exemplar did exist, we would have guided tours to it by the hundreds.

Considering the nature of American urbanization as it has been occurring over the past 40 or 50 years, is our new community policy to be designed to create something brand-new, something experimental? Or are we to subject ourselves to the market as an incentive mechanism? Are we to create the market? Are we to design deliberately for the population overspill in our still-expanding urbanized areas? Just what are the determinants?

Of one thing I am certain: It is our responsibility to bend the trends in urbanization as they have taken place and change the whole direction and quality of the development incentive mechanisms that have been responsible for the creation of millions of dollars' worth of the kind of suburbia we now know is no longer good for us. Without a national planning program, the real estate rape of the United States will continue.

Title VII adds a new dimension to old programs. It does not eliminate or change them. It is a supplement which has not been tried. It is a new incentive mechanism for development, with new forms of controls and new stipulations on the quality of development. Title VII's great advantage is that it does not consider the sole goal of its incentive mechanisms to be anything that can be sold for the highest price.

But every kind of new community, wherever it is, should first come within the overall controls of a national policy that specifically stakes out those parts of the country in which no urbanization should occur. The current process has resulted in the irretrievable loss of vast stretches of beaches and many of our finest mountain and forest areas. The "second home" subdivisions arising in the Cascades, the Olympics, the Rockies, and the Appalachians are all part of a catastrophic real estate boom with which national urban growth policy must come to grips.

An urban growth policy that does not encompass the wheeler-dealer along with the developer who desires to build a well-planned new town, dooms the latter to failure purely on the basis of competition and salesmanship—unless the designers of the new towns can beat them to the draw.

The greatest development incentive we have in the United States is the lack of genuine land-use planning and controls, which has permitted and encouraged freewheeling destruction. An urban growth policy must include land-use controls that encourage a developer to do the right thing. A developer in turn must be willing to expose the details of the design and layout of his property to a public review mechanism.

It should be understood clearly that control mechanisms are not only internal but external. There needs to be stringent protective devices for the environment in which the new town is to be located. The

A PLAN FOR
URBAN GROWTH

Report of the National Policy Task Force,

The American Institute of Architects

entire region requires every type of ecological and environmental planning on a continuing basis so that the total context within which the new town exists is maintained in a kind of perpetual trust. Unless this is done, the new town will be swallowed up (as Reston and Columbia may be very shortly) by urbanization from outside sources or by parasitical urbanization beyond the control of the developer.

The entire land-control mechanism at the local, regional, and state level is so primitive, so inadequate, and so confused legally, administratively, and from the physical design standpoint that much more attention must be given to it. Under the American system, the police power is not written into the Constitution and is not a federal responsibility but a local one. The whole question of how to make use of the police power at the local level for the purposes we envisage is crucial to their success. It must be considered in depth.

THIS REPORT IS ABOUT AMERICA at its growing edge. It outlines a set of policies that can enable this nation—as a responsible member of a threatened world of nations—to shape its growth and improve the quality of its community life.

The strategic objective of these policies is a national mosaic of community architecture designed to be in equilibrium with its natural setting and in sympathetic relationship with its using society.

In brief, the report urges that:

1. Changes be made in a number of the "ground rules" (e.g., tax policy, governmental organization, etc.) that presently shape the development of American communities.

2. The nation develop the capacity to build and rebuild at neighborhood scale (the "Growth Unit"), ensuring open occupancy, environmental integrity, and a full range of essential facilities and services.

3. Federal, state, and local governments—in partnership—set the pace and standards for growth policy through a special impact program affecting 60 of the nation's urban regions and a third of the nation's expected growth between 1970 and 2000.

THE CIRCUMSTANCES WE ARE DEALING WITH

The nation's population has grown and urbanized dramatically over the last generation. By conventional measures, most of us have prospered. Personal and family incomes generally have increased. Housing conditions have improved. National opinion polls consistently find that most of us feel the quality of our personal lives is better. And amid the flurry of sudden growth, we have staked out a substantial range of free choice.

But a lot of things have us worried and dissatisfied—and properly so.

Millions of Americans have not had this range of free choice. Machines have pushed men off the land and into deteriorating cities where they have been imprisoned by rising prejudice and dwindling opportunity. Others have been left behind, trapped in the forgotten hamlets and hollows of rural America.

The nation has been polarizing into richer and poorer, black and white, growing suburbs and declining cities, neighborhoods of higher and lower status, and some with no status at all.

Giant urban regions have sprawled into being without the armature of public utilities and services that make the difference between raw development and livable communities.

Jobs have been separated from housing, forcing families to spend more money on highway transportation than on homes and more time on the road than with each other.

Land, money, and building costs have priced more and more Americans out of the conventional housing market—not just the poor, but the middle class as well. Construction has lagged for the lower-income groups and larger families. Abandonment of existing stock in the older cities has picked up at a threatening rate. Mobile homes have "saved the day" for growing numbers of Americans (though not the minorities), but they have scattered their residents out past the range of regular community life and services.

Our growth has broken loose from the regenerating cycle of nature. The accumulating wastes of this growth—phosphates, plastics, pesticides, heat, hydrocarbons—contaminate our soil, air, and water, and cast a growing cloud over our nation and our future.

Land has become a negotiable commodity and tossed carelessly into the game of speculation for profit. Once in the market, not only its use but its very existence is subordinated to the highest bidder and shortest-term gain.

The comforts and hardships, the benefits and costs of national growth have not been shared equitably. Our tax structure frequently has dumped some of the highest costs on those least able to pay. The education of the nation's children and the general level of community services have been left to the happenstance of local tax ratables and the small politics that exploit them. They breed fiscal zoning, and fiscal zoning has put a damper on the social and economic mobility of the poor and working class.

The social distortions in the development of our communities are reflected in our built environment. For much of what we have built, largely since World War II, is inhuman and potentially lethal. We have created a community architecture that, in its lack of efficiency, its inattention to human scale and values, and its contribution to chaos, adds up to a physical arena adverse to "the pursuit of happiness," one of the fundamental rights that stirred us to create a nation. Surely it is as important to bring our physical fabric into conformity with this goal as it is to do so with our social fabric. We cannot long endure an environment that pollutes air, water, food, and our senses and sensibilities.

At the same time that our growth has created an environmental crisis, the governmental process for dealing with growth has been scissored into bits and pieces. Whatever energies and resolves Americans can muster to shape their growth and salvage their environment are dissipated in an almost infinite chain of separate and conflicting consents which have to be negotiated in order to do the public's business. Just when the nation

most needs its enterprise, creativity, and overriding sense of community, stymie and cynicism become the order of the day.

Now another generation of dramatic growth is about to begin. The numbers of Americans in the 25 to 44 age group—traditionally those who create new households—are increasing at a rate nearly *nine* times that of the past decade. These new households will not likely beget children at the bulging rate of postwar, but they will inevitably touch off a new burst of community formation and urban growth. It is doubtful that these new householders will fit easily into old patterns. Many of them will not want to. Families will be smaller. Wives will be working. Their tolerance of environmental pollution and bureaucratic incompetence will be lower. They will be demanding more for their money and especially the money they are asked to pay in taxes.

And young adults are not the only Americans pressing for places to live—to live better and in many respects to live differently. More and more Americans are living longer. During the 1970s an ever-growing proportion of our population will have raised their families, retired from their jobs, and started looking for communities that will serve their changing needs. There will be another round of kids with mothers asking for day care, new waves of migrants and immigrants searching for something better than ghettos to live in, and alumni of the ghetto—increasing millions of them—who have learned from tragic experience not to let even poverty trap them in bad neighborhoods forever and again.

TOWARD A NATIONAL GROWTH STRATEGY: THE POLITICS AND PROMISE OF DIVERSITY

Sharpening awareness of the flaws in the way we've grown accounts for the rising

demand for a national growth policy. Our nation's search for such a policy is a welcome sign of a maturing society, a more civilized and humane America. But just because so many seem to be asking for a national growth policy, that doesn't mean they all want the same policy. And just toting up everybody's unhappiness about how we've grown—and maybe goofed—doesn't necessarily add up to a policy that's better or more consistent or more salable to the American public.

Not until these differences in need and life-style are admitted and understood will we really be on our way toward more productive policies for national growth. These diversities are the facts of life which politicians—especially the President and the Congress—have to deal with if the nation is to have governing policy and not just years of fruitless debate.

In fact it well may be that a diversified nation that values free choice above all may have to live with a national growth policy that is less than coherent, that contains more inconsistencies than it resolves, that turns the power of conflicting forces into creative energy—and that succeeds because it strives toward unity but does not mutilate its freedoms in an all-out effort to achieve it.

We submit this report in that spirit. We are a single profession with our own creative diversities. We have spoken assertively, but only to enrich the national debate, not dominate it. We have tried to convert what we think are legitimate discontents into constructive ideas of how to make America better. And we have taken the risk of translating generalities (which is easy) into specifics (which is tough).

BELIEFS AND PREMISES WE START WITH

1. A national growth policy is first of all an expression of national values.

2. The values we most cherish are the

worth of the individual and his freedom of choice. These values have been stated constantly in national legislation, but not so regularly honored.

3. We believe, therefore, that national growth policy actually should commit the nation to these values, not merely restate them. What has been missing is the public competence that makes both our values and our policies credible: laws with teeth; programs with money behind them; public officials with the power to act and willingness to fulfill a leadership role. Private freedom and public competence are not incompatible. One needs the other.

4. The goals of national growth policy and the problems it should be concerned with have more to do with the quality of life than with numbers. We do not share two of the usual fears: that American population is too large and that not enough houses will be built to meet our growing demand. During the past decade Americans have spontaneously and freely limited reproduction. The birthrate is now at an all-time low. Earlier estimates of how much America would grow in the next 30 years now seem too high. The total well may be as low as 60 million—a number we certainly can care and provide for. Meanwhile, housing starts have picked up. The prospects are that the nation's stated housing goal (2.6 million annually during the 1970s) may be met. And these goals actually may turn out to be too high.

It is not the numbers we should be concerned about but the quality of living and the choice of life-styles that are opened to Americans—whoever they are and however many there may be. This is what we believe Americans mean when public opinion polls regularly report that a majority of them say they would prefer to live in smaller communities. Not that they won't abide living in large metro-

politan areas. Despite what they say, most of them have chosen to move and stay there. But they are searching for communities that are more livable; neighborhoods that are safe; neighborhoods that are within easier reach of jobs and a richer mix of community life and services; neighborhoods small enough to have some identity of their own, where no one need be anonymous while attaining the privacy Americans always have yearned for.

5. It follows, we think, that the measuring rod of national growth should be the quality of our neighborhoods, and the assurance that neighborhoods—even when they change—will not deteriorate. The neighborhood should be America's Growth Unit. We have made it the theme of this report.

6. By concentrating on the neighborhood as a Growth Unit, national policy can relate to growth and regrowth wherever it may occur—in rural areas, in smaller towns and outlying growth centers, in metropolitan areas and their central cities, in freestanding new communities. No national policy would be politically salable that did not speak to every condition of America. No national policy would be comprehensive if it did not.

7. Our own guess is that most of America's expected growth from now until the end of the century will occur within existing metropolitan areas—whether all of us would like that to happen or not. The economics and the politics of radically changing that pattern are too difficult. They well may be impossible. Marginal changes, yes. And since we too have a general prejudice in favor of "more balanced growth" and against overloading the environment (as we have done, possibly, in some of the Great Lakes and coastal regions) we should be

of a mind to encourage these changes.

But realities force us to be realistic. We therefore conclude that American growth policy should concentrate on improving the present and future conditions of our existing metropolitan areas.

8. Within these areas we believe the first priority should go toward improving the condition of the older core cities, more especially the condition of those trapped in poverty and the squalor of declining neighborhoods. Until we deal with the deep-seated factors in American life that give rise to such conditions, all growth in America is vulnerable, no matter how much concern and money are lavished on it, no matter how carefully it may be segregated from those neighborhoods where the contagion of decline is more evident.

9. Growth and regrowth—building new communities and restoring old ones—must go together. We think it folly to try urban renewal in the older, denser neighborhoods before moving and relocation room is made ready elsewhere. That means, we think, a deliberate policy of building new neighborhoods on vacant land before renewal of older neighborhoods is begun.

10. We believe that no national growth policy will work unless there is a broader base for financing the facilities and services necessary for more livable communities. The local property tax is no longer enough. We have exhausted it, and now it is crippling us.

There are many possible ways of achieving this broader base of financing. Our own preference is for the federal government to assume far more of the costs of social services such as health and welfare, and more of the costs of utilities. We believe the states also should assume a greater share of local costs, especially of schools, and should do so through a combination of broad-based taxes whose impact is less regressive and its yield more responsive to changes in the general level of the economy.

11. Similarly, we are convinced that an effective national growth policy will require broader perspectives and, in many cases, larger governmental jurisdictions. We welcome signs that the states are readying themselves to participate more actively in community development—even when, as in the case of zoning, taxation, and other matters, they have to be prodded into action by the courts. The states are essential to the development of a national growth policy precisely because their jurisdictions (and hopefully their views) are broader, and because they constitutionally control the ground rules of local government and community development.

We also welcome the signs of new life at the metropolitan level. A promising example is the emergence of regional planning, development, and financing in the Minneapolis/St. Paul area. If indeed most of America's growth is to occur in these areas, some form of regional control must evolve—and soon.

12. And while these broader capacities are developing, we also see the need for more citizen control and participation at the neighborhood level. Neighborhoods have been swallowed up in the growth and change of urbanizing America. The exact forms and functions of neighborhood government can vary, but national growth policy cannot do without the sturdiness and savvy of grass-roots support. We see no contradiction in simultaneous transfer of power upward to broader-based levels of government and downward to the neighborhoods. It is not power that is being subtracted, it is capability that is being added.

13. It also follows from our concern with the neighborhood Growth Unit that the architects who design it, the developers who package and build it, the doctors and teachers and lawyers and merchants who serve it should be given every honorable encouragement to work at this scale. Urban America may be massive, but it has accumulated in a formless way from a myriad of actions and designs that were of less than neighborhood scale. Thought and habit patterns will have to change if we are to build more livable neighborhoods—neighborhoods that fit as building blocks into metropolitan, regional, and national societies.

14. We wonder whether the time has come to consider less affluent standards of housing in favor of higher standards of neighborhood environment, facilities, and services—if indeed the choice must be made. Less affluent, at least, than is explicit in the spiraling requirements of floor space and lot sizes and building codes that are being written defensively into suburban and other exclusionary legislation. The rising cost of exclusion is even higher than the rising cost of building. The product may well be more luxurious houses but less desirable, certainly less open communities.

15. Finally, we are convinced that an effective national growth policy requires that land development increasingly be brought under public control. This is true particularly of land that lies in the path of growth or that otherwise is crucial to the community's well-being—open space, floodplains, coasts and shores, etc.

We favor public acquisition and preparation of land in advance of development. We believe that the appreciating value of urbanizing land should be recycled into the costs of developing, serving, and maintaining it. We believe that, in many cases, leasing rather than outright

sale would be desirable for land acquir and assembled by public action.

BUILDING AT NEIGHBORHOOD COMMUNITY SCALE: THE GROWTH UNIT

The Growth Unit is first of all a concept a general way of saying that America's growth and renewal should be designed and executed not as individual building and projects but as human communitie with the full range of physical facilities and human services that ensure an urb life of quality.

GROWTH UNIT

■ 20 persons/acre
▨ variable densities
⛶ open space
○ recreation
● community facilities

The Growth Unit does not have fixed mensions. Its size in residential terms normally would range from 500 to 3,00 units—enough in any case to require a elementary school, day care facilities, community center, convenience shopping, open space, and recreation.

Enough, too, to aggregate a market for housing that will encourage the use of new technology and building systems. Also enough to stimulate innovations in building maintenance, health care, cable TV, data processing, security systems, and new methods of waste collection and disposal. Large enough, finally, to realize the economies of unified planning, land purchase and preparation, and the coordinated design of public spaces, facilities, and transportation.

This general scale is consistent with likely trends during the 1970s that will encourage the filling in of open land and the renewal of older neighborhoods within existing metropolitan areas—as well as the expansion of outlying communities (Growth Centers) within the population range of 25,000 to 250,000. It also coincides with the trend toward "miniaturization" which seems to characterize emerging patterns of consumer behavior and demand and which is producing a new range of facilities such as community health centers, neighborhood city halls, and convenience shopping centers.

Life-styles, housing types, and residential densities could vary according to local markets and circumstances.

Larger communities—up to and including freestanding new towns—should be built as multiples of these Growth Units, allowing of course for an emerging hierarchy of additional services and facilities, such as high schools, community colleges, hospitals, regional shopping centers, mass transit, and utility systems.

The neighborhood Growth Unit relates just as much to the rebuilding of America's older cities as it does to new growth on open land. We have learned the hard way that urban renewal and the rehabilitation of older neighborhoods cannot succeed when done piecemeal, house by house, problem by problem.

The job is much bigger than that, and the Growth Unit is a more appropriate scale and way of doing it.

The Growth Unit is based firmly on the principle of open occupancy and equal access to facilities and services. Moreover, by linking growth and regrowth both outside the central cities and within them, the nation can find an orderly way out of its segregated living patterns and the haunting tragedy of its older cities.

Finally the Growth Unit offers a valid measuring point for environmental performance. It can be planned and judged as a "package" rather than a disjointed accumulation of activities, some of which do and some of which do not meet going standards of ecological innocence.

USING THE GROWTH UNIT IN A NATIONAL GROWTH STRATEGY

Concentrating on the Growth Unit is a practical and incremental way of approaching a national growth policy. But it is not a retreat from major and even radical changes—as those who recently have ventured into large-scale development painfully can attest. Architect after architect, developer after developer, large company after large company have tried their hands at building new communities at larger scale. Only a few have survived—and even for them the experience has been bloody. Listed below are some of the constraints and hazards, changes and reforms we think are necessary if this nation is to achieve the capacity to produce livable neighborhoods without all the traumas (and mischief) that presently are involved.

1. *Housing and Land-Use Policy.* Growth Units of the sort we propose will not be built at the rate and scale we propose unless there is an assured flow of credit at stabilized rates of interest over a sustained period of time; unless low- and

moderate-income families are subsidized directly (through income supplements, housing allowances, Section 235 and 236 type interest reductions, etc.) at levels equivalent to the housing subsidies now provided higher-income homeowners in the form of tax deductions of mortgage interest and local property tax payments (plus what economists call "imputed rents"); and unless state governments retrieve sufficient control over local building, zoning, and health regulations to insure an adequate supply of land for large site development—and also land permanently reserved for open space, ecological balance, and communal use.

2. *Front Loading.* Building at neighborhood scale requires front money equal at least to 40 per cent of the total investment, with no appreciable return on that early investment coming until the fifth to 15th year. Few are in a position to advance that kind of money and wait so long for a return. Public money and guarantees are still scanty and hard to come by. Except in New York State, they are available only through one limited program of the federal government. These public supports will have to be expanded greatly, at both federal and state levels.

3. *Aggregating Sites.* The assemblage of large sites is a problem, but probably less so than obtaining the many consents necessary to develop them: zoning, building codes, etc. For the private developer, time is money. One major developer is reported to have incurred interest costs of $5,000 per day over a year while awaiting the necessary consents. Too many developers have been led into dubious practices in an effort to offset these costs and find ways around these constraints.

The passage of legislation authorizing planned community development promises some relief. Probably more important will be an arrangement allowing for someone other than the developer to hold the land until the consents have been negotiated and the developer can move immediately to build.

4. *The Public Infrastructure.* Another barrier is the shortage of public funds for the necessary infrastructure and community services. We propose that the federal and state governments plan and construct networks of utility corridors, including transit, water, sewage, electricity. These would constitute the skeleton of utilities on which Growth Units could be fastened.

At the level of a single project the scale of development we propose requires a long-term and disciplined schedule of public spending geared closely to the efforts of the builder.

5. *Removal of Tax Disincentives.* Both federal and state tax systems are replete with impediments and disincentives to building and rebuilding at neighborhood scale. The Internal Revenue Code encourages a quick-build-and-sell posture for the developer. It discourages his staying around to make certain that the costs and concerns of management and upkeep are given attention equal to that given the cost of construction.

6. *Tax Incentives.* Building communities is far more complex than the single missions that become manageable profit centers for a business enterprise. Congress might declare the building of ·Growth Units to be in the national interest and make special tax and other provisions to enable American enterprise—under tight performance standards—to make the long and broad commitments the job requires.

7. *Property Tax.* America's dependence on the local property tax is especially hurtful. By tying practically all costs of community development to local ratables, it causes undue hardships to the

builder and the citizen alike. The apparent answer is to move toward broad-based taxation at state and federal levels. It also suggests moving certain costs from local to state and federal governments.

8. *Revenue Sharing.* Any sharing of revenue by the federal government with the states should be conditioned on certain reforms, including a restructuring of the property tax system, zoning and building codes, and reallocation of infrastructure costs.

9. *Governmental Structures and Process.* Governments in America—federal, state, and local—are not organized to facilitate the kind and scale of development we propose. Major changes and innovations are in order:

● At the federal level, some analogue of a national development corporation capable of negotiating the necessary bundle of federal grants and consents; dealing with counterpart state, local, and private development agencies, and tapping national money markets.

● At the state level, development corporations emulating and going beyond the pioneering example of New York.

● At the metropolitan level, public and public/private corporations subject to regionwide planning and participation and oriented both to redevelopment of the inner city and to new development on open land.

10. *Categorical Grant Programs.* The tradition of categorical funding that long has been followed in American government needs to be modified. Above all, the Highway Trust Fund, we think, must be converted to a general fund for community development and greatly expanded. If this self-regenerating fund is not refashioned to serve our highest priority needs, the nation will place itself in bondage to the automobile and superhighway.

USING THE GROWTH UNIT IN COMMUNITY DESIGN

A national strategy based on the Growth Unit requires the use of tactical stepping stones in the design of communities that will be in harmony with human needs and the natural environment. Such a strategy must be a long-term commitment. Its integrity must be maintained consistently, although it may require continuous updating to accommodate changes we cannot foresee. Commitment to a long-term strategy based on such fundamental principles as freedom of choice and the worth of the individual demands tactics that emphasize flexibility and diversity.

Community design based on the Growth Unit should embrace the following principles:

1. *Equilibrium.* The design should be economical in its consumption of natural resources. It should minimize the emission of harmful effluents and encourage emissions that tend to replenish natural resources. The need for transportation should be reduced by intermingling residential and other uses. Community services (such as health care, education, and security) should be consciously designed as systems and subsystems.

2. *Symbiosis.* The design should provide a beneficent and nourishing relationship between the physical environment and its using society. The surest means of attaining this relationship is to encourage community participation in the design process.

3. *Satisfaction of Spiritual Needs.* The design must satisfy the individual user's need for reassuring symbols that speak to him from the natural setting and from architecture within this setting. It must satisfy his need for symbols of place and personality which distinguish one person and one community from another—his

need for an environmental order that de-
notes purpose in life.

4. *Expansion of Locational Options.*
Just as the national strategy emphasizes
freedom of choice of location, design of
Growth Units should reduce barriers
based on economics or race or age. This
means that transportation, industry, and
commerce must be placed with attention
to their social consequences.

5. *Expansion of Qualitative Options.*
The design mosaic must provide a rich variety of living environment matching the
variety of life-styles within our society.

6. *Open-Space Preservation.* Community design must preserve open space at
all geographic scales from the national to
the local. Certain areas should be pre-
cluded from development either because
of natural features that are hazardous to
residents or where development would
threaten ecological balance or recreational values.

7. *Historic Preservation.* Our historic
heritage must be preserved from destruction or erosion if a sense of individual and
community identity is to survive. Preservation of historic buildings and communities will require the discovery of new uses
as original uses become obsolete. Some
historic structures may have to be altered
and modernized to accommodate contemporary functions. We must also look to
the values in contemporary architecture
that may in time have historic significance.

8. *Public Investment as a Key to Development.* Public utilities and facilities can
be used to determine settlement patterns,
both nationally and at the level of the
single Growth Unit. The network of transportation and communications corridors
should be the essential basis for comprehensive planning within the proposed
communities and for their external connection with the existing community fab-

ric. It should be designed and put in
place incrementally in accordance with
the largely private development of housing, commerce, and industry. Since this
infrastructure is relatively permanent, it
should be generous in its dimensions in
order to permit accommodation of future
technological developments. It should be
seen as the opportunity for expression of
great civic art and architecture.

9. *Amendable Architecture.* The design should provide a physical fabric that
is amendable by its occupants to accommodate changes in life-styles, technology, and economic circumstance.

10. *Reduced Cost of Shelter.* Design
should seek to reduce the cost of housing.
Offsite manufacture is one method of pursuing this goal, but care must be taken to
produce a kit of parts that can be assembled in many differing ways to provide environmental variety. The design should
take maximum advantage of the reduction in governmental constraints which
must be a part of a national growth strategy. Better quality and workmanship can
be attained once such constraints are removed. The unearned increment in the
value of the land should be recaptured by
the public, instead of becoming part of
the inflated cost of shelter, as it does now.

11. *Experiment with Change.* We must
deliberately experiment with change.
This, in turn, will require that public
funds be available to finance experimentation. Each Growth Unit can be a
laboratory for new applications of technology and design. Procedural experimentation could involve the using community and public/private and multidisciplinary development teams in an open
"trialogue." The behavioral sciences can
be involved in the development of a more
sophisticated basis for establishing user
needs. New ways of determining costs
and benefits could take into greater ac-

count intangible factors and qualitative
benefits.

THE GROWTH UNIT AND THE URBAN
CRISIS*

The neighborhood Growth Unit applies to
all America. But some parts of the nation's society and landscape have been
and will continue to be especially impacted by growth. We believe a more specific and concentrated response should
be made to the problems of the nation's
declining central cities and their fast-
growing metropolitan areas.

There are approximately 65 metropolitan areas in this country with 1970
populations of 500,000 or more. These
65 urban regions accounted for half the
nation's total population, more than half
of the nation's black population, and 60
per cent of the nation's total growth during the decade 1960-70.

Currently, 80 per cent of America's
growth is taking place within existing
metropolitan areas. In all probability the
metropolitan areas cited above will continue to absorb the lion's share of national
growth and the problems that go with it.

Without foreclosing (actually it could
be planned as part of) a national strategy
that might attempt to shift growth from
these urban regions, we propose that the
federal government join immediately
with the affected state and local governments in developing growth plans for
these critical areas.

These plans should include the following elements:

1. Governments involved immediately
should assemble one million acres of land
for community development within the
core cities and in the metropolitan periphery. (We would estimate the cost of acquiring this at $5 billion.) The appreci-

---

*This builds on a forthcoming paper by Bernard
Weissbourd

149

ating value of this land—realized by lease and sale over the next 30 years—would be enough to cover its original cost plus a large proportion of the costs of preparing the land for development.

2. A third of the nation's growth (20 million) during the next 30 years could be accommodated on these one million acres at average densities of 25 persons per acre—far under the present densities of troubled core cities, and within range of current consumer choice and economic feasibility.

3. The building block of this development would be the neighborhood Growth Unit—500 to 3,000 dwellings, 2,000 to 10,000 persons—built either singly or in multiples which over time would be fitted together into larger satellite communities.

4. The development of these Growth Units should be staged to provide relocation and elbowroom for the restoration of older neighborhoods in the core area. Open occupancy would be insured—with the end result that no one sector of the metropolitan area would be, or feel, overwhelmed.

5. The social mix of these neighborhoods would be further insured by housing subsidies and allowances covering housing rental costs exceeding 25 per cent of family income. These subsidies also would be available to families filtering into existing housing throughout the metropolitan area.

6. The federal, state, and local governments would join in planning and paying for the necessary infrastructure—particularly transportation and utility corridors which would weave these Growth Units into the existing fabric of metropolitan life: jobs, education, health care, etc.

7. The economics (and for that matter the politics) of these selected metro-

politan areas should be pooled—benefits (such as new ratables) as well as costs. As a matter of first principle, new growth should not be allowed to occur as an escape from, or at the cost of, the revitalization of older neighborhoods.

8. Zoning and building codes for these Growth Units should be developed jointly by the three levels of government, with the states taking a strong initiative.

NATIONAL GROWTH STRATEGY AS AN INVITATION TO CREATIVITY

Community building of the sort we propose is a many-sided challenge.

1. A challenge to developers, planners, and architects to anticipate and give creative expression to the emerging lifestyles of a richly diversified American people. The trends clearly are moving in the direction of smaller families with working mothers. The trends seem also to be moving toward residential densities lighter than those of the central city but heavier than those of existing suburbs. They also are moving toward the requirements, certainly an expectation, of a rich array of critical services, such as day care, health, and continuing education. They also are pointing toward a greater degree of privacy and security. The art will be to put all these together into a working and livable community. The Growth Unit invites that art.

2. A challenge to those committed to the integrity of the environment—to produce increments of growth that are less hostile to man and nature, that continuously reduce the pollution of land, air, and water, and that maintain open spaces and greenbelts for recreation and tranquility.

3. A challenge to all of us who must exact more and more resources which—at least relatively—are dwindling.

Multipurpose space and reusable resources will be the order of the day and will require all the inventiveness and ingenuity we can command.

4. A challenge to restructure the financing and delivery of critical services, especially health, education, and security in the face of escalating costs and consumer dissatisfaction. We believe strongly, for instance, that electronic information systems should be incorporated routinely as part of the community's infrastructure. There also is the prospect that imaginative use of cable television can reshape public education.

5. A challenge to each of the special skills, disciplines, and professions that historically have worked in isolation and are now being forced by the logic of complexity to meld their activities.

6. A challenge to develop new forms of joint enterprise, both within the private sector and between business and government.

7. A challenge to find new ways of resolving the dilemma of dividing trends, on the one hand toward more distant government of greater resources and scope and on the other toward neighborhood control.

It is not easy to develop governing policy for a diverse nation in the full cry of its existence. It would be much easier to let the cup pass and continue to build the world's first throwaway civilization.

But if we are to achieve some coherence and not let freedom vanish into chaos, we have no alternative but to deal with all the tumbling forces and facts of the here and now, and then find levers that have the power not only to move but to win majority consent.

We have chosen the neighborhood Growth Unit as one such lever. It is within the grasp and values of every American. What we urge is that the nation see and

grasp it as part of a national strategy—
to make of this country what it can and
must be: a society confident and united
enough to enjoy the richness of its diversity. Livability of that kind does not come
by accident. Even free choice requires
design.

TASK FORCE MEMBERS

Archibald C. Rogers, FAIA, chairman;
chairman of the board of RTKL Inc., Baltimore; first vice-president and president-
designate (1974) of The American Institute of Architects. He developed planning guidelines for a team approach to
highway planning, which led to the establishment of the Urban Design Concept
Team assembled to plan Baltimore's expressway system.

Ieoh Ming Pei, FAIA, principal of
I.M. Pei and Partners, New York City.
His firm was responsible for the planning
and design of Philadelphia's Society Hill
redevelopment, a renewal plan for Okla-
homa City's central business district,
Montreal's Place Ville Marie, and a master plan for the redevelopment of downtown Boston.

Jacquelin Robertson, AIA, currently
director of New York City's Office of Mid-
town Planning. He formerly headed the
urban design group within the city's planning commission.

William L. Slayton, Hon. AIA, executive vice-president of the Institute. He is
a former commissioner of the Urban Renewal Administration, Housing and
Home Finance Agency, and later president of Urban America Inc.

Paul N. Ylvisaker, professional adviser, dean of the School of Education,
Harvard University. He was formerly
commissioner of community affairs for
the state of New Jersey and later professor of public affairs and urban planning at
Princeton University.

MECHANISMS

Execution of the Growth-Unit concept requires governmental mechanisms or institutions. Their creation requires federal-
incentive legislation and state-enabling
or institution-creating legislation. These
mechanisms can be in several forms.
Those discussed below are examples.

At the metropolitan scale, one needs a
metropolitan planning and development
agency to deal with the rebuilding of the
worn-out portions of the metropolitan
area, with control over the direction and
form of peripheral growth, and with
building the interstices, infilling those
areas leapfrogged by development.

The metropolitan planning and development agency should be responsive, in
an electoral way, to the residents of the
metropolitan area. Methods of election
and representation would be determined
by the interests of the individual state.

Although such a metropolitan planning
and development agency should exercise
the metropolitan planning function, it
must also have authority, with teeth, to
see that its development plan is actually
carried out. Development follows urban
umbilical cords—transportation, communications, and utilities. To direct
growth, one must control the infrastructure. Thus this agency must have authority over the location and timing of
major infrastructure development—
major roads, mass transit, major water
and sewer lines, airports, open space,
state and federal office buildings, publicly owned or financed hospitals, and
any other public investment that influ-
ences economic development and determines the pattern and character of future
urbanization.

*The metropolitan planning and devel-
opment agency* must also have the authority of eminent domain to do the following:

1. Acquire vacant or quasi-vacant land
in the urbanized portion of the metropolitan area to encourage the building of
Growth Units in these areas. This is the
infilling process.

2. Acquire land in the deteriorated portions of the metropolitan area at a scale to
enable the building of Growth-Unit redevelopment.

3. Acquire land in the path of development at least to diminish speculation in
land and to establish the character of future development.

4. Acquire raw land on the somewhat
removed periphery of the urbanized
area in order to build Growth Units or
multiples of Growth Units.

Once such land is acquired, the planning and development agency should
prepare broad-based plans for its development and install the necessary utilities
and public facilities. It should then lease
or sell the land to those developers who
agree to build in accordance with the prescribed plan and who also agree to provide housing for a specified spectrum of
economic groups. The rate of land disposition should be geared to the rate of
urban growth for the metropolitan area.
The metropolitan planning and development agency would, by this method of
land acquisition and disposition, determine the pattern and character of future
growth.

A metropolitan planning and development agency should be able through this
process to acquire sufficient land so that
the prices of its offerings keep in line the
speculative land values of private holdings in other portions of the metropolitan
area.

The metropolitan planning and development agency also should be given authority over the location of housing for
low- and moderate-income families. Real
freedom of choice requires not only that

there be housing for all races and income groups throughout the metropolitan area, but that it be in sufficient quantity to assure the actual availability of housing units.

Within the inner city the metropolitan planning and development agency should concentrate on relatively long-range (15 to 20 years) Growth-Unit development plans, recognizing that the transformation of inner-city areas takes time and that housing must be available prior to displacement if large-scale land acquisition and development are to take place. Emphasis should be on early installation of good public facilities, particularly schools, to improve the area's public investment character. When rebuilding takes place it must be for all income groups and all races. Replication of the socioeconomic character of the area before clearance is not the objective. Although Fort Lincoln in Washington, D.C., is not a clearance area, it is a good example of this approach. Such areas must be rebuilt to attract middle- and upper-middle-income families as well as low, and white as well as minority families.

In order to maintain control over development, the metropolitan planning and development agency should have control over all major zoning decisions in the metropolitan area. There also should be a uniform building code for the metropolitan area.

Such a metropolitan planning and development agency would not serve as a municipal government, carrying out normal municipal services such as police, fire, street repair, and library services. Existing political jurisdictions would continue their municipal governmental functions, but they would be relieved of the functions previously itemized. In fact, one would hope for the establish-

ment of some form of neighborhood quasi-governmental institutions within the central city to deal with neighborhood municipal functions on a neighborhood (Growth Unit) scale.

And finally, but most important, is the necessity of equalizing the property tax throughout the metropolitan area to remove locational bias for economic development.

At the state level it might well be desirable to create a state urban development corporation much like the New York State Urban Development Corporation, with the authority to acquire raw land for the construction of new towns, but not within the jurisdiction of metropolitan planning and development agencies where such agencies exist.

Also it is important that the state, with federal assistance, assume the cost of financing public education to relieve the cities of this considerable burden. Each state will determine its means of financing.

The states also ought to adopt enabling legislation which encourages the creation of Planned Unit Developments, assisting private holders of substantial acreage to develop such areas along the guidelines of the Growth Unit.

The state should also adopt statewide performance-oriented building and other codes relating to the construction, maintenance, and safety of structures.

At the federal level, the government should take over the costs of welfare, thus relieving the state and many local governments of the welfare burden. Here again, there is no prescription for the means of financing.

To encourage the states and localities (metropolitan areas) to undertake these kinds of development programs, the federal government should provide incentive grant legislation. Assistance in the fi-

nancing of major infrastructures should be given to those metropolitan areas where an adequate governmental mechanism has been established to carry out a development plan.

In addition, as a means of encouraging metropolitan areas to proceed with such action as quickly as possible, the federal government should provide financing for the acquisition of one million acres in the 65 metropolitan areas where the population exceeds a quarter million. The location of this acreage should be determined by the metropolitan area agency (or the state in the absence of such an agency) and some of it, of course, will consist of present federal holdings.

In the field of housing the federal government should intensify its experiments with the subsidy of the family rather than the housing unit, and try to transform housing subsidy programs to remove the stigma of housing built specifically for the poor or lower-middle-income groups.

The federal government also should provide incentives similar to those in Title VII for new towns, to encourage metropolitan planning and development agencies and statewide urban development corporations to acquire land by eminent domain or direct purchase to provide for the building of Growth Units and new towns. These incentives could provide assistance in financing land acquisition and subsidizing the installation of the necessary public utilities and facilities.

Title VII of the present Housing and Urban Development legislation leaves the location and timing of new-town developments to the happenstance of private developer landholdings rather than to public decision. Federal legislation should emphasize, in fact require, that the incentives be granted only to those developments that are in accord with the metropolitan development plan—a development plan created by an agency with the authority to see that the plan is actually carried out.

A possible additional mechanism at the federal level is a national urban development corporation working with a national development bank to build several experimental Growth Units or new towns to learn firsthand the difficulties and potentials of various kinds of development. The Minnesota Experimental City is a good example of this possibility.

These mechanisms also must be geared to making the process of private development a simpler operation than it frequently is with the constraints now established by local government. The role of the planning and development agency will provide the private developer with the assurance of being able to acquire land at nonspeculative prices. He also will have the assurance that he will be building in a planned development and need not fear the impact of uncontrolled adjacent development. But in addition the private developer should be free, within the constraints of the Growth Unit's overall plan, to build as he sees fit. An aim of the metropolitan planning and development agency should be to establish the simplest process possible for the processing of the necessary plans and building permits.

Within this mechanism some special financial incentives should be included to encourage experimental Growth-Unit developments. Such incentives might be in the form of governmental assumption of some of the financial risks plus adequate funds for substantial research in this area.

In some instances states may feel it more desirable to retain for themselves greater authority over urban development in the urbanized areas within the state and may wish to establish centralized authority over zoning, land development, review of plans, and so on.

There is no one specific mechanism for controlling and directing urban growth and rebuilding, but the principle of public determination of where such development takes place is essential. It also is essential that there be public control over the distribution of housing for a spectrum of economic groups throughout the metropolitan area, for otherwise there would be no assurance that actual freedom of choice in housing location and style would be provided.

Mechanisms also should be established to deal with the expansion of smaller communities. Here it probably is necessary to use a state urban development corporation and the state's planning capacity to create development plans for smaller communities, and then acquire land and develop Growth Units.

And finally there needs to be a more careful examination of the existing mechanisms of rebuilding inner-city areas. We have reached the point where the constraints for rebuilding are so great that it is virtually impossible to rebuild inner-city areas at a scale sufficiently adequate to change their character. We have seen examples of relatively small-scale redevelopment in inner-city areas fail because the character of the entire neighborhood was not changed. The principle of citizen participation is very important, but citizen participation should not be translated into veto power by the local citizens. The sample principle applies, of course, to those suburban communities that, through the zoning ordinance, have vetoed housing for minorities and the poor in their communities.

There should be a mechanism that provides technical assistance to an area's residents to aid them in evaluating and proposing plans for the development and redevelopment of their area. But such plans must also be reviewed in light of the development program for the entire metropolitan area. Adequate consultation and consideration of the views of the residents of any area that is to be redeveloped, or where development is to take place, must be given. The process should be one of full consideration and review, but the governmental agency must have the clear authority to carry out the development program. This probably will be the most difficult mechanism to establish, yet our cities will continue to disintegrate unless we find a mechanism that permits their rebuilding at a scale that creates entire new neighborhoods (Growth Units) that are open and attractive to all races and all income groups.

This sketches out the mechanisms needed for implementation of the concept of the growth unit. The details will vary among the states, but these are the essential principles. If America is to be effective in controlling the character and direction of its urban growth and rebuilding, then it must have such mechanisms.

BIBLIOGRAPHY

BOOKS

ADVISORY COMMISSION ON INTERGOVERN-MENTAL RELATIONS. *Urban and Rural America: Policies for Future Growth.* Washington, D.C.: U.S. Government Printing Office, 1968.

ALLEN, MURIEL I. (ed). *New Communities: Challenge for Today.* Washington, D.C.: American Institute of Planners, 1968.

BACON, EDMUND N. *Design of Cities.* New York: Viking, 1967.

BERRY, B., and HORTON (eds). *Geographic Perspectives on Urban Systems.* New Jersey: Prentice-Hall, 1969.

BRECKENFELD, GURNEY. *Columbia and the New Cities.* New York: Ives Washburn, Inc., 1971.

BROWN, A.J., and H.M. SHERRARD. *An Introduction of Town and Country Planning.* New York: American Elsevier Publishing Company, 1968.

CAMERON, GORDON C. *Regional Economic Development, The Federal Role.* Washington, D.C.: Resources for the Future, 1970.

CANTY, DONALD (ed). *The New City: A Program for National Urbanization Strategy.* New York: Frederick A. Praeger, 1969.

CLAPP, JAMES A. *New Towns and Urban Policy.* New York: Dunellen, 1971.

CURTIS, VIRGINIA (ed). *Land-Use Policies.* Chicago: American Society of Planning Officials, 1970.

DAVID, PHILIP. *Urban Land Development.* Homewood, Illinois: Richard D. Irwin, Inc., 1970.

DERTHICK, MARTHA. *New Towns in Town.* Washington, D.C.: Urban Institute, 1972.

DE VISE, PIERRE, et al. (eds). *Slum Medicine: Chicago's Apartheid Health System.* Chicago: University of Chicago Press, 1969.

EDWARDS, GORDON. *Land, People and Policy: The Problems and Techniques of Assembling Land for the Urbanization of 100 Million New Americans.* Trenton: Chandler-Davis Publishing Company, 1969.

EICHLER, EDWARD P., and MARSHALL KA-PLAN. *The Community Builders.* Berkeley: University of California Press, 1967.

ELDRIDGE, H. WENTWORTH (ed). *Taming Megalopolis.* 2 Vols. Garden City: Doubleday and Company, 1967.

FUCHS, VICTOR R. *Productivity Differentials Within the Service Sector.* New York: Columbia University Press, 1967.

GANS, HERBERT J. *People and Plans; Essays on Urban Problems and Solutions.* New York: Basic Books, 1968.

GIMLIN, HOYT. *New Towns.* Washington, D.C.: Editorial Research Reports, 1968.

GOODMAN, PAUL, and PERCIVAL GOODMAN. *Communitas: Means of Livelihood and Ways of Life.* New York: Random House, Inc., 1960.

GOTTMANN, JEAN. *Megalopolis, The Urbanized Northeastern Seaboard of the United States.* New York: The Twentieth Century Fund, 1961.

HANSEN, NILES M. *Rural Poverty and the Urban Crisis.* Indiana: Indiana University Press, 1970.

INTERNATIONAL CITY MANAGERS' ASSOCIATION. *New Towns: A New Dimension of Urbanism.* Chicago: ICMA, 1966.

LINDHOLM, R.W. (ed). *Property Taxation in the U.S.A.* Madison: University of Wisconsin Press, 1967.

MAYER, ALBERT. *The Urgent Future.* New York: McGraw-Hill Book Company, 1967.

MCKEEVER, J. ROSS (ed). *Community Builders Handbook.* Washington, D.C.: Urban Land Institute, 1968.

MORRISON, PETER A. *Urban Growth, New Cities, and "The Population Problem."* Santa Monica, California: Rand Corporation, 1970.

MUMFORD, LEWIS. *The City in History.* New York: Harcourt, Brace and World, Inc., 1961.

NEUTZE, RICHARD. *Economic Policy and the Size of Cities.* Canberra: National University of Australia, 1965.

OSBORN, FREDERIC J., and Arnold Whittick. *The New Towns: The Answer to Megalopolis.* New York: McGraw-Hill, Inc., 1963.

PERLOFF, H.S. (ed). *Planning for Environmental Quality.* Washington, D.C.: Resources for the Future, 1969.

PERLOFF, H.S., and L. WINGO (eds). *Issues in Urban Economics.* Baltimore: Johns Hopkins University Press, 1968.

PRED, ALLAN. *The Spatial Dynamics of U.S. Urban-Industrial Growth, 1800-1914.* Cambridge: M.I.T. Press, 1966.

REPS, JOHN W. *The Making of Urban America.* Princeton: Princeton University Press, 1965.

RICHARDSON, H.W. *Regional Economics.* New York: Praeger, 1969.

ROLLINS COLLEGE. *New Towns: A Comparative Study.* Winter Park, Fla.: Center for Practical Politics, 1970.

SCHNORE, LEO F., and H. FAGIN (eds). *Urban Affairs and Policy Planning.* California: Sage Publications, 1968.

SEYMOUR, L. WOLFBEIN. *Employment and Unemployment in the United States.* Chicago: Science Research Associates, Inc., 1964.

STEIN, CLARENCE S. *Toward New Towns for America.* Chicago: Public Administration Service, 1951.

TETLOW, JOHN, and ANTHONY GOSS. *Homes, Towns, and Traffic.* New York: Frederick A. Praeger, 1968.

THOMAS, RAY. *London's New Towns: A Study of Self-Contained and Balanced Communities.* New York: Committee for Economic Development, 1969.

TWENTIETH CENTURY FUND, *New Towns: Laboratories for Democracy.* New York: Twentieth Century Fund, 1971.

U.S. DEPARTMENT OF LABOR, BUREAU OF LABOR STATISTICS. *Patterns of U.S. Economic Growth.* Washington, D.C.: U.S. Government Printing Office, 1970.

UNWIN, RAYMOND. *Town Planning in Practice.* New York: Charles Scribner's Sons, 1919.

VON HERTZEN, HEIKKI. *Building a New Town; Finland's New Garden City, Tapiola.* Cambridge, Mass.: M.I.T. Press, 1971.

WHYTE, WILLIAM H. *The Last Landscape.* New York: Doubleday and Company, 1968.

WINGO, LOWDEN. *Issues in Urban Economics.* Baltimore: Johns Hopkins, 1968.

ARTICLES IN PERIODICALS

ABBOTT, SIDNEY. "New Hope for New Towns," *Design and Environment,* Spring 1972, 28ff.

ABEN, NORMAN A. "Transportation Inputs in New Town Planning," *Traffic Quarterly,* XXIII (April 1969), 243-261.

ALONSO, WILLIAM. "The Historic and the Structural Theories of Urban Form: Their Implications for Urban Renewal," *Land Economics,* XL (1964), 227-31.

————— "The Mirage of New Towns," *The Public Interest,* No. 19 (Spring 1970), 3-17.

American Builder. "New Towns: The Arguments . . . For . . . Against," June 1966, 94-97.

American Builder. "Sales Manager of '66: Our Product Sells Itself," February 1967, 10.

American City. "A 'New Town' on an Island," September 1970, 110-112.

American County Government. "Modern Zoning for Reston," May 1967, 16-19.

ANDERSON, J.W. "A Brand New City for Maryland," *Harper's Magazine,* November 1964, 100-106.

APGAR, MAHLON, IV. "New Business from New Towns?" *Harvard Business Review,* XLIX (January/February 1971), 90-109.

ARCHER, R.W. "From New Towns to Metrotowns and Regional Cities," *American Journal of Economics and Sociology,* XXVIII (July 1969), 257-270.

————— "From New Towns to Metrotowns and Regional Cities, Pt. 2," *American Journal of Economics and Sociology,* XXVIII (October 1969), 385-398.

Architectural Forum. "New Approach to New-Town Planning," September 1964.

Architectural Forum. "New Town," September 1967, 44-52.

Architectural Record. "Belconnen Town Center, Canberra, Australia," February 1970, 132-135.

Architectural Record. "A New Town that Conserves the Landscape," April 1967, 151-158.

Architectural Record. "Nun's Island, Phase 1, Montreal, Quebec," Mid-May 1970, 100-102.

ASHLEY, THOMAS J. "New Communities and Property Taxation," *Journal of Soil and Water Conservation,* XXV (July/August 1970), 132-136.

————— "A New Urban Growth Strategy for the United States," *Urban and Social Change Review,* Spring 1971, 50-52.

————— "The Urban Growth and New Community Development Act," *Mortgage Banker,* XXXI (February 1971), 20ff.

Barclay's Bank Review. "Britain's New Towns," XLV (February 1970), 3-7.

BARUCHEL, JOHN J. "A New Way of Life Four Minutes from Downtown," *Journal of Property Mangement,* July/August 1970, 156-163.

BECKMAN, NORMAN. "Development of National Urban Growth Policy." *American Institute of Planners,* XXXVII, No. 3 (May 1971), 146-160.

BERRY, BRIAN. "Geography of the U.S. in the Year 2000," *Transactions of the Institute of British Geographers,* I, No. 1 (1970), 20-31.

BERZOK, ROBERT M. "New Towns Seen as Alternatives; Detroit Group Studies Urban Growth Issues," *National Civic Review,* LX (June 1971), 350-351.

Better Homes and Gardens. "The New Town: A Proving Ground for Bold New Ideas," September 1969, 70-73.

BORCHERT, T.R. "American Metropolitan Evolution, 1967," *The Geographic Review,* LVII, No. 3 (July 1967), 301-332.

Building Research. "New Town: Philosophy and Reality," January/February 1966, 9-34.

Buildings. "Miami Lakes: A Very Different New Town," January 1969, 44-46.

Buildings. "New Towns: Who Wants Them? Who Builds Them? How Are They Doing?" April 1967, 64-67.

BOYKIN, HAMILTON H. and JAMES C. BRINCEFIELD, JR. "New Town Money Comes Easier with Uncle Sam's Guarantee," *Real Estate Review,* Spring 1972, 62-71.

BRADFORD, D.F., R.A. MATT, and W.E. OATES. "The Rising Cost of Local Public Services: Some Evidence and Reflections," *National Tax Journal,* XXII, No. 2 (June 1969), 20-24.

BROWN, ERICH H. and JOHN SALT. "New City on the Oxford Clay," *Geographical Magazine,* XLI (August 1969), 830-838.

BRYAN, JACK. "'Main Street' Revived in Midwest New Town," *Journal of Housing,* July 1972, 282-289.

——— "New Town/In Town; New Town/Out of Town," *Journal of Housing,* April 1972, 119-131.

——— "Philadelphia Is Turning Old Town into New Town," *Journal of Housing,* June 1972, 229-235.

Bulletin. "New Towns and Urban Rehabilitation," March 1971.

BURCHARD, JOHN. "Some Antidotes for Ugliness," *American Institute of Architects Journal,* XLIII, No. 4 (April 1965), 29-34.

BURNETT, F.T. "Open Space in New Towns," *Journal of the Town Planning Institute,* LV (June 1969), 256-262.

Business Management. "Emerging Idea: Instant Towns," December 1966.

Business Week. "Brave New Towns That Aged Awkwardly," January 9, 1971, 22-24.

Business Week. "Can 'New Towns' Meet a Budget?" November 18, 1967, 103-104.

Business Week. "The Corporate Land Rush of 1970," No. 2139 (August 29, 1970), 72-77.

Business Week. "A Firmer Foundation for New Towns," January 9, 1971, 22.

Business Week. "A Gallic Answer to Urban Congestion: A $1-Billion 'New Town' of Office Towers and Apartments Rise in Paris," November 7, 1970, 74ff.

Business Week. "The Irvine Ranch Fights Regulation," July 3, 1971, 57-58.

Business Week. "'New Town' Rises Back at the Ranch," September 23, 1967, 176-182.

Business Week. "New Towns: Lessons Europe Is Teaching Us," November 22, 1969, 130-131.

Business Week. "New Towns Rise on the Hill," February 7, 1970, 96-97.

Business Week. "A New Type of 'New Town' Breaks Ground for Planners," July 19, 1969, 123-136.

Business Week. "The Race Is on for New Towns," March 13, 1971, 130-132.

Business Week. "Soul City's Need Is Green Power," January 17, 1970, 106.

Business Week. "A Strong Boost for 'New Towns'," May 31, 1969, 50.

Business Week. "Where City Planners Come Down to Earth," August 20, 1966, 100-102.

Business Week. "Why New Towns Boom or Fall Flat," November 15, 1969, 149.

CAMPBELL, ARTHUR C. "New Towns Down South: Sponsors Vary Widely, From T.V.A. to McKissick," *South Today,* II (March 1971), 3-4.

CARBINE, MICHAEL E. "New Towns and the Search for an Urban Solution," *Manpower,* July 1969.

CARRUTH, ELEANORE. "Private Developers Are Making the Big Move to New Towns," *Fortune,* LXXXIV (September 1971), 95ff.

Changing Times. "Can New Cities Remake America?" May 1970, 19-22.

Changing Times. "Tomorrow's Cities: Go Up, Spread Out or Start Over?" April 1970, 19-22.

Civil Engineering. "Planning U.S. Cities for the Year 2000," September 1970, 54-56.

Columbia Today. "The Architectural Committee," February/March 1970, 8-15.

Columbia Today. "How Columbia Manages Its Amenities While Gearing for Public Control," March 1971, 11-15.

Columbia Today. "The Nebulous Art of New Community Management," March 1971, 8-10.

CORRIGAN, ANNE WOODWARD. "England's New Towns," *Manpower,* II (February 1970), 11-14.

COX, HARVEY. "Dream City (Almost)," *Commonweal,* January 20, 1967, 426-427.

CZAMANSKI, STANISLAW. "Industrial Location and Urban Growth," *The Town Planning Review,* XXXVI, No. 3 (October 1966), 14-31.

DANIELS, L.K. "New Equation: Nature Center, Community Involvement," *American Forests,* LXXVI (November 1970), 20ff.

DARWENT, S.W. "Growth Poles and Growth Centers—A Review," *Environment and Planning,* I, No. 1 (1969), 1-9.

DAVIS, GEORGIA K. "Title VII: A Spur to the Building of New Communities," *AIA Journal,* August 1971, 41-43.

DOWNS, ANTHONY. "Alternative Forms of Future Urban Growth in the United States," *American Institute of Planners Journal,* January 1970, 3-11.

Downtown Idea Exchange. "New Towns Downtown," February 1, 1969, 1.

DRIGGS, GARY. "Building a Planned Community Through a Service Corporation," *Federal Home Loan Bank Board Journal,* August 1972, 4-9.

EINSWEILER, ROBERT C., and JULIUS C. SMITH. "New Town Located in a Municipality: Jonathan Saves Money and Chaska Increases Tax Base," *American Institute of Planners Notebook,* June/July 1971.

Engineering News-Record. "New Communities Aired in Hearings," CLXXXIII (July 31, 1969), 13.

FERNSTROM, JOHN R. "New Towns: An American Decision," *Industrial Development,* September/October 1969, 17-19.

FISCHER, JOHN. "The Easy Chair; Planning for the Second America," *Harper's Magazine,* CCXXXIX (November 1969), 21ff.

Florida Planning and Development. "Building New Cities," November 1966, 6-7.

FLYNN, ANNE. "New City for the '70's," *American City,* October 1970, 84-86.

FOER, ALBERT A. "Democracy in the New

Towns: The Limits of Private Government," *The University of Chicago Law Review,* XXXVI (Winter 1969), 379-412.

Forbes. "Long Perilous Path," CIV (August 15, 1969), 42.

Fortune. "What's New About New Towns?" February 1966.

GALENSON, W. "Economic Development and the Sectoral Expansion of Employment," *International Labor Review,* LXXXVII, No. 6 (June 1963), 505-509.

GLADSTONE, ROBERT. "New Town's Role in Urban Growth Explored," *Journal of Housing,* January 1966.

GLADSTONE, ROBERT, and HAROLD F. WISE. "New Towns Solve Problems of Urban Growth," *Public Management,* May 1966, 128-139.

GLADSTONE, ROBERT M. "Does Building a City Make Economic Sense?" *Appraisal Journal,* July 1966, 407-412.

GODSCHALK, DAVID R. "Comparative New Community Design," *American Institute of Planners Journal,* November 1967, 371-386.

Government Executive. "New Cities—How Strong a Role Can the Federal Government Play," III (August 1971), 51-53.

Guarantor. "Park Forest South: New Town of the 70's," Autumn 1972, 2-5.

HACK, GEORGE D. "The New Town Concept," *Current Municipal Problems,* XII (November 1970), 158-161.

HALL, EDWARD N. "The Air City," *Traffic Quarterly,* January 1972, 15-31.

HANSEN, NILES M. "Urban Alternatives for Eliminating Poverty," *Monthly Labor Review,* XCII, No. 8 (August 1969), 46-48.

HARRIS, CHAUNCY D. "The Market as a Factor in the Localization of Industry in the United States," *Annals of Association of American Geographers,* XLIV, No. 4 (December 1954), 315-348.

HARRIS, THOMAS G., JR. "Howard County Plans Its Future: Columbia," *American County Government,* May 1967, 20-33.

HARVEY, ROBERT O., and W.A.V. CLARK.

"Controlling Urban Growth: The New Zealand and Australian Experiment," *The Appraisal Journal,* XXXII, No. 4 (October 1964), 551-558.

HELBOCH, RICHARD W. "New Towns in the United States," *Professional Geographer,* July 4, 1972, 242-246.

HERMAN, HAROLD, and MICHAEL L. JOROFF. "Planning Health Services for New Towns," *American Journal of Public Health,* April 1967.

HERRERA, PHILIP. "The Instant City," *Fortune,* June, 1967, 135-138.

HIRSCH, WERNER Z. "Expenditure Implications of Metroplitan Growth and Consolidation," *Review of Economics and Statistics,* XLI, No. 3 (August 1959), 232-241.

————— "Interindustry Relations of a Metropolitan Area," *Review of Economics and Statistics,* XLI (November 1959), 360-369.

HOFFMAN, ELLEN. "New Towns for Old Cities," *Progressive,* XXXIV (September 1970), 31-35.

HOPPENFELD, MORTON. "A Sketch of the Planning-Building Process for Columbia, Maryland," *American Institute of Planners Journal,* November 1967, 298-408.

House and Home. "Jonathan, Minn.: First Private New Town Backed by a HUD Guaranteed Loan," XXXVII (May 1970), 36.

House and Home. "New Approach to New-Town Planning," December 1964, 82-89.

House and Home. "New Towns: Are They Just Oversized Subdivisions—With Oversized Problems?" June 1966, 92-103.

House and Home. "Nun's Island," December 1969, 56-63.

House and Home. "The Old-Fashioned Subdivision Is Getting a Brand-New Look," May 1970, 74-87.

House and Home. "The Story of a Market Success—and a Financial Failure," August 1967, 52-57.

HOWARD, PHILIP. "Reston Revisited," *Design and Environment,* Spring 1972, 22-27.

HUD Challenge. "New Communities," August 1972.

HUD Challenge. "New America," November/December 1970, 10-12.

HUGHES, JAMES. "New and Better Towns," *Steelways,* September/October 1967, 20-23.

Industrial Development. "New Towns: A Vital Component of a Strategy for More Balanced Growth in Urban and Rural America," May/June 1969, 4-6.

Industrial Development. "New Towns Sprouting Like Lapel Buttons at a Love-In," CXXXIX (March 1970), 2-6.

Journal of Housing. "First 'New Community' Receives HUD Guarantee," XXVII (February 1970), 67.

Journal of Housing. "HUD Funds Four More New Towns," XXVIII (March 1971), 114-115

Journal of Housing. "Israel New Town Honored by American Jury," XXVII (April 1970), 188-192.

Journal of Housing. "Urban Growth and New Communities—Title VII of the Housing and Urban Development Act of 1970," XXVIII (January 1971), 21-22.

KAIN, J.F. "Housing Segregation, Negro Employment, and Metropolitan Decentralization," *Quarterly Journal of Economics,* LXIII, No. 2 (May 1968), 167-199.

KEEGAN, JOHN E., and WILLIAM RUTZICK. "Private Developers and the New Communities Act of 1968," *Georgetown Law Journal,* LVII (June 1969), 1119-1158.

KEENE, JENNESS. "Foster City: To the Brink and Back to Fiscal Health," *House and Home,* February 1970, 4-5.

KELLAWAY, A.J. "Migration to Eight New Towns in 1966," *Journal of the Town Planning Institute,* LV (May 1969), 196-202.

KENNEDY, FRANK. "Welfare Island: A Totally Designed Environment," *Design and Environment,* Winter 1970, 20-37.

KIESLING, H. "Measuring a Local Government Service: A Study of School Districts in New York State," *Review of Economics and Statistics,* XLIX, No. 3 (1967), 356-367.

KIMBROUGH, JOHN T. "New Towns and Regional Development: Project Scioto," *Appalachia,* November/December 1970, 5-9.

KINSEY, DAVID N. "The French Z.U.P. Technique of Urban Development," *American Institute of Planners Journal*, XXXV (November 1969), 369-375.

KLABER, EUGENE HENRY. "New Cities," *Nation's Cities*, August 1966, 16-17.

KLUTZNICK, PHILIP M. "Needed: A Sensible and Sane National Urban Growth Policy," *Mortgage Banker*, XXXI (November 1970), 58ff.

KRAEMER, K.L. "Developing Governmental Institutions in New Communities," *Urban Lawyer*, I (Fall 1969), 268ff.

KUNKEL, J.H. "The Role of Services in the Annexation of a Metropolitan Fringe Area (of Flint, Michigan)," *Land Economics*, XXXVI, No. 2 (May 1960), 208-212.

LAMBETH, EDMUND B. "New Towns: Can They Work," *Washington Monthly*, I (October 1969), 20-25.

LAMPARD, ERIC E. "The History of Cities in the Economically Advanced Areas," *Economic Development and Cultural Change*, V (January 1955), 86-102.

LAWSON, SIMPSON. "A 'New Town' Planned for the Urban and Rural Poor: The University of Louisville Develops a Controversial Strategy to Change the Flow of Migration," *City*, IV (June/July 1970), 35-38.

———— "New Towns in Old Cities," *City*, V (May/June 1971), 40-41.

Lawyers Title News. "New Villages to Be More Important Than New Cities," March 1970, 8-10.

Lawyers Title News. "Nun's Island, Quebec," May 1970, 7-10.

LEAVITT, WILLIAM. "An Idea for a City— Born of the Space Age," *Air Force and Space Digest*, LIII (January 1970), 42-44.

LEROYER, ANN M. "The New Towns Movement in Great Britain and the United States," *Urban and Social Change Review*, Spring 1971, 53-58.

LICHFIELD, NATHANIEL, and PAUL F. WENDT. "Six English New Towns: A Financial Analysis," *Town Planning Review*, XL (October 1969), 283-314.

LIEBERMAN, MYRON. "New Communities: Business on the Urban Frontier; A Special Issue," *Saturday Review*, LIV (May 15, 1971), 20ff.

Life. "A City Made to Human Measure," LXX (January 8, 1971), 76-83.

LIGHT, LOIS. "Instant Utopia: Everybody Talks About the Overcrowded Cities; British Columbia Has Done Something About It," *Imperial Oil Review*, LIII (June 1969), 22-25.

LILLEY, WILLIAM, III. "Parties, Agencies Scrambling to Shape Future of New Communities Program," *National Journal*, April 4, 1970, 726-730.

LISTON, LINDA. "The Case for the Airport New Town," *Industrial Development*, July/August 1969, 3-9.

———— "Need for New Towns Spurs State Legislative Action," *Industrial Development*, November/December 1969, 15-18.

LO, JONATHAN. "The Manipulation of Property Tax and a Determinant of Changing Land Use Patterns in the Urban Fringe," *Annals of Regional Science*, I, No. 1 (December 1967), 74-79.

LOGUE, EDWARD J. "The Need for Urban Growth Policies," *American Institute of Architects*, May 1971, 18-22.

Look. "Jim Rouse's Satellite City," February 10, 1970, 55-58.

MARGOLIES, JOHN S. "New Town for New York City," *Architectural Forum*, October 1969, 40-45.

MARS, DAVID. "Localism and Regionalism in Southern California," *Urban Affairs Quarterly*, XI, No. 4 (June 1967), 47-74.

MAURER, NEIL. "Thoughts on New Towns," *AIA Journal*, January 1972, 35-36.

MAYER, ALBERT. "Greenbelt Towns Revisited," *Journal of Housing*, January 1967.

———— "Greenbelt Towns Revisited," *Journal of Housing*, February/March, 1967.

———— "Greenbelt Towns Revisited," *Journal of Housing*, April 1967.

———— "It's Not Just the Cities," *Architectural Record*, December 1969, 105-110.

———— "New Towns and Fresh In-City Communities," *Architectural Record*, August 1964, 129-138.

MCDADE, THOMAS. "New Communities in America," *Urban Land*, January 1965, 6-8.

MCKNIGHT, HENRY T. "Converting Farm Land to New Towns," *Farm and Land Realtor*, February 1972, 1-7.

MCMAHAN, JOHN W., and DAVID L. PETERSON. "New Towns are the Ultimate Real Estate Investment," *Real Estate Review*, Spring 1972, 56-61.

MENZIES, IAN. "Toward Balanced Development of New Towns and Old Cities," *Urban and Social Change Review*, Spring 1971.

MILLER, RICHARD A. "Turning Small Towns into New Ones," *Architectural Forum*, February 1962.

MOLINARO, LEO A. "Truths and Consequences for Older Cities," *Saturday Review*, May 15, 1971.

MONTGOMERY, ROGER. "Synanon City," *Architectural Forum*, November 1970, 52-55.

MOORE, DANIEL W. "Planning for a New Town," *American Society of Civil Engineers Journal of Urban Planning and Development Division*, April 1971.

MORRIS, DOUGLAS, and LUTHER TWEETERS. "The Cost of Controlling Crime: A Study in Economies of City Life," *Annals of Regional Science*, V, No. 1 (June 1971), 33-49.

MORRIS, M.D. "New Towns in the Desert," *American City*, November 1970, 94-96.

MORRIS, ROBERT L. "New Towns and Old Cities," *Nation's Cities*, April 1969, 8-11.

———— "New Towns and Old Cities," *Nation's Cities*, May 1969, 19-22.

———— "New Towns and Old Cities," *Nation's Cities*, June 1969, 39-42.

MULLARKEY, MARY J. "The Evolution of a New Community: Problems of Government," *Harvard Journal on Legislation*, VI (May 1969), 462-483.

MYERS, PHYLLIS. "Columbia's Institutions," *City*, III (October 1969), 33-38.

MYERS, SUMNER, and ROBERT SCHWARTZ.

"New Towns Are Our Mandate for Urban Innovations," *Architectural Forum*, June 1970, 38-41.

NAHB Journal of Homebuilding. "21st Century Enclosed City of 50,000 Underway in Alaska," October 1970, 28-31.

Nation's Business. "New Towns and Industrial Parks Change Europe," October 1970, 97-98.

Nation's Business. "Rise of the New Cities," August 1968, 72-78.

NATOLI, SALVATORE J. "Zoning and the Development of Urban Land Use Patterns," *Economic Geography*, XLVII, No. 2 (April 1971), 171-184.

New Republic. "Starving New Communities," CLXIV, (May 29, 1971), 9.

Newsweek. "The New-City Blues," July 14, 1969, 46-51.

Newsweek. "A New Town in Town," LXXVIII (July 19, 1971), 40ff.

NORCROSS, CARL. "A Look at Crofton Maryland—New Ideas in Creating a Fine Environment," *Urban Land*, December 1964, 3-7.

————— "What Buyers Think of Reston," *Urban Land*, February 1966, 7-8.

O'NEILL, J. L. "Columbia, Gem of America's New Towns," *American Home*, LXXIII (May 1970), 95ff.

O'NEILL, RICHARD W. "New Towns; Everything We Know Now Says They Won't Work; But There Are a Lot of Things We Don't Know," *House and Home*, XXXVIII (September 1970), 61.

OTTEN, ALAN L. "The New Town Idea Is Vastly Overrated," *Nation's Cities*, December 1970, 15, 26.

Parks and Recreation. "New Towns, a Boon to the Quality of Life," V (October 1970), 13.

PASCAL, ANTHONY. "Where Will All the People Go? How Much Will They Dump When They Get There?—Population Distribution, Environmental Damage and the Quality of Life," *Annals of Regional Science*, V, No. 1 (June 1971).

PAUMIER, CY, JR. "The Case of a New Town," *AIA Journal*, November 1970, 33-36.

PERLOFF, HARVEY. "New Towns Intown," *American Institute of Planners Journal*, May 1966, 155-161.

PETER, J. "Jim Rouse's Satellite City," *Look*, XXXIV (February 10, 1970), 55-57.

Petroleum Today. "Can Life Be Beautiful? Probably More Beautiful Than It Usually Is: Instant Cities, Called New Towns, Give An Idea of What the Future Could Hold," XI (Winter 1970), 12-15.

PICKARD, JEROME P. "HUD Survey and Analysis of Large Developments and New Communities Completed or Under Construction in the U.S. Since 1947," *Urban Land*, January 1970, 11-12.

Practical Builder. "What's New About New Towns?" July 1966, 73-83.

Prescott, James R. "The Planning for Experimental City," *Land Economics*, XLVI (February 1970), 68-75.

Professional Builder. "The Apartment New Town," November 1970, 146-149.

Professional Builder. "Big Ticket Bonanza," April 1972, 104-109.

Professional Builder. "Fertile Climate for New Towns Promises Opportunity for Builders," October 1970, 13-15.

Professional Builder. "New Communities: The 'Now' Approach to Land Development," April 1972, 96-103.

Professional Builder. "Taking the Debt Sweat Out of New Towns. 'Jonathan' Opens Doors with HUD Guarantee," April 1970, 55.

Progressive Architecture. "Corporations as New Master Builders of Cities," L (May 1969), 150-161.

Progressive Architecture. "Lake Anne Village Center: A Planned Community Nucleus," May 1966, 193-201.

Progressive Architecture. "New Towns and Major Spaces," June 1965.

PROKOSCH, WALTHER. "Joppatowne—A Marine-Oriented Community in Maryland," *Urban Land*, June 1965, 7-11.

REED, J. DAVID. "The Impact of a Dominant Industry on a Metropolitan Area: A Case Study of Wichita, Kansas," *Journal of Regional Science*, V, No. 1 (1971), 62-83.

RIBOUD, JACQUES. "New Towns for a New Civilization," *Town and Country Planning*, June 1970.

RICKS, B. "New Town Development and the Theory of Location," *Land Economics*, XLV (February 1970), 5-11.

RICKS, R. BRUCE. "Location of New Towns: The Use of Low-Priced Land May Serve to Reduce Development Profits," *Federal Home Loan Bank Board Journal*, June 1970, 10-15.

ROBINSON, WILLIAM K. "Kingswood—A Recreation-Oriented Community in Ohio," *Urban Land*, June 1965, 3-6.

ROGIN, RICHARD. "New Town on a New York Island," *City*, V (May/June 1971), 42-27.

ROPER, HUGH. "The Plan is a Beginning: Some Further Thoughts on Milton Keynes," *Journal of the Town Planning Institute*, LVI (April 1970), 129-133.

ROUSE, JAMES W. "A Garden for People to Grow In," *Lawyers Title News*, January 1966, 88-99.

————— "Great Cities for the Great Society," *Mortgage Banker*, July 1965, 8-13.

————— "How to Build a Whole New City from Scratch," *Savings Bank Journal*, October 1966, 26-32.

SALLEY, MARJORIE A. "Public Transportation and the Needs of New Communities," *Traffic Quarterly*, January 1972, 33-5.

SAUNDERS, G. W., JR. "New Towns to Cure Urban Sprawl Described," *National Underwriter*, XXXV (December 12, 1969), 50-51.

Savings and Loan News. "HUD Tests New Strategies for Mass Housing Systems," XCII (January 1971), 41-47.

Savings and Loan News. "300 Million People in 30 Years . . . Where Will They Live?" XCI (June 1970), 46-49.

SCHILLER, R. K. "Location Trends of Specialist Services," *Regional Studies*, V (April 1971), 1-10.

SCOTT, STANLEY. "Urban Growth Challenges New Towns," *Public Management*, September 1966, 253-260.

SIMON, ROBERT E., JR. "Planning a New Town—Reston, Virginia," *Planning 1964*, 1965, 150-157.

————— "Real Property in the Urban Society. Firm President Traces Planning of New Town," *Virginia Law Weekly*, XVIII, No. 5 (October 14, 1965).

SIMONDS, JOHN O. "Miami Lakes New Town," *Parks and Recreation*, V (October 1970), 29ff.

SLAYTON, W.L. "Don't Oversell New Towns," *American City*, LXXXVI (May 1971), 8.

SPAGNOLA, PATRICIA. "New Towns," *Pennsylvania Department of Internal Affairs Bulletin*, August 1965.

STAMBLER, H.V. "New Directions in Area Labor Force Statistics," *Monthly Labor Review*, XCII, No. 11 (August 1969), 51-54.

SUNDERLAND, LOWELL E. "Why Columbia Succeeded Where Others Failed," *Mortgage Banker*, XXX (June 1970), 10ff.

————— "Yankee Discipline," *Columbia Today*, December 1969/January 1970, 14-18.

TALBOT, ALLAN. "Analysis: New Towns Are Not a New Idea, But They Could Become Part of a New Strategy to Deal With Urban Growth," *City*, May 1968.

TANNENBAUM, ROBERT. "Planning Determinants for Columbia—A New Town in Maryland," *Urban Land*, April 1965, 3-6.

THOMPSON, WAYNE E. "Prototype City—Design for Tomorrow," *Public Management*, July 1966, 212-217.

TIEBOUT, CHARLES. "Economics of Scale and Metropolitan Governments," *Review of Economics and Statistics*, XLII, No. 4 (November 1960), 442-444.

————— "A Pure Theory of Local Expenditures," *Journal of Political Economy*, LXIV (October 1956), 416-424.

TILLMAN, DAVID A. "New Town Plant Sites: Unproven Experiment or Utopia?" *Industrial Development*, March/April 1972, 33-34.

Time. "The City: Starting From Scratch," March 7, 1969.

Town and Country Planning. "New Towns Come of Age," January/February 1968.

TRUPP, PHILIP. "Langley Park and Columbia: Looking for a Way of Life," *Washingtonian*, January 1971, 22-28.

TURNER, ALAN. "A Case for New Towns," *AIA Journal*, November 1970, 28-32.

TURNER, ALAN, and JONATHAN SMULIAN. "New Cities in Venezuela," *Town Planning Review*, XLII (January 1971), 3-27.

UNDERHILL, JACK A. "European New Towns: One Answer to Urban Problems?" *HUD Challenge*, March/April 1970, 19-23.

U.S. New and World Report. "New Cities: A Look at the Future," January 26, 1970, 64-65.

Urban and Social Change Review. "New Towns and Urban Policy," IV (Spring 1971), 50-62.

VON ECKARDT, WOLF. "Fresh Scene in the Clean Dream," *Saturday Review*, LIV (May 15, 1971), 21-23.

————— "New Towns 73 Years Later," *Saturday Review*, LIV (February 6, 1971), 61.

————— "Planning for 'Publick Concerns.' A Brave New Town in Northern Virginia Continues the Traditions of City Planning Brought to These Shores by Enlightened Colonists," *Arts in Virginia*, Winter 1967, 16-29.

Washington University Law Quarterly. "Symposium—New Towns," February 1965.

WEAVER, ROBERT C. "Federal Proposals May Solve City Problems," *Public Management*, June 1966, 154-159.

WEISSBOURD, BERNARD, and HERBERT CHANNICK. "An Urban Strategy," *Appraisal Journal*, January 1970, 100-117.

WELLS, A.W. "Compulsory Land Acquisitions for New Communities and Redevelopment in Great Britain and the United States," *Journal of International Law and Economics*, VI (June 1971), 77ff.

WHEAT, JANIS K. "New Town Blossoms in Virginia Farmland," *National Geographic School Bulletin*, XLVIII (October 20, 1969), 90-93.

WILLMOT, PETER. "Social Research and New Communities," *American Institute of Planners Journal*, November 1967, 387-397.

WOODS, WILLIAM K. "An Urbanologist's Notebook, Part 1," *North American Review*, CCLV (Spring 1970), 27-33.

————— "An Urbanologist's Notebook, Part 2," *North American Review*, CCLV (Summer 1970), 61-73.

WRIGHT, GORDON. "New Towns Going Straight? A Chicago Developer Lays One on the Line," *House and Home*, July 1972, 32.

YLVISAKER, PAUL N. "New Towns—Old Cities," *Jersey Plans*, Spring 1968, 19-25.

ZEHNER, ROBERT B. "Neighborhood and Community Satisfaction in New Towns and Less Planned Suburbs," *American Institute of Planners Journal*, November 1971, 379-385.

OTHER MATERIAL

ALLEN, MURIEL L. (ed). *New Communities: Challenge for Today.* AIP Background Paper No. 2. Washington, D.C.: American Institute of Planners, October 1968.

ALONSO, WILLIAM. *The Economics of Urban Size.* Working Paper No. 138. Berkeley: University of California center for Planning and Development, 1970.

————— *The Question of City Size and National Policy.* Working Paper No. 125. Berkeley: University of California Center for Planning and Development, 1970.

ALONSO, WILLIAM, and MICHAEL FAJANS. *Cost of Living and Income by Urban Size.* Working Paper No. 128. Berkeley: University of California Center for Planning and Development, 1970.

ALONSO, WILLIAM, and ELLIOTT MEDRICH. *Spontaneous Growth Centers in Twentieth Century American Urbanization.* Working Paper No. 113. Berkeley: University of California Center for Planning and Development Research, January 1971.

BRANDENBURG, JOHN G. *The Industrialization of Housing: Implications for New Town Development.* Chapel Hill, North Carolina: university of North Carolina Center for Urban and Regional Studies, 1970.

BRITISH INFORMATION SERVICES. *The New Towns of Britain.* Central Office of Information Reference Pamphlet 44. New York, 1969.

CLAPP, JAMES A. *The New Town Concept: Private Trends and Public Response.* Exchange Bibliography 122. Monticello, Illinois: Council of Planning Librarians, April 1970.

Development Potentials of a New Community Near Chesterton, Indiana. Evanston, Illinois: Barton-Aschman Associates, Inc., May 1970.

DUNCAN, OTIS. "Service Industries and the Urban Hierarchy," *Papers of the Regional Science Association,* V (1959), 105-120.

FODOR, LAZLO, and IVAN ILLES. "Problems of Metropolitan Industrial Agglomeration: The Budapest Case," *Papers and Proceedings of the Regional Science Association,* XXII (1969), 65-84.

FRASER, JACK B. *New Towns: What Architects Should Know About Them.* Washington, D.C.: American Institute of Architects, October 1969.

FRIEDMANN, JOHN. *Draft Proceedings.* Colloquium on the Toronto Urban Field, ed. Gerald Hodge. University of Toronto: Center for Community and Urban Studies, April 30/May 1, 1970.

FRIEDMANN, JOHN, and JOHN MILLER. "The Urban Field," *Journal of the American Institute of Planners,* XXXI, No. 4, November 1965, 312-319.

GARN, HARVEY A. *New Cities, New Communities and Growth Centers.* Working Paper 113-30. Washington, D.C.: Urban Institute, March 1970.

GEDDES, ROBERT L. (ed). *Innovations and New Communities.* Princeton, New Jersey: Princeton University School of Architecture and Urban Planning, 1970.

GILDEA, JAMES J. *GE-UNC New Towns Financial Feasibility Model.* Chapel Hill, North Carolina: University of North Carolina Center for Urban and Regional Studies, May 1971.

GLIEGE, JOHN G. *New Towns: Policy Problems in Regulating Development.* Tempe, Arizona: Arizona State University Institute of Public Administration, 1970.

GULF RESTON, INC. *Reston: Density Control Under the Residential Planned Community (RPC) Chapter of the Fairfax County Zoning Ordinance.* Reston, Virginia: Planning and Engineering Staff, October 1970.

HARVARD UNIVERSITY GRADUATE SCHOOL OF DESIGN. *New Communities: One Alternative: A Harvard Study of New City.* Cambridge, Massachusetts, June 1968.

JACKSON, SAMUEL C. "The Tough Issues in an Urban Growth Policy." In remarks of Hon. Archer Nelsen, *Congressional Record,* CXVI, July 2, 1970.

KAIN, J. F. *Urban Form and the Cost of Urban Services.* Discussion Paper No. 6. Cambridge: Harvard University Program of Regional and Urban Economics, 1966.

KELLY, MICHAEL. *Planning the Government of a New Town.* (Unpublished paper). New Haven, Connecticut: Yale Law School, February 1967.

LITCHFIELD PARK PROPERTIES. *From Farmland to City: Litchfield Park, Arizona.* Litchfield Park, Arizona: Victor Gruen Associates.

MAYER, ALBERT. *Greenbelt Towns Revisited.* Washington, D.C.: U.S. Department of Housing and Urban Development, October 1968.
————— "Urgent Need for New Towns," *National Conference Housing Yearbook,* 1967.

MACMILLAN, JAMES A. *Public Service Systems in Rural-Urban Development,* unpublished Ph.D. dissertation. Iowa State University, 1968.

MCKEEVER, J. ROSS. *What's New In Europe's Urban Development,* special report. Washington, D.C.: Urban Land Institute, 1969.

MEMPHIS AND SHELBY COUNTY PLANNING COMMISSION. *Shelby Farms.* Memphis, Tennessee: Harland Bartholomew and Associates, 1970.

New Communities in Metropolitan Areas: An Analysis. Washington, D.C.: Metropolitan Washington Council of Governments, 1970.

New Towns: A New Dimension of Urbanism. Chicago: International City Managers' Association, 1966.

New Towns Round Table: A Conference Held at the National Housing Center, Washington, D.C., June 29-30, 1964. Washington, D.C.: National Association of Home Builders, 1964.

New York State Looks at New Communities. New York: New York State Urban Development Corporation, 1969.

Regional New Towns: Alternatives in Urban Growth. Detroit: Metropolitan Fund, Inc, May 1970.

ROCKEFELLER, DAVID. "The Need For a Solution of Massive National Social Problems," in remarks of Jacob K. Javits, *Congressional Record,* CXVI, February 17, 1971.

SCHWIND, PAUL J. *Migration and Regional Development in the United States, 1950-1960,* Department of Geography Research Paper No. 133. Chicago: University of Chicago, 1971.

THOMAS, RAY. "Aycliffe to Cumbernauld: A Study of Seven New Towns in Their Regions," *Political and Economic Planning,* Broadsheet 516, XXXV. London; 1969.

TORNQUIST, GUNNAR. "Contact Systems and Regional Development," *Lund Studies in Geography,* Ser. B, No. 35, 1970.

ULMANN, E. L., and M. DACEY. "The Minimum Requirements Approach to the Urban Economic Base," *Papers and Proceedings of Regional Science Association,* VI, 1960, 175-194.

U.S.D.A. "A New City—A New Opportunity," *Extension Service Review,* XLII, February 1971, 10-11.

Urban Planning and Land Policies. Washington, D.C.: Government Printing Office, 1939.

WALKER AND DUNLOP. "The New City: An Attempt to Plan for Urban Growth," *Portfolio,* May/June 1970, 1-2.

WASHINGTON CENTER FOR METROPOLITAN STUDIES. *Reston: A Study in Beginnings.* Washington, D.C., 1966.

WIEGAND, CAMERON. *The New Town and Transportation Planning: General Overview With a Case Study of Columbia, Md.* Washnngton, D.C.: Urban Transportation Center, Consortium of Universities, 1970.

WINSBOROUGH, HAL H. "Variations in Industrial Composition with City Size," *Papers of the Regional Science Association*, V, 1959, 121-129.

Working List of Open Space Communities. Washington, D.C.: National Association of Home Builders, Land Use and Engineering Department, March 1970.

REPORTS AND HEARINGS

ADVISORY COMMISSION ON INTERGOVERNMENTAL RELATIONS. *Urban and Rural American Policies for Future Growth.* A Commission Report. Washington, D.C.: U.S. Government Printing Office, April 1968.

HIGHWAY RESEARCH BOARD. *Planned Communities: 5 Reports.* Highway Research Record No. 97. Washington, D.C.: National Research Council, 1965.

U.S. CONGRESS (House), COMMITTEE ON BANKING AND CURRENCY. *Papers Submitted to Subcommittee on Housing Panels on Housing Production, Housing Demand and Developing a Suitable Living Environment.* 92nd Cong., 1st Sess. Washington, D.C.: U.S. Government Printing Office, June 1971.

U.S. CONGRESS (House), SUBCOMMITTEE ON HOUSING OF THE COMMITTEE ON BANKING AND CURRENCY. *Housing and Urban Development Legislation—1970.* Hearings, 91st Cong., 2nd Sess. Washington, D.C.: U.S Government Printing Office, 1970.

U.S. CONGRESS, JOINT ECONOMIC COMMITTEE. *Regional Planning Issues.* Hearings before the Subcommittee on Urban Affairs of the Joint Economic Committee, Part 1. Washington, D.C.: U.S. Government Printing Office, October 1970.

U.S. CONGRESS (Senate), SUBCOMMITTEE ON HOUSING AND URBAN AFFAIRS OF THE COMMITTEE ON BANKING AND CURRENCY. *Housing and Urban Development Legislation of 1970.* Hearings, 91st Cong., 2nd Sess.,

Parts 1 and 2. Washington, D.C.: U.S. Government Printing Office, 1970.

U.S. DEPARTMENT OF HOUSING AND URBAN DEVELOPMENT. *St. Charles Communities: Report to HUD.* Washington, D.C.: Interstate General Corporation, November 1971/January 1972.

WURSTER, CATHERINE BAUER. "Framework for an Urban Society," *Goals for Americans: Report of the President's Commission on National Goals.* New York: Prentice-Hall, Inc., 1969.

NEWS ARTICLES

American City. "A 'New Town' on an Island . . . Offers Suburban Living Within Minutes of Downtown Montreal," September 1970, p. 110ff.

BASSETT, GRACE. "New Town Closeup," *San Francisco Examiner,* June 21, 1970, p. A1.

BIRCHFIELD, JAMES. "Columbia Report— The New City Continues Rapid Growth," *Washington Star,* June 18, 1971, p. D1.

———— "New City's Aims Achieved," *Washington Star,* April 30, 1971, p. D1ff.

CHABRIER, YVONNE. "Getting Involved Out in Reston," *Potomac,* June 8, 1969, p. 22ff.

CONTI, JOHN V. "An Architect Views a Crowded Space Ship," *Wall Street Journal,* March 11, 1970.

FAVRE, GEORGE H. "New Impetus for 'New Towns,'" *Christian Science Monitor,* October 6, 1970, p. 2.

———— "New Town Bucks U.S. Trends," *Christian Science Monitor,* October 9, 1970, p. 8.

HUXTABLE, ADA LOUISE. "Vision of a New Town on Welfare Island Is Unveiled Here," *New York Times,* October 7, 1970, p. 49ff.

KARMIN, MONROE W. "Creating Communities: New Towns Likely to Blossom Across U.S.: An Unexpected Law is Hastening the Trend," *Wall Street Journal,* CLXXVII, March 5, 1971, p. 26.

KEATLEY, ROBERT. "Selling a Big New Town to 'Provincial' Staten Island," *Wall Street Journal,* CLXXVII, March 11, 1971, p. 6.

KERNAN, MICHAEL. "The Green Dream," *Washington Post,* February 14, 1971, p. K1ff.

———— "The Green Dream—II," *Washington Post,* February 5, 1971, pp. C1-C2.

MAYER, ALBERT. "A New Look at the 'New City,'" *Village Voice,* XVI, August 5, 1971, p. 15ff.

———— "Dreamy Living in the 'New City,'" *Village Voice,* XVI, July 22, 1971, p. 6ff.

RUHE, BENJAMIN. "City Builder (Robert E. Simon)," *Washington Star Sunday Magazine,* May 8; 1966, pp. 4-8.

STOUT, JARED. "Residents Cautiously Hopeful About Reston," *Washington Post,* January 2, 1969, p. B1ff.

SULLIVAN, RONALD. "A City of 200,000 is Envisioned in Jersey Meadow," *New York Times,* November 24, 1970, p. 1ff.

VON ECKARDT, WOLF. "The 'Real Life' Takes Over in Secluded Reston," *Washington Post,* July 20, 1969, p. L1ff.

———— "Reston Adds Low-Income Units to the Mix," *Washington Post,* April 6, 1970, p. B1ff.

Wall Street Journal. "HUD Gives Guarantees of $54 Million to Build Two New Communities; Sites Near Chicago, Washington Benefit Under Plan to Provide Moderately Priced Housing," July 2, 1970, p. 14.

Washington Post. "Columbia: New Town Three Years Later," June 20, 1970, pp. E1, E16.

Washington Post. "New Town 'Test Lab' Envisioned," August 14, 1971, p. D1.

WATSON, DOUGLAS. "Reston, Columbia Pay Little Heed to Social Status," *Washington Post,* January 14, 1971, p. F1.

WEDEMEYER, DEE. "The New Towns Are Suceeding," *Washington Star,* August 21, 1970, p. D1ff.

WELSH, JAMES. "D.C. Area's Third New Town Planned in Charles County," *Washington Star,* May 18, 1970, p. A9ff.

163

INDEX